COSMOPOLITAN MEDIATION?

MANCHESTER
UNIVERSITY PRESS

New Approaches to Conflict Analysis

Series editor: Peter Lawler, Senior Lecturer in International Relations, Department of Government, University of Manchester

Until recently, the study of conflict and conflict resolution remained comparatively immune to broad developments in social and political theory. When the changing nature and locus of large-scale conflict in the post-Cold War era is also taken into account, the case for a reconsideration of the fundamentals of conflict analysis and conflict resolution becomes all the more stark.

New Approaches to Conflict Analysis promotes the development of new theoretical insights and their application to concrete cases of large-scale conflict, broadly defined. The series intends not to ignore established approaches to conflict analysis and conflict resolution, but to contribute to the reconstruction of the field through a dialogue between orthodoxy and its contemporary critics. Equally, the series reflects the contemporary porosity of intellectual borderlines rather than simply perpetuating rigid boundaries around the study of conflict and peace. *New Approaches to Conflict Analysis* seeks to uphold the normative commitment of the field's founders yet also recognises that the moral impulse to research is properly part of its subject matter. To these ends, the series is comprised of the highest quality work of scholars drawn from throughout the international academic community, and from a wide range of disciplines within the social sciences.

PUBLISHED

Karin Fierke
*Changing games, changing strategies:
critical investigations in security*

Helena Lindholm Schulz
*Reconstruction of Palestinian nationalism:
between revolution and statehood*

Cosmopolitan mediation?

Conflict resolution and the Oslo Accords

DEINIOL JONES

Manchester University Press
MANCHESTER AND NEW YORK

distributed exclusively in the USA by St. Martin's Press

Copyright © Deiniol Jones 1999

The right of Deiniol Jones to be identified as the author of this work has been asserted by him in accordance with the Copyright, Designs and Patents Act 1988.

Published by Manchester University Press
Oxford Road, Manchester M13 9NR, UK
and Room 400, 175 Fifth Avenue, New York, NY 10010, USA
http://www.man.ac.uk/mup

Distributed exclusively in the USA by
St. Martin's Press, Inc., 175 Fifth Avenue, New York,
NY 10010, USA

Distributed exclusively in Canada by
UBC Press, University of British Columbia, 6344 Memorial Road,
Vancouver, BC, Canada V6T 1Z2

British Library Cataloguing-in-Publication Data
A catalogue record for this book is available from the British Library

Library of Congress Cataloging-in-Publication Data applied for

ISBN 0 7190 5518 0 *hardback*

First published in 1999
06   05   03   02   01   00   99   10   9   8   7   6   5   4   3   2   1

Typeset in Photina by Servis Filmsetting Limited, Manchester
Printed in Great Britain by Bookcraft (Bath) Ltd, Midsomer Norton

For Sophie

CONTENTS

Acknowledgements — ix

Introduction — 1

1 Mediation in social philosophy	9
'Mediation' is itself disputed	10
Power-politics and social theory	14
Facilitation and social theory	16
2 Mediation as critical normative practice	23
Fragmentation in a globalised world	23
Shifting technological dynamics	26
International mediation as an institution	29
Mediation and questions of agency	31
3 Geostrategic mediation	34
The critique of the immutability thesis	35
History, states and facts	40
Geostrategy in the Middle East	47
4 Facilitation, problem-solving and mediation	58
Conflict and the hermeneutic dimension	59
The facilitation of human need	63
Communicative ethics and the practice of facilitation	66
Questions of action and practice	70
5 Cosmopolitan mediation	80
Habermas and the roots of critical international relations	82
Contemporary cosmopolitanism	87
The application to international mediation	90
Three problems facing cosmopolitan international theory	92
6 From Madrid to Oslo: the origins of Norwegian facilitation	105
The origins of Norwegian facilitation	106
The resources of small states	112
The opportunity and pressure of defeat	113

The problem of Gaza	117
Pressures on the Palestinian population	121

7 From Oslo to where? The radical intimacy of the hearth — 129

The case for the Accords: the dynamic of mutual recognition	130
Mutual recognition and the power to exclude the validity claims of statehood	133
How the text negates mutual recognition	138
Performative contradiction: coherence vs. shattered identity	140
The radical intimacy of the hearth	143
An international conference?	147
Concluding remarks	149

Conclusion — 157
Select bibliography — 165
Index — 169

ACKNOWLEDGEMENTS

I would like to acknowledge the support and invaluable encouragement of the following people: Peter Lawler, Andrew Linklater and Paul Cammack. Their belief in the value of the project steered me to its completion.

I would also like to thank Nicola Viinikka and Pippa Kenyon at Manchester University Press for their kind support and patience over the last few months.

The ESRC provided the financial support for this research. The Norman Chester fund in the Department of Government at Manchester University offered some financial finishing touches.

The origins of the book lie in the broad intellectual culture of the Department of Government at the University of Manchester. For the completion of the project I offer love and thanks to Sophie Hannah, who gave me the best research environment that anyone could ever ask for.

Introduction

In his *Keywords*, Raymond Williams notes that the term 'mediation' has 'long been a relatively complex word in English' and that 'it has been made very much more complex by its uses as a key term in several systems of thought.'[1] As Williams points out, the term 'mediation' has been used in a political sense to describe the reconciling of political adversaries and in a religious sense to refer to the act of reconciling the principles of God and man. The meaning of mediation is traditionally complex, and in this book we shall see that it is. Unfortunately, perhaps, I wish to complicate things further by demonstrating how new thinking about international relations creates an alternative shade of meaning in the concept of international mediation. This book intends to link new concepts to the study of international mediation so that those connected with the study of international relations, and even those engaged in the practice of international mediation, can think about the topic using ideas drawn from a broader sociological and political perspective. My hope is that the critical meaning of mediation, which I shall present in this book, will become a 'keyword' in the new post-positivist/realist international relations vocabulary.

Anyone familiar with the theory of international relations knows that the powerful realist theory and its more strident neo-realist front-line defence have come under a barrage of criticism in recent years and that a number of new theoretical positions have consequently emerged.[2]

Realism, or structuralist neo-realism, provides a coherent picture of the international world. Its emphasis on nation-states, the pursuit of power, structural anarchy and the theoretical and moral divide between the 'domestic' and the 'international' provide a compelling if somewhat depressing view of the nature of international politics. Despite realism's theoretical competency, its themes and arguments have been called into serious question in the contemporary literature. Focusing on the developed West, liberal international political economy has argued that the structural anarchy of international relations is softened by the economic interdependence which exists between the world's communities.³ Taking into account the relationships between the developed and the developing world, Marxist political economy claims that economic inequalities underpin the structure of the international system and it has reminded the theory of international relations of the themes of emancipation and revolutionary historical change.⁴ Historical sociology has taken the broad sweep of history into account and has noted how international systems and structures have changed over epochs and through time through the engines of state-building and military development.⁵

The walls dividing the international and the domestic have been breached. Attempts have been made to extend John Rawls's distributive theory of justice out into the world of international relations.⁶ Using communitarianism and cosmopolitanism, the theory of international relations has described the tensions between the obligations owed to the world community and the obligations owed to the immediate community.⁷ Feminist and environmental perspectives have been developed which point out particular failings of the world (dis)order.⁸

From a more sociological or philosophical perspective, critical theory has argued that the construction of knowledge is rooted in practice and concludes that theory cannot merely be about 'objective' explanation and description. Here, the categories of ideology, normativity and emancipation move to the foreground of analysis.⁹ Postmodernism has criticised grand narratives of history, the existence of essentialist categories of analysis, and it has focused on the role played by a power-infused language and discourse in the construction and defence of international orders.¹⁰ At present, the post-positivist critique of realism gives rise to a constellation of perspectives as the hegemony of realism breaks down into a fragmented multiplicity of views.

This book will introduce critical and cosmopolitan international theory to the study of international mediation. Accordingly, it will examine the work of Jürgen Habermas and his interpreters in the theory of international relations: theorists such as Andrew Linklater and David Held.¹¹ From a critical or cosmopolitan perspective, as we shall see, mediators can be charged with certain normative goals: enlarging the boundaries of political community, overcoming sectional and factional differences, expanding the domain of moral responsibility which ought to exist between international actors, and promoting relations which conform to certain ideals of international order – in particular, respect for a democratically constructed international law. In this light, a central part of international politics retains a link to certain Enlightenment goals and aspirations. Put boldly, objective moral knowledge is possible and the idea of 'progress' in international politics is given some sense and meaning.

These normative questions are pressing ones and it is hard to see how the theory of international mediation has avoided them for so long. After all, mediation is a prominent part of the international political agenda and events associated with it have not escaped widespread public attention. The immediate

Introduction

post-Cold War world has been marked by two great and defining international events which were both connected with the theory and practice of international mediation. The conflict in the former Yugoslavia and the 1993 Oslo Accords signed by the Palestine Liberation Organisation (PLO) and the Israeli government were both significant events of the post-1989 world order, and both events reveal a history of mediation. In the Yugoslavian case the United Nations (UN), the European Union (EU) and the United States all spent time intervening in an attempt to stop the violence; the Dayton Agreement was the product of the latter's efforts. In the Middle East, a US mediation eventually gave way to a more 'successful' mediation conducted by certain Norwegian actors. Since 1993, the USA has continued to justify its role in the conflict between Israel and Palestine by pointing to its indispensable 'mediation'. Mediation is a significant and defining part of international politics. In this light, it is absurd to suppose that it should escape serious critical analysis.

Chapter one presents the current state of mediation theory. After discussing the importance of international mediation, and the topics complexity, the power-political/geostrategic and facilitative/problem-solving paradigms are identified and described. The chapter describes how ideas of rationality which are deeply embedded in our culture also inform the study of international politics and international mediation.

Chapter two argues that the theory of mediation should take a critical turn. The chapter introduces the concept of 'crisis'. The twin forces of fragmentation and globalisation mean that all international actors need to develop policies which address international conflict, policies which would include concepts of international mediation. Chapter two also documents the existing state of weapons technology, a critical situation which renders the problem of international conflict even more acute. Finally, mediation is presented both as an institution and as a form of international agency. As an institution, mediation serves the task of historical and cultural reproduction in a time of crisis. As a form of agency, mediation needs to respect the conditions of plurality which exist in the world. In future chapters, these institutional and discursive questions turn the theory of mediation towards cosmopolitan ethics.

Chapter three engages with power-political or geostrategic analyses. Questions of agency and normativity are pitted against the power-political emphasis on states, immutable international structures, technical and empirical knowledge. The idea of the mediator as manipulator and problem-solver is criticised. Manipulation is always based on relations of hierarchy, domination and control. Critical theory argues, however, that stable international politics must incorporate the values of intersubjectivity, rationality, truth and justice. Geostrategic approaches sacrifice regional dynamics for a greater global vision, a vision which views all international action as an unceasing struggle for power, mastery and domination. Consequently, all the tensions and crises associated with a 'macro' global competition for power are 'pumped' into the 'micro' regional conflict with obvious adverse consequences for the regional situation. Kissinger's 'disengagement' policies of the early 1970s, and the idea that Israel is a regional 'strategic asset' of the United States in a wider global confrontation, are testimony to the dangerous, inflated ambitions of geostrategic approaches.

Chapter four engages in a critique of the facilitative approach. The emphasis on hermeneutic understanding, the model of conflict resolution based on the fulfilment of human needs/drives and the idea of action as theoretical reflection is contrasted with the ideas of critique, rational will-formation and the importance of ensuring that words and deeds never part company. The facilitative problem-solving workshop is described as a well-meaning flight from the burdens of genuine political action. Its normative understanding is deficient, its pretence at neutrality is potentially dangerous and its concentration on symbolic and psychological issues can obscure or postpone a confrontation with the substantive issues of an international dispute. (The critique of the facilitative approach will find its echo in the analysis of the Oslo Accords, which is developed in chapters six and seven). Facilitation theory attempts to develop a normative perspective, but it needs critical insights to boost its theoretical and practical energies. For example, contemporary facilitation theorists try to develop an affinity with Habermasean political ethics. However (a) facilitation becomes subsumed into a wider democratic project as a result and (b) a critical or cosmopolitan approach to international mediation is more robust and potentially wide-ranging than the problem-solving workshop when we turn to questions of policy. A cosmopolitan form of political practice, with its roots in an abstract version of the right, cannot be reduced to facilitation exercises.

Chapter five – on cosmopolitan international theory – presents the normative standpoint of critical theory. The roots of critical approaches in the work of Jürgen Habermas are discussed, and critical theory is contrasted with Marxism, Kantianism, postmodernism and instrumentalism. We analyse Habermas's views on the primacy of language orientated towards understanding. And Habermas's model of 'discourse ethics' is presented as a critical standpoint from which practices of mediation can be normatively assessed. The work of the mediator is then discussed with reference to the work of Andrew Linklater and David Held. The mediator is charged with upholding democratic dialogue, enlarging moral responsibility and with creating and stabilising international relationships which incorporate the mutual recognition of validity claims. The mediator aims at the creation of 'democratic public law' and a 'dialogic community'.

There are problems facing a cosmopolitan ethic. First, cosmopolitanism needs to engage in historical analysis if it is to avoid charges, articulated by postmodernism, of presuming to speak with a sovereign voice – a voice beyond politics and contestation. Second, cosmopolitanism, in attempting to overcome the normative deficit of facilitation theory, may ignore, to its cost, the latter's emphasis on incremental and hermeneutic procedures. Third, cosmopolitanism may overestimate the extent to which there exist moral and political resources of a cosmopolitan nature. Is Nietzsche correct, for example, when he argues that 'error' and not progress is the central condition of modern life?

A case study is presented and discussed in chapters six and seven. The critical approach to international mediation is applied to the Norwegian facilitation of the Oslo Accords which occurred in the first half of 1993. Between January and August 1993, a Norwegian academic and the Norwegian foreign ministry helped the PLO and the Rabin/Peres government of Israel to sign an agreement which granted the Palestinians self-government in parts of the Gaza Strip and West Bank. The Oslo Accords make an explicit claim to normative validity; they contain, for example, Letters of Mutual Recognition. In addition, much is made of the emancipatory nature of the Norwegian facilitation process. The Oslo process and Accords offer a good example for the critical approach to international mediation. The idea that the Oslo Accords created a 'peace process' is a central tenet of the received view of the relationship between Israel and Palestine. However, the difficulties with this argument are revealed through a cosmopolitan analysis. Mutual recognition requires national rights for both parties to the dispute, yet the Oslo process has conspicuously failed in this regard. The bulk of the analysis stops at 1993 and does not really trace the subsequent history. However, the case study will remain important. First, the basic contours of the political situation created in the Accords of September 1993 will be seen to have defined the situation throughout the 1990s. Second, the case study demonstrates how international mediation can be studied in the light of critical or cosmopolitan theory.

Chapter six sets the historical context. The origins of the Oslo Accords in the post-Cold War and post-Gulf War political climate are discussed. The financial and political bankruptcy of the PLO and the pressures being placed on Palestinians in Israeli Occupied Territory motivated the Palestinian acceptance of mediation. For their part, Israel was keen to shed its responsibility for the Gaza Strip which was, in the words of one commentator, on the verge of an anti-colonial war. The Norwegians had close historical ties with the Labour Party in Israel and the opportunity to facilitate emerged with the deadlock in the official Washington negotiations and the victory, in Israel, of a Labour government. The Norwegian facilitation offered 'the perfect camouflage' to break the political deadlock and it eased into being the post-Cold war international order in this particular part of the Middle East.

Chapter seven subjects the Oslo Accords and the Norwegian facilitation to critical analysis. Using the themes developed in earlier chapters – especially chapter five – I argue that the Oslo Accords and the Norwegian facilitation *reproduce* rather than overcome structures of inequality and domination. Too many of the claims of Palestinian nationalism were marginalised by the Oslo process and

Accords, which were dominated by the Israeli national security agenda – i.e., the security of an Israel expanded into territory captured during the Six-Day War of 1967. The Oslo process was premised on what critical theory calls a 'performative contradiction'. The use of language in the process and Accords covers up and legitimises what would otherwise be seen as naked, if not brutal, strategic action. In their normative appeals, the Oslo process and Accords free ride on the commitments to truth, rationality and justice embedded in cosmopolitan ethics.

Unfortunately, the Norwegian facilitation is *intrinsically* related to the political process which marginalised the claims of Palestinian nationalism. Norwegian facilitation exists in a space between the international and the domestic. As a peace process, therefore, it is well suited to formulating an agreement which also exists between the international and the domestic. And it is also well suited to maintaining the Palestinians in a space between the domestic and the international – i.e., in Israeli-occupied territory. In the interests of moral and practical learning, the Palestinians need a peace process which bolsters their international standing, not a secret peace process which hides them away in an international political no man's land. It is widely believed that Palestinian statelessness lies at the root of the Israeli–Palestinian conflict. As the Norwegian facilitation helped perpetuate Palestinian statelessness, it follows that it was not an exercise in international conflict resolution and not an exercise in moral and practical learning in international relations. The Oslo Accords, process and the Norwegian facilitation all fail the crucial critical and cosmopolitan tests which specify the importance of instituting the intersubjective testing of normative validity claims.

In the conclusion, I attempt to sum up the lessons to be learnt from this book, which has implications for a number of areas in international politics: namely, the theory and practice of third-party intervention, the Middle East peace process, the practice of facilitation and the theory of international relations itself. The lessons are by no means uniform. In chapter five, I argue that historical and contextual enquiry is important to the critical theory of international relations. This is because the lessons to be learned from its application are by no means straightforward. The themes of a critical theory of international relations can mean different things in different contexts. For example, the cosmopolitan thrust does not negate the importance of issues of state sovereignty. In the Palestinian–Israeli conflict, for example, mutual recognition and extending moral responsibility highlight the importance of states and national rights. In addition, the lessons for the practice of facilitation in international politics are not obvious. My critique of the Oslo process casts doubt on the efficacy of facilitation when certain struggles for national independence make up a conflict. I do not wish to argue that facilitative policies are completely bankrupt.

In essence, the critical approach to international mediation involves recognising the dual meaning of mediation articulated by Raymond Williams. Here,

Introduction

mediation brings actors together and it also reconciles those actors to ideals of living together. Importantly, though, what this means in practice is itself mediated through historical understanding. There are, then, three forms of reconciliation involved in the critical theory of international mediation: a reconciliation between disputing actors, a reconciliation of those actors to the need to live in accordance with normative political principles derived from a cosmopolitan ethic, and a reconciliation of those principles to the details and contexts of particular circumstances.

Despite the difficulties, the abiding image of the mediator which I want to convey is a cosmopolitan image. This image differs in quality from both the geostrategic and facilitative models. The geostrategic mediator is like Hobbes's *Leviathan*. It is a power which overwhelms the disputants and which attempts to rule by the sword. In the facilitative approach, the third party shrinks in size and is in turn overwhelmed by the disputants, who now appear like Leviathans themselves. The cosmopolitan approach contrasts with both images. The cosmopolitan approach borrows aspects of both images, yet transcends them at the same time. The cosmopolitan mediator strives to attain the stature of a Leviathan. But, like the traditional figure of justice, the cosmopolitan mediator appears with the sword in one hand and the scales of justice in the other.

NOTES

1. R. Williams, *KeyWords: A Vocabulary of Modern Culture* (London: Fontana Press, 1988), p. 204.
2. See E. H. Carr, *The Twenty Years Crisis* (London: Macmillan, 1962), H. Morgenthau, *Politics Among Nations* (New York: Alfred A. Knopf, 1978) and K. Waltz, *Man, the State and War: A Theoretical Analysis* (New York: Columbia University Press, 1959) for the classic exposition of realism. After the boundaries of the discipline were breached by interdependence theory, world-order studies and international political economy, Waltz published his neo-realist defence – *Theory of International Politics* (New York: Random House, 1979).
3. This position is most obviously associated with the work of Robert Keohane. See, for example, R. Keohane (ed.), *Neorealism and its Critics* (New York: Columbia University Press, 1986).
4. See R. Cox, 'Social Forces, States and World Order: Beyond International Relations Theory', in Keohane (ed.), *Neorealism*.
5. R. Little, 'International Relations and Large-Scale Historical Change' in A. J. R. Groom and M. Light (eds), *Contemporary International Relations: A Guide to Theory* (London, New York: Pinter Publishers, 1994).
6. C. R. Beitz, *Political Theory and International Relations* (Princeton and Guildford: Princeton University Press, 1979).
7. A. Linklater, *Men and Citizens in the Theory of International Relations*, 2nd edn (London: Macmillan, 1990).
8. M. Light and F. Halliday, 'Gender and International Relations' and M. Hoffman, 'Normative International Theory: approaches and issues' in Groom and Light (eds), *A Guide to Theory*.
9. M. Neufeld, *The Restructuring of International Relations Theory* (Cambridge: Cambridge University Press, 1995).

10 See, for example, J. George, *Discourses of Global Politics: A Critical (Re)Introduction to International Relations* (Boulder: Lynne Rienner, 1994).
11 Further bibliographic details will be given as the thesis moves on. Key texts, however, include the following: J. Habermas, *Moral Consciousness and Communicative Action* (Cambridge: Polity Press, 1990); A. Linklater, *Men and Citizens*; D. Held, *Democracy and the Global Order* (Cambridge: Polity Press, 1995).

1

Mediation in social philosophy

MEDIATION IS A form of conflict resolution in international politics which stresses the vital role of a third party in the process of creating peace and facilitating agreement between erstwhile disputing actors. The use of mediation as a tool of interstate politics has a long history. Scholars have traced its use back to the classical world.[1] The Catholic Church made use of it during the Dark and Middle Ages. Mediation formed part of Renaissance diplomacy and it was also institutionalised in the Congress of Vienna, the nineteenth-century European system of international governance.[2]

In the contemporary world, the idea and practice of mediation loom large. In the interest of creating and maintaining international peace, the charter of the United Nations commits its signatories to the use of mediation in the event of serious interstate dispute. Article 33 of the UN charter requires all parties to a dispute that is likely to 'endanger the maintenance of international peace' to submit to a mediation process. International mediation is a crucial responsibility of the UN Secretary-General. The charters of regional organisations, such as the Organisation for African Unity and the Organisation for Security and Cooperation in Europe also refer to mediation as a tool of regional interstate conflict resolution.[3]

Mediation plays a prominent role in contemporary international affairs. Whenever some historic or epoch-making international event makes the news headlines a mediator has often played a role in the shaping of events. The prominence of this type of international politics, where a few individuals make decisions which affect the lives of millions, entails the need for serious critical analysis and debate within the theory of international relations.

There is a need to peer beyond what Noam Chomsky calls 'language in the service of propaganda'.[4] As George Orwell writes in his essay 'Politics and the English Language': '[a]djectives like epoch-making, epic, historic, unforgettable, triumphant, age-old, inevitable, inexorable, veritable, are all used to dignify the sordid processes of international politics.'[5] Typically, and unfortunately, these are all phrases used in connection with mediated 'peace-processes', 'new world orders' and the like. The problem is that these Orwellian-like phrases are ideological or honorific terms and they obscure more than they illuminate. The media may parrot the phrase 'peace process' as if in a trance. However, the meaning of such phrases is not obvious. As the work of Vivienne Jabri testifies, the concept 'peace' is as controversial as the concept of justice or any of the more routine and hotly disputed political concepts.[6] Despite the existence of this conceptual ambiguity, the phrase 'peace process' is used very loosely – to refer, for example, to the mere fact that some sort of negotiations are taking place. The theory of international relations is rightly charged with giving some sense to the empty tokens of popular conflict resolution discourse.

Despite mediation's relationship with what Orwell calls the 'sordid processes of international politics', serious commitments to maintaining international order are going to have to rely, at least in part, on relatively informal mediation processes. This is a second reason to study international mediation. In his recent diagnosis of the modern world, Eric Hobsbawm reflects on the importance of mediation for the global order by contrasting the system of international governance which characterised the nineteenth century with the absence of international governance and the chaos of the late twentieth century. He writes:

> for the first time in two centuries, the world of the 1990s entirely lacked any international system or structure. The very fact that, after 1989, dozens of new territorial states appeared without any independent mechanism for determining their borders – without even third parties accepted as sufficiently impartial to act as general mediators – speaks for itself.[7]

The creation and maintenance of an international order is still constrained by the existence of sovereign entities, despite the onset of 'globalisation', whatever this may mean. In this international context, which is, at best, only what the English school called an 'anarchical society', mediation is a diplomatic process that could operate both within and against an international environment which is basically hostile to the rule of international law.[8] Admittedly, this is a rather vague assertion, but there is some truth in it. In the absence of any clear form of global government, mediations, sanctioned by the norms of an international order, could represent an informal diplomatic tool capable of pursuing just and workable political settlements to contemporary international conflicts.

'Mediation' is itself disputed

There is no universal definition of the term 'mediation'. The nature of mediation seems to differ across the vicissitudes of time and space. Nearly every term in Christopher Moore's definition of mediation, for example, is contested by other mediation theorists. Moore writes:

[m]ediation is the intervention into a dispute or negotiation by an *acceptable, impartial* and *neutral* third party who has no *authoritative decision-making power* to assist disputing parties in *voluntarily* reaching their own *mutually acceptable settlement* of issues in dispute.[9]

The meaning of the term is not as straightforward as Moore would like to think. Take, at the outset, the emphasis on 'neutrality'. Kolb and Babbit note that mediator neutrality is frequently and openly violated and that this does not necessarily interfere in the overall process. Touval and Zartman actually go so far as to promote partiality, declaring that neutrality can actually be detrimental to the possibility of agreement.[10] Cobb notes how mediators can 'fix' or regulate the story or history of a dispute.[11] Pruitt and Carnevale note the existence of 'emergent' mediation, where the mediator arises from an ongoing and not necessarily neutral political climate. Here, as Kolb and Babbit succinctly state, 'neutrality is an alien concept'.[12]

The idea that the mediator can have no 'authoritative decision-making power' and that their presence is always 'acceptable' to disputing parties also masks some political possibilities. It contradicts the potential power that mediators may have to force solutions in so far as they embody the authority of international, transnational or regional organisations.[13] Thomas Princen notes how the Vatican, in its role as mediator, can 'lean' on its formal authoritative power and 'influence' agreement.[14] In such situations, actors are forced to accept a mediator's decision-making presence. They do so, as those actors belong to organisations whose laws and constitutions contain obligations which promote authority in the event of conflict.

Finally, the emphasis on 'voluntarism' and 'mutual acceptability' can be called into question. Mediators can, and do, work with political pressure to force compromise. Kolb states that the mediator is often a 'spin doctor', that peculiarly contemporary form of political actor, working on 'impression management' through the 'intentional and unconscious [manipulation] of symbolic resources'.[15] Similarly, Touval and Zartman refer to the mediator as a 'manipulator' – working with 'leverage', 'sticks' and 'carrots'. Whether it is possible 'voluntarily' to accept the pressures of 'sticks' and 'carrots' ('throffers' as they have been called in political theory) is debatable. Nevertheless, it should be clear that the presence of overt manipulation (does this include deception?) calls into question the naive idea that the mediator relies *exclusively* on consent, voluntarism and mutual acceptability.[16]

This view of mediation as a rather complex form of international politics is bolstered by a recognition of the plurality of actors who can be involved in a mediation. Mediations have been conducted by private individuals, what are termed scholar/practitioners, 'formal' individual mediators, regional organisations, transnational organisations, international organisations, small states, large states and superpowers.

Furthermore, mediations are no longer conducted solely by the central states in the international system. The overwhelming number of intermediary activities during the period 1815–1914 were carried out by national governments – usually the 'great powers' of Europe. Bismarck's 'honest-broking' during the Balkan crisis of 1876 is an obvious example of a great power mediation which defined the European international politics of the latter third of the nineteenth century. In more recent times, however, mediation is seen as one of the primary tasks of non-state actors, such as regional, transnational and international organisations. Non-state actors are playing an increasing role in the mediation of international conflict. Future mediation theory may well concentrate its investigations on the role of the UN or the EU.[17]

As well as the mediators or the third parties themselves, mediation procedures obviously include the actors who are in dispute. These, too, are various in nature. In the literature on mediation it is noted that prominent disputants in mediation procedures have included community leaders, academics, large states, small states, sub-national groupings, superpowers, churches and national liberation movements.

Also, it is argued that the post-Cold War world has built within it, but not exclusively, a dynamic of 'fragmentation'. This 'fragmentation' will ensure a diversity of possible disputants. Note, for example, the number of political groups which have emerged out of the ruins of the Soviet Union.[18] Within a fragmenting international environment, it is recognised, as Kolb and Babbit write, that 'the adversaries are not clearly bounded'.[19] The likely disputants in any future mediation may not even be groups that are recognised to exist at the present time. Of course, the usual catalogue of international actors – states, international organisations and so on – are likely to be involved. However, it would seem that the list of possible future disputants may include many different types of actor: revolutionary groups, sub-national groupings, supra-national groups, liberation movements, nationalist movements, and political formations, such as pressure groups, which coalesce around a particular set of issues only to disappear once those issues are resolved.

In dealing with this plethora of problems and circumstances, mediators can, it is argued, pursue a variety of activities and roles. Again, we can see why mediation resists easy categorisation. Susskind and Babbit make the distinction between 'unassisted' and 'assisted' forms of dispute resolution.[20] Mediation is obviously a form of 'assisted' negotiation. Disputants are said to need assistance for a number of reasons.

Rothman emphasises the existential-psychological difficulties which can stand in the way of rational discussion between two parties.[21] Here, the task of the third party is to ease fears about the intentions and nature of the 'other'. Pruitt and Carnevale, and many of the articles in a collection edited by Folger and Jones, discuss the cognitive-psychological aspects of disputant interaction. Their analyses focus on issues of stereotyping and (mis)perception and how these phenomena distort the process of communication.[22] Kelman and his 'problem-solving workshop' approach combines both the existential-psychological and the cognitive-psychological perspectives.[23] Touval and Zartman, and the articles contained in Faure and Rubin, all focus on various communication problems – getting the message across – such as a lack of sensitivity to cultural differences or the appropriate manner of presenting political proposals to groups different to one's own.[24] Here the mediator acts as a translator of information which passes between different political cultures and contexts – whether they be 'ethnic' or merely the differences between different bureaucratic organisations. Susskind and Babbit also note the problems of misinformation, accuracy and poor mutual understanding.[25] Moore highlights the fact that there may be no actual protocol for a negotiation and that the task of the mediator is often to establish basic lines of communication.[26]

On top of these 'facilitative' roles, Fisher, Moore, and Ury and Patton all emphasise more active and substantive mediations. They write that the mediator is a 'formulator' of creative and imaginative proposals which, interjected into negotiations at specific points, are designed to avoid the problems of political stalemate and impasse.[27] In this more substantive mode, mediators are charged with constructing and structuring an agenda/negotiation script. The content of this script is designed to be perceived by all parties to be a fair (or realistic) method of addressing the issues at hand.

At the closing stages of a mediation, Fisher and Moore note the important and vital role that mediators can play in monitoring and guaranteeing agreements once they have actually been made.[28] In this latter sense, rather like Hobbes's *Leviathan*, mediators serve as a repository of trust. Finally, mediation may also be necessary to overcome a basic unwillingness on the part of disputants to negotiate and resolve conflict. Here, as Touval and Zartman write, 'mediators are players in the plot of relations around the conflict, with some interest in its outcome'.[29] Via 'leverage' – i.e., 'sticks' and 'carrots' – parties to a dispute might be 'persuaded' that 'negotiation' is the best option.

It should be clear that recognising a mediator cannot be accomplished with few definitional guidelines as an aid. International mediation is a very complex phenomenon. Fortunately for our theoretical and investigatory purposes, mediation is also an idea and practice which is held together by certain family resemblances. These family resemblances are commonly recognised to be divided into two main sub-groups: a power-political/geostrategic paradigm and a facilitative/problem-solving paradigm. This division offers some concrete and recognisable shape to both theory and practice.

The precise nature of mediation is hard to pin down. Mediation has always been something of a mysterious art, with as many theories of practice as there are practitioners. Perhaps this disciplinary uncertainty is not such a bad thing. As Bercovitch puts it:

> [t]he myriad of possible mediators and the range of mediatory roles and strategies is so wide as to defeat many attempts to understand . . . the essence of mediation . . . Assigning an exclusive role or a strategy to one kind of mediation is neglectful of the dynamics of the process. It is also detrimental to the search for common and divergent dimensions of mediation across social contexts.[30]

Despite the flexible nature of the concept of mediation the broad distinction between power-political and facilitative approaches should be remembered. The distinction aids the understanding and renders a rather murky field of enquiry a little clearer.

Power-politics and social theory

The geostrategic/power-political approach is strongly influenced by the concept of strategic rationality, although not consciously so. The concept of strategic rationality is a sociological term. Nevertheless, as a broad category, it accurately describes the broad practical and theoretical orientations of many different approaches. The concept of strategic rationality is effectively summarised by Stephen White. He writes:

> Action is conceptualised as the intentional, self-interested behaviour of individuals in an objectivated world, that is, one in which objects and other individuals are related in terms of their possible manipulation. The rationality of action is correspondingly conceptualised as the efficient linking of actions seen as the means to the attainment of individual goals.[31]

As this approach tends to avoid deep-contextual issues, power-political mediators are pessimistic about what can be achieved in a mediation process. Touval and Zartman admit that there is no attempt to effect a 'deep reconciliation of the parties'. The condition of international anarchy renders the ambition of harmony hopelessly idealistic. The aims of mediation are minimal. As Touval and Zartman define the key power-political injunction – 'manage a conflict, by dampening or removing its violent means and manifestations'.[32] Power-political mediators aim to achieve a 'negative peace', i.e. the absence of war or a Hobbesian civil society.

For this approach, international conflicts are more intractable and harder to solve when they involve broader moral or cultural issues. As Kressel and Pruitt write, 'mediation is more difficult when issues of principle are involved'.[33] The power-political approach argues that the mediator ought to 'repackage' normative commitments so that they appear in a more tradeable and manageable form. Touval and Zartman write: 're-defining the issues . . . to include items that can be traded against each other is often the key to a mediator's success.'[34] They recognise the reality of action in the pursuit of cultural or moral ends. But value-rational action has hazardous consequences and the prudential mediator should 'repackage' these issues in a more acceptable form. For Touval and Zartman, culture and morality have to be systematically rationalised if they are to be properly managed.

Many mediation theorists adopt strategic rationality as the principle of research. Touval and Zartman write, for example, that: '[o]ur discussion in this article is based on the assumption that the context of international relations, and particularly its power politics, has a major effect on international mediation.'[35] They add that: 'the desire to mediate is . . . intertwined with motives best described within the context of power politics. For understanding these motives a rational-actor approach is most useful, one that employs cost-benefit considerations.'[36] For Touval and Zartman, social coordination is achieved via what they call 'leverage', and 'leverage' is exercised in the deployment of economic, political (in the executive or administrative sense) and even military resources.

Bercovitch and Rubin make a similar claim about the characteristics of international social integration. They write: '[m]ediators like other political actors engage in mediation and expend resources *because they expect to gain something from it* . . . This is how we should consider and study international relations.'[37] As actors pursue money, executive and administrative power, international political action, according to Bercovitch and Rubin, ought to be coordinated via money and power. This is efficient and it is 'realistic'. Pruitt and Carnevale adopt a similar approach. They write of a 'dominant theoretical paradigm' in which competing parties 'are brought together by a desire to resolve a divergence of interest . . . *Their aim is to maximise self-interest*, though they may not be very good at doing so' – hence the need for mediation.[38] Admittedly, Pruitt and Carnevale express an awareness of the limitations of the realist approach. They write, for example, that, '[i]t ignores the social context of negotiation, overlooking such important phenomena as social norms'.[39] Nevertheless, the analysis of mediation that they put forward explicitly makes use of the strategic approach. Carnevale makes use of a 'strategic choice model' to predict and understand the future course of a mediator's behaviour.[40]

Other mediation theorists who are less clearly influenced by strategic rationality nevertheless demonstrate an acquaintance with its main themes and base at least some of their analyses on its precepts. Mitchell writes: 'it is plain that . . . institutions undertaking an intermediary role in the conflict do so because they obtain some *reward* for doing so.' He adds that 'these "rewards" can take a variety of forms' and that they differ 'according to the institution undertaking the role'.[41] On top of the more traditional realist pursuit of economic, political and military resources, Mitchell adds a set of more 'bureaucratic' motivations such as the search for expansion, influence and prestige. Thus we arrive at what political theorist Alessandro Ferrara calls, '[t]he hegemony of the type of social action rooted in the modern profit-orientated enterprise and in the bureaucratized state apparatus'.[42]

Facilitation and social theory

A contrasting approach to the power-political approach is commonly referred to as the facilitative or problem-solving approach. Like its opposite number, the facilitative approach works within a particular understanding of the social scientific context. We shall discuss this context before moving onto the more pragmatic details.

Broadly put, the facilitative approach works with the idea of contextual rationality. Situations defined by contextual rationality are those:

> in which the overriding motivation has an intrinsically intersubjective or social character in that it expresses a recognisable orientation to the values of some community as they are manifested in some basic moral, religious or social norms. It is in relation to this sort of orientation that we are often willing to consider even an action endangering self-preservation as possibly rational.[43]

As Habermas has argued, actors have a practical interest in historical and hermeneutic understanding, as well as a technical interest in the strategic or instrumental empirical analytic sciences.[44]

In this view, the relationship of actors to the world is more complicated than the idea of strategic rationality would lead us to believe. Actors are beings with culturally specific ideas, beliefs about the world, points of meaning and diversity. There is a substantive world of symbolic meaning, as well as a world of political and economic self-interest. The former is messy, intricate and complex, and evades the order and symmetry of the latter. As the philosopher Wittgenstein put it:

> Our language can be seen as an ancient city: a maze of little streets and squares, of old and new houses, and of houses with additions from various periods; [only at the periphery is it] surrounded by new boroughs with straight streets and uniform houses.[45]

The facilitative approach responds to the more substantive intricacies of social life embodied in the contextual view. Contextual meaning cannot be understood via the abstract structuralist focus on social systems. Social thought and action, as Habermas argues, should focus on broad questions of meaning, questions of cultural reproduction, social integration and individual identity.[46] The currency of meaningful social exchange and understanding, in this context, is not executive and administrative power, but is, instead, ordinary language. Only ordinary language can capture such things as moral relationships, cultural differences and the various tones and shades of individual or collective meaning and identity. The language of system and structure is blind to these experiences.

Contextual action requires a different set of skills to action within the system. In the place of deductive cognition, an actor, too, must judge. In the place of abstraction an actor must learn the power of immersion. In the place of universalising, the actor must learn to attend to particulars. Instead of manipulation, enquiry must learn the values of autonomy. And in place of mute strategic and instrumental action, enquiry must learn how to speak and how to listen.

In international conflict, mediators have to deal with this realm of symbolic reality and meaning. Thus, there exists an approach to mediation which is based on 'the realisation that conflict is a socially created and communicatively managed reality occurring within a socio-historical context that both affects meaning and behaviour and is affected by it.'[47] From this perspective, clear and concise communication is the ideal. Conflict results from a poor mutual understanding of the various and competing contexts of meaning. Ongoing, wide-ranging and perspicuous communication is thus the *raison d'être* of the facilitative approach to international mediation.

Unfortunately, the international world is beset by problems of poor communication and misunderstanding. As Thomas Princen writes:

> [i]n a complex world, leaders employ 'short cuts to rationality'. Established beliefs resist change even with new information; decisions are made on the basis of a single important value dimension; historical analogies to recent important cases weigh heavily; other states are assumed to be more unified and rational than available information indicates; one's benign intentions are assumed to be appreciated by others; and the role of accidents and confusion is discounted.[48]

In this scenario, the facilitator acts as a conduit of accurate information, aiming to reassure actors of their long-term, mutual rationality and thus generating virtuous cycles of cooperation. Through communication, actors can climb out of the state of nature. The mediator deals with the cognitive limitations of an overburdened political understanding. Hoffman thus writes of the 'educational role' of the mediation process, as the facilitator tutors disputing actors in the finer points of individual context, meaning and identity.[49]

Often it is existential, and not just cognitive psychological barriers, which fuel conflict. In such circumstances the nature, identity, rationality and context of the 'other' is deliberately distorted in order to maintain polar oppositions of individual identity – though perhaps on an 'unconscious' level. The problem, here, is not cognitive but rather existential psychology. The concept of contextual meaning runs deeper than simple 'factual' misunderstanding. It cuts right into the essence of individual, group or national identity. All actors have a need for mutual recognition. If this need is ignored or perceived as ignored then hostility towards the 'other' is the result. Once these more hostile impressions are formed and embedded within the broad cultural psyche, existential commitments to the now crystallised identities mean that distortions are hard to remove. Such existential processes, as facilitation theory points out, make conflict resolution extremely difficult.

Rothman writes that international conflict inevitably involves the 'demonization of the other' where 'all negative, violent, aggressive words and deeds of the other side against one's own group are viewed as characteristics of the nature of the evil other'.[50] In the absence of meaningful political participation between different groups, stories or narratives are constructed which bind actors to a common group loyalty.[51] The absence of legitimate mutual recognition results in fear and mistrust. Frequently, narratives are constructed that crystallise around fixed and polar conceptions of identity – oppositions of good and evil. Individuals in situations of serious international conflict lead fearful and lonely lives. In such situations actors console themselves with stories of their own virtue and the wickedness of others. As Sarah Cobb writes, '[w]ith great regularity, disputants construct the "others(s)" as responsible for the negative outcome, which has two discursive consequences: (1) the construction of the self as victim, and (2) the construction of other as victimizer.'[52] Fear of the 'other' is magnified by ideologies or religions that 'demonise' others and serve to bind insecure and lonely individuals to a common and often extreme world-view. Hostility towards others, in this situation, is part and parcel of the creation of political identity. Myths help stabilise this identity but they do so by being impervious to rational modification. And maintaining the obscuring myth is more important than uncovering an ideology that could put an end to conflict.

The third-party facilitator is an actor without any sort of power in the traditional realist sense. However, the fact of realist powerlessness translates into a new form of power – a facilitative or communicative power. This form of power can work where realist forms of power fail. The third-party facilitator is not a major international actor, a linchpin of the international system. Neither is it a major and contending state. Consequently, the third-party facilitator develops a peculiar freedom of its own. This freedom involves the time and patience necessary to overcome deeply entrenched cycles of hostility and mistrust.

Unencumbered by the cares and worries which affect the larger state, the third-party facilitator roams the globe seeking out forms of influence and prestige based on the power of communication. This point was made by Jan Egeland, a Norwegian facilitator of the Oslo Accords. He writes: 'it was Norway's close ties with Israel that made Norway so interesting for the PLO. Conversely our direct contact with Yasser Arafat made Israel choose us as their back channel.'[53] The Norwegian foreign policy elite, unencumbered by large international problems of their own, had wonderful opportunities to develop imaginative and creative foreign policies.

Away from the international limelight, facilitators have the ability to provide low-profile, secluded settings for exploratory negotiations. Jan Egeland, the facilitator in the Oslo back channel, made this point in a speech to the JFK School at

Harvard in March 1995. Egeland spoke of the 'perfect camouflage' that the Norwegians could offer to Israeli and Palestinian negotiators keen to hide their activities from hostile constituencies 'back home'.[54] Who would think that the Norwegians could be hosting discussions which aimed at solving one of the great international problems of the twentieth century?

How do facilitators gain the necessary trust and confidence? Facilitators are not 'big players' on the international scene with 'interests' of their own. Facilitators use their weak international status to pursue their activities. As there is nothing at stake for the facilitators, there is no incentive to cheat and lie. They have two motivations, which stem from their weakness as international actors. First, a desire to appear basically neutral in the eyes of others. Second, a desire to ensure a peaceful international order. Being a powerless international actor in a competitive international arena means that the stance of neutrality is strategically rational, as is the maintenance of a peaceful international order. The facilitator thus claims an interest only in the peaceful resolution of the international dispute. From a larger state this type of claim would arouse immediate suspicion. However, disputing parties may believe the facilitator's claims as they can appreciate the prudential reasoning of the facilitator. Offering low-risk communication in a trusted environment is in the strategic interest of the facilitator, and disputing states, being strategically rationally actors themselves, recognise and appreciate this fact.

Thus the facilitator, like the psychoanalyst, does not attempt to impose a solution on the disputants. Like a magician, the facilitator only invokes the spectre of communicative power. The facilitator will create the conditions and parameters of debate and then will employ all the known facilitative techniques designed to protect the state of communication. Within this framework, substantive solutions are always supposed to arise from the bottom up – from the participant's perspective. In the process of political enlightenment there are only participants. This freedom to generate self-sustaining solutions is important. It enhances disputant autonomy. But, more importantly, it has a knock-on effect in that subsequent agreements and political arrangements are self-supporting and sustaining. As Hoffman puts it, '[a] facilitated resolution promotes compliance because the solution is derived from the parties themselves'.[55]

NOTES

1 F. A. Adcock, D. J. Mosley, *Diplomacy in Ancient Greece* (London: Thames and Hudson, 1975).
2 G. Mattingly, *Renaissance Diplomacy* (Boston: Houghton Mifflin, 1955), A. J. P. Taylor, *The Struggle for Mastery in Europe* (Oxford: Clarendon Press, 1954).
3 S. G. Amoo and W. I. Zartman, 'Mediation by Regional Organizations: The Organization of African Unity in Chad', in J. Bercovitch and J. Z. Rubin (eds), *Mediation in International Relations: Multiple Approaches to Conflict Management* (London: The Macmillan Press,

1992); 'The CSCE and the Changing Role of Nato and the European Union', *Nato Review*, 3:42 (1994).
4 N. Chomsky, *Chronicles of Dissent: Interviews with David Barsiman* (Stirling, Scotland: AK Press, 1992).
5 G. Orwell, 'Politics and the English Language', in *The Penguin Essays of George Orwell* (London: Penguin, 1984), p. 352.
6 V. Jabri, *Discourses on Violence* (Manchester: Manchester University Press, 1995).
7 E. Hobsbawm, *The Age of Extremes* (London: Abacus, 1994), p. 559.
8 For an account of the 'anarchical society' see H. Bull, *The Anarchical Society* (Basingstoke: The Macmillian Press, 1977).
9 C. Moore, *The Mediation Process: Practical Strategies for Resolving Conflict* (San Francisco/London: Jossey-Bass, 1986). p. 14. My emphasis.
10 See D. M. Kolb and E. F. Babbit, 'Mediation Practice in the Home Front: Implications for Global Conflict Resolution', in J. A. Vasquez, J. J. Johnson, S. Jaffe and L. Stamato (eds), *Beyond Confrontation, Learning Conflict Resolution in the Post-Cold War Era* (Michigan: University of Michigan Press, 1995), pp. 63–86; S. Touval and W. I. Zartman, 'International Mediation: Conflict Resolution and Power Politics', *Journal of Social Issues*, 41:2 (1985), pp. 27–45; S. Touval and W. I. Zartman, 'Introduction', in Touval and Zartman (eds), *International Mediation in Theory and Practice* (Boulder, Colorado: Westview Press, 1985), pp. 7–17.
11 S. Cobb, 'The Narrative Perspective on Mediation: Toward the Materialization of the Storytelling Metaphor', in J. P. Folger and T. S. Jones (eds), *New Directions in Mediation: Communication Research and Perspectives* (London: Sage Publications, 1994).
12 D. G. Pruitt, and P. J. Carnevale, *Negotiation in Social Conflict* (Buckingham: Open University Press, 1993). The quotation is from Kolb and Babbit, 'Mediation Practice on the Home Front', p. 65.
13 See, for example, Amoo and Zartman, 'Mediation by Regional Organizations', pp. 131–48 and J. O. C. Jonah, 'The United Nations and International Conflict: The Military Talks at Kilometer Marker-101', both in Bercovitch and Rubin (eds), *Mediation*. A distinction is often made within the literature between 'process' and 'content' mediatory interventions – see, for example, Bercovitch, 'The Structure and Diversity of Mediation in International Relations', in *ibid*, p. 16. Given that mediators make substantive interventions in disputes, it is difficult to see how a regional or international actor acting as a mediator could avoid making 'authoritative' substantive interventions. As Jonah writes of the UN mediation of the kilometer 101 talks, '[w]hile the third party must always be impartial, its should not hesitate to use its comprehensive understanding of the issues involved to intervene in the negotiating process . . . The UN team's awareness of these considerations enabled it to offer compromise suggestions at the crucial point in the negotiations' – see Jonah, 'The United Nations and International Conflict'. Did the fact that these 'suggestions' came from the UN endow them with any authority? Surely, this is so.
14 T. Princen, 'Mediation by the Vatican', in Bercovitch and Rubin (eds), *Mediation*, pp. 162–5.
15 D. Kolb, 'Expressive Tactics in Mediation', *Journal of Social Issues*, 41:2 (1985), p. 24.
16 Tonval and Zartman, 'International Mediation'. For a discussion of whether or not 'throffers' interfere with liberty, see H. Steiner, 'Negative Liberty' in D. Miller (ed.), *Liberty* (Oxford: Oxford University Press, 1991).
17 Article 33 (Chapter VI) of the Charter of the United Nations, for example, states that 'The parties to any dispute, the continuance of which is likely to endanger the maintenance of international peace and security, shall, first of all, seek a solution by negotiation, enquiry, mediation, conciliation, arbitration, judicial settlement, resort to regional agencies or arrangements, or other peaceful means of their own choice.' The UN has played,

and is playing, a prominent role in the mediation of disputes – see, for example, T. M. Franck and G. Nolte, 'The Good Offices Function of the U.N. Secretary-General', in A. Roberts and B. Kingsbury (eds.), *United Nations, Divided World* (Oxford: Oxford University Press, 1988).
18. R. Clutterbuck, *International Crisis and Conflict* (Basingstoke: The Macmillan Press, 1993) and S. Smith, *The Nationalities Question in the Soviet Union* (Harlow, Essex: Longman Group, 1993).
19. Kolb and Babbit, 'Mediation Practice on the Home Front', p. 88.
20. 'Overcoming the Obstacles to Effective Mediation of International Disputes', in Bercovitch and Rubin (eds), *Mediation*, p. 36.
21. J. Rothman, *From Confrontation to Cooperation* (London: Sage Publications, 1992).
22. R. Little and S. Smith, *Belief Systems and International Relations* (Oxford: Basil Blackwell, 1988). For further analysis of this problem, see Folger and Jones (eds), *New Directions in Mediation*.
23. H. C. Kelman, 'Informal Mediation by the Scholar/Practitioner', in Bercovitch and Rubin (eds), *Mediation*.
24. G. O. Faure and J. Z. Rubin (eds), *Culture and Negotiation* (London: Sage Publications, 1993).
25. 'Overcoming Obstacles'.
26. Moore, *The Mediation Process*, p. 19.
27. See R. Fisher, 'Pacific, Impartial Third-Party Intervention in International Conflict: A Review and an Analysis', in Vasquez et al. (eds), *Beyond Confrontation*; Moore, *The Mediation Process*, and R. Fisher, W. Ury and B. Patton, *Getting to Yes* (London: Business Books, 1981).
28. Fisher, 'Pacific, Impartial Third-Party Intervention', and Moore, *The Mediation Process*, ch. 14.
29. Touval and Zartman, 'International Mediation', p. 32.
30. Bercovitch, 'The Structure and Diversity of Mediation', pp. 6–7.
31. S. White, *The Recent Work of Jürgen Habermas* (Cambridge: Cambridge University Press, 1988), p. 10.
32. Touval and Zartman, '*International Mediation*', p. 44.
33. K. Kressel and D. G. Pruitt, 'Themes in the Mediation of Social Conflict', in Vasquez et al. (eds), *Beyond Confrontation*, p. 187.
34. Touval and Zartman, 'International Mediation', p. 35.
35. *Ibid.*, p. 28.
36. *Ibid.*, p. 32.
37. Bercovitch and Rubin (eds.) *Mediation*, p. 9. My emphasis.
38. Pruitt and Carnevale, *Negotiation in Social Conflict*, p. 8. My emphasis.
39. *Ibid.*
40. *Ibid.*, p. 172.
41. C. R. Mitchell, 'Motives for Mediation', in Mitchell and Webb (eds), *New Approaches to International Mediation* (Westport, Connecticut: Greenwood, 1988), p. 33.
42. A. Ferrara, *Modernity and Authenticity: A Study of the Social and Ethical Thought of Jean-Jacques Rousseau* (Albany, New York: New York State University Press, 1993), p. 49.
43. White, *The Recent Work*, p. 15.
44. J. Habermas, *Knowledge and Human Interests*, trans. J. Shapiro (Boston: Beacon Press, 1971).
45. L. Wittgenstein, *Philosophical Investigations* (Oxford: Blackwell, 1953), para 18.
46. J. Habermas, *The Theory of Communicative Action* (Cambridge: Polity Press, 1991).
47. Folger and Jones (eds), *New Directions*, p. ix.
48. T. Princen, *Intermediaries in International Conflict* (Princeton: Princeton University Press, 1992), p. 27.

49 M. Hoffman, 'Defining and Evaluating Success', *Paradigms: The Kent Journal of International Relations*, (Winter 1995) p. 8.
50 Rothman, *From Confrontation*, pp. 15–16.
51 This process is recognised in the mediation literature. See Folger and Jones (eds), *New Directions*. Rothman, in *From Confrontation* talks about this process with reference to the relationship between Israel and Palestine. Perhaps more generally, Hannah Arendt, in *The Origins of Totalitarianism* (London: Allen and Unwin, 1967), has argued that race ideologies serve to bind 'lonely' individuals, i.e. individuals not united by a meaningful political culture.
52 Cobb, 'Narrative Perspective', p. 57.
53 J. Egeland, *The Norwegian Channel: The Secret Peace Talks between Israel and the PLO*. Paper presented to the JFK School in Harvard, 23 March 1995, p. 4.
54 *Ibid.*, p. 5.
55 M. Hoffman, 'Third Party Mediation and Conflict Resolution in the Post-Cold War World', in J. Baylis and N. J. Rengger (eds), *Dilemmas of World Politics* (Oxford: Clarendon Press, 1992), p. 272.

2

Mediation as critical normative practice

WE IMMEDIATELY ALTER the conditions and parameters of our discussion if we situate the theory and practice of mediation in the following context: protracted social conflict, fragmentation plus globalisation and the existing state of weapons technology. These conditions, inherent in the contemporary international world, mean that mediators are frequently involved in what we might call critical normative practice. I use the term 'critical' here in two senses. First, mediation seeks to alter existing social realities through political understanding and action based on that understanding. Second, I use the term 'critical' to refer to a situation of crisis – a political context which is threatening and which must in some way be overcome.

Fragmentation in a globalised world

I begin with a concept familiar to conflict analysis, a concept rightly viewed by many as a first principle of conflict research. This is the concept of 'protracted social conflict'. Jay Rothman writes: 'Protracted social conflicts are characterized by long-standing seemingly insoluble tensions that fluctuate in intensity over extended periods of time.'[1] Such conflicts, as Rothman adds, 'seem to defy solution'. They become a danger point in international relations. This point may be stable for periods of time, but it always threatens to erupt, alter and disrupt the wider political dynamics of the world. Rothman discusses the Israeli–Palestinian conflict in such terms. We shall return to this conflict, correctly characterised by Rothman, in later chapters.

A 'protracted social conflict' is a crisis in the international system when the current set of political realities cannot cope with a given set of problems and a collapse or radical and unwelcome change in history becomes a likelihood. As Habermas writes:

> crises arise when the structure of a social system allows fewer possibilities for problem solving than are necessary to the continued existence of the system. . . .

> Crises in social systems are not produced through accidental changes in the environment, but through structurally inherent system-imperatives that are incompatible and cannot be hierarchically integrated.[2]

An example of a political structure which 'cannot be hierarchically integrated' would be the call for a Jewish state (Israel) on the West Bank of the River Jordan – as the latter is populated by nearly one million Palestinian Arabs. The pieces of the political jigsaw just do not fit together and crisis is the result.

Crises are not reducible to the lack of systemic integration. Crises also have a harmful effect on the subjectivity and identity of those caught up in the failing social structure, and in the final instance it is this subjective experience that brings the crisis to a head and gives it an oppressive reality. Habermas continues: 'only when members of a society experience structural alterations as critical for continued existence and feel their social identities threatened can we speak of crises.'[3]

Rothman states that this condition of subjective insecurity is at the root of the Israeli–Palestinian conflict. He argues that this century-old conflict has created 'pervasive despair and desperation' among those trapped in the failing social structure and that this despair unleashes itself in patterns of violence.[4] I will argue that this situation applies particularly to Palestinians living in the West Bank and Gaza. In later chapters we will consider the conditions of the Gaza Strip immediately prior to the Oslo process. As we shall see, trapped in a failing structure following the Gulf War, the PLO and the Israeli Labour government sought to quell the escalating violence and the crisis in the Gaza Strip through the medium of the Oslo Accords.

As crisis impinges on the political consciousness of subjects caught up in it, it inevitably gives rise to political and normative speculation; that is, crisis creates and invokes criticism. Thus 'structurally inherent contradictions can, of course, be identified only when we are able to specify structures important for continued existence.'[5] Questions of identity and purpose are inevitably raised by perceptive political actors who see the failing structures of political power and who search for an alternative order. All existing structures are called into question. As Camus writes of *The Rebel*:

> It is to himself, and to himself alone, that he returns in order to find law and order. Then the time of exile begins, the endless search for justification, the nostalgia without an aim, the most painful, the most heart-breaking question that of the heart which asks itself: where can I feel at home?[6]

Protracted social conflicts present what John Burton calls 'an evolutionary dilemma'.[7] A stark and inescapable choice arises: do actors move with the forces of permanence or the forces of change? Risks are attached to either option. Permanence equals continuing crisis; change equals a leap into the unknown.

Within the international system as a whole, crises are not 'internal' to themselves. That is, they have consequences which may echo around the globe, and as they become more serious they threaten to draw in international actors who are not otherwise directly involved. Rothman writes that protracted social conflict threatens to 'spill over, from domestic into regional and international arenas"[8].

The problem, as many writers now acknowledge, is that both fragmentation *and* globalisation exist as twin forces of the international system.[9] Linklater and Macmillan write:

> In recent times the significance of national boundaries has been eroded by various processes operating above and below national governments. Globalisation and fragmentation are transforming the nature of political community across the world.[10]

Of course, discussion of these terms is, as Ian Clark writes, 'anything but straightforward'.[11] However, it is possible to specify at least one way in which these forces interact. This demonstrates why all international actors need develop policies of international conflict resolution, including policies of international mediation. The situation in question occurs when the consequences of fragmentation travel down globalised networks of power and communication from the source of conflict adversely to effect and draw in actors who exist in the wider web of international relations.

Clark writes as though globalisation and fragmentation work in different, opposing directions. He illustrates, for example, their 'contradictory nature', 'their two opposed tendencies', or the fact that they move in 'both directions'.[12] However, fragmentation and globalisation can work in harmony. Here, the consequences of fragmentation 'use' globalisation to project themselves across the world. Indeed, Clark recognises the phenomenon in the First World War, which he correctly describes as 'the essence of fragmentation', a 'monumental collapse of the international system'. However, the consequences of this fragmentation travelled throughout the globe via globalised networks of power and communication. The British state, for example, mobilised millions of men throughout the world via the clarion call of empire. Clark describes this process as follows:

> It is hard to imagine a more tangible expression of globalisation on the lives of ordinary people: if globalisation means the compression of all life and the creation of networks to transfer impacts from one part of the system to another then the First World War certainly attained this condition over a greater span than had any similar military encounters over the centuries.[13]

Thus we have to consider a situation where the forces of fragmentation move out from their original source through globalised networks of power and communication to make themselves felt on the wider international scene. Particular conflicts will vary in their capacity to 'travel'. Some conflicts may prompt regional or continental specific responses and only mild interest from powers further afield. Other conflicts will demand the full attention of powers beyond the continent or region in question. Which crises ought to demand greater international attention is a contested issue, and it will continue to be so. As one writer describing the 'World-America' of the twenty-first century writes:

> Crises and tensions in the rest of the world will be evaluated in terms of the threat they pose to the harmonious functioning of the empire. The corollary of this outlook is that conflicts and human dramas without 'strategic significance' may simply be ignored. The 'new order' does not set out to eliminate disorders that remain strictly local.[14]

The fact that the consequences of fragmentation can travel across the globe through globalised networks of power and communication means that all states or international actors have an interest in developing policies which address regional conflict. Decisions about what crises are important should not be left to the mind of one power alone, no matter how strong and influential that power may be. When superpowers make mistakes, for example, the consequences are amplified. Thus, as Hannah Arendt writes, 'It is true, for the first time in history all peoples on earth have a common present: no event of any importance in the history of one country can remain a marginal accident in the history of any other.'[15] In this context, the absence of an international outlook is a sign, as Nietzsche would put it, that 'the genius for organisation is lacking'.[16] Andrew Linklater puts the point like this:

> if societies were largely self-contained and incapable of doing harm to one another then the boundaries of moral communities could converge with the boundaries of actual communities but the reality is quite different and societies are inevitably drawn into complex dialogues about the principles of international coexistence.[17]

Shifting technological dynamics

The possibility that conflict and fragmentation can travel around global networks of power and communication is made more acute when we realise the nature of the forces that can move out from the centre of conflict into the wider international web. In this section, I detail the technologies of war. When, to quote the poet Yeats, 'the centre cannot hold, mere anarchy is loosed upon the world', we may witness a darkening cloud of military technology on the horizon. What forces of destruction and devastation are abroad in the world? This question can be answered by examining, albeit briefly, aspects of the current state of military technology. A consideration of the current state of weapons technology makes the problem of international conflict even more acute.

Consider three broad types of military technology: conventional or mechanized weapons, chemical weapons and, finally (and ultimately), nuclear weapons. All these weapons relate to successive phases in the growth of modern industrial, scientific and technological innovation. As Hugh Crone writes, 'any advance in technology has been followed almost immediately by the application of that technology to war'.[18] To put the point more sharply, all military technologies ever invented have at some time been used.

Conventional weapons – tanks, planes, ships, guns and missiles – and the battery of iron and steel wielded by the mass-conscripted army represent the traditional or classic image of war in modernity. Such forces, born in the age of modern revolutions, persist. Thirty million people are under arms full time in the world – more than 10 per cent of the number of men aged 18–22.[19] Mass conscription with no conscientious objection occurs in many countries. (Eric Hobsbawm calls this 'the democratisation of the means of violence'.[20]) The production of conventional weapons is tied in with industry and the development of the nation-state. Most of the conventional arms trade moves from the industrialised and stable countries of the North and West, where the arms are produced, to the more unstable countries of the South and East, where the arms are consumed.

The type of war produced by conventional arms can be seen in the first and second Gulf Wars and is highly destructive of both human life and material infrastructure. In fact, given modern technological development in this field of weapons, it might be misleading to call this type of conflict, 'conventional war', which sounds too reassuring. In many ways, modern conventional weapons are as destructive as their more unconventional counterparts – the chemical, the biological and the nuclear.

Conventional war ranges from First-World-War-like attrition to Second-World-War-like Blitzkrieg. These two types of warfare have made an appearance in the Persian Gulf in recent years. The first Gulf War between Iran and Iraq consumed $55 billion worth of imported arms and resulted in more than a million dead. The second Gulf War was over in a matter of weeks, as the computer-guided and more sophisticated iron and steel of the North rained in from the sky and overwhelmed the men and machinery of the South.

Conventional wars retain that blood and steel character of the first industrial age – developed in the mass armies of Napoleon and revealed to the world for the first time in full majesty during the First World War. Analysts predict that the nationalist, conventional war fought over resources remains a future likelihood in many parts of the globe.[21]

The chemical industry is a product of the second industrial revolution of the late nineteenth century, which saw the development of electricity, flight, the combustion engine and telecommunications. Governments quickly considered the use of toxic chemicals in war. In 1899 the Hague Convention banned projectiles whose sole use was the dispersion of asphyxiating gases. This resolution proved immaterial. In April 1915 the Germans released 150 tonnes of chlorine from gas cylinders against the Allied lines – many more tonnes were released against the Russians. The age of chemical warfare had begun.[22]

The Geneva Protocol of 1925 aimed to prohibit 'the Use in War of Asphyxiating, Poisonous or Other Gases, and of Bacteriological Methods of Warfare'. Crone writes that, this Protocol is still the 'definitive' international statement on chemical weapons. The agreement is old and flawed. No real methods of implementation or enforcement are written into it. Perhaps more importantly, countries are not prohibited from acquiring weapons as a standby against attack. Since 1925, it is known that Italy, Japan and Iraq have used chemical weapons in war, and perhaps there are others.[23] Many countries around the world have stockpiles of chemical weapons, including, in all likelihood, the principle states of the democratic West.

Since 1915, the chemicals and their means of their delivery have been 'improved'. Modern chemical warfare would consist of nerve agents, delivered using rocket technology, whose function is to attack the operation of the muscles. There are counter-measures. However, these measures are military rather than civilian in nature and are themselves technologically sophisticated. As Crone points out, 'to survive a nerve gas attack would require a high degree of training and discipline'.[24] And as the phenomenon of Gulf War syndrome has demonstrated, the ability of the military to prepare an adequate defence against chemical weapons is under question.[25] Without doubt, the only effective civilian defence against chemical attack is banning the use of chemical weapons or preventing the outbreak of serious conflict in the first place, and, possibly, through mediation.

The same is true, of course, of nuclear weapons. The advent of nuclear science marks a new phase in the technological development of the modern world. Based on the physics of the early twentieth century, whose nature troubled even those who were involved in its development, nuclear science snaps the link between the natural and human world. As Hannah Arendt writes, '[s]cientifically, the modern age which began in the seventeenth century came to an end at the beginning of the twentieth century; politically the modern world in which we live today was born with the first atomic explosions.'[26]

It is not possible to translate the theoretical essence of nuclear science into ordinary experience, as it is with Newtonian physics. Nuclear science is for extraordinary use. Consequently, it is the introduction of cosmological processes onto the surface of the planet which delineates this new age. Previously, technology had reproduced or enhanced natural processes which could exist alongside human life. It is possible, for example, for an individual to witness Newtonian processes, naturally occurring, in his or her back garden. With nuclear science, however, processes inherent in the dawn of galaxies can be reproduced in the English countryside.[27] Nuclear technology is, to use Arendt's phrase, a form of 'action into nature'.[28] And handling the repercussions of this technology is, and will prove to be, the labour of Sisyphus. Having made its appearance in the world, the responsibility for controlling its use will fall on the shoulders of countless future generations.

Nuclear weapons are a product of the age of totalitarianism and they carry the qualities of that age into the present. As they are, as Hobsbawm writes, 'the child of anti-fascism', they are a lingering reminder of the collapse of international politics in this century.[29] At the end of the century of totalitarianism, this 'child of anti-fascism' has grown into a second nuclear age, dominated by problems of horizontal weapons proliferation. The Nuclear Non-Proliferation Treaty, signed in 1968, has subsequently attracted the membership of 141 states (by 1990). The regime is contradictory and haphazard. First, the Permanent Members of the UN Security Council impose obligations on others, yet their own enterprise is often unrestrained. (Witness, for example, French nuclear trials in the Pacific in 1997). Second, and most importantly, there are no real enforcement mechanisms.

Thousands of nuclear weapons hundreds of times more powerful than the Hiroshima bomb still exist on the earth. And although remote, the nuclear option exists as long as the weapons and the science exist. The nuclear stand-off between India and Pakistan in the spring of 1998, for example, is a testimony to the continuing dangers. As is the development of nuclear technology in Israel and the possible acquisition of nuclear technology in Iran.

The modern world, and each successive phase in the growth of science, technology and industry, have bequeathed to us a certain type of military technology. Unlike older industries and technologies, which die out and are replaced by others, modern military technology seems just to 'hang around' and accumulate. Although these technologies remain largely dormant at the present time, a series of critical international events could yet see their reappearance in the world. In terms of a theory of international mediation, certain institutional and discursive questions follow from this analysis.

International mediation as an institution

As an institution, mediation can play a vital role in the historical and cultural reproduction of international society in a time of crisis.

All international actors are caught in the philosophy and reality of the moment. Life only exists on the planet because the universe is large enough to accommodate the infinitely improbable. And at any one point in space and time human life itself consists of a unique constellation of circumstances, forces, movements, peoples and events. Thus the unique is constantly being created and re-created in the human world through the form and drama of the historical moment.

I refer to what the philosopher Hannah Arendt calls the human conditions of 'natality' and plurality. Underlying the homogenising forces created by both nature and socialisation is a fundamental metaphysical reality which could only be destroyed in a world totally devoid of human life. Birth brings the new into the world. And, as Arendt writes, '[i]n man, otherness which he shares with everything that is, and distinctness, which he shares with everything alive, become uniqueness, and human plurality is the paradoxical plurality of unique beings'.[30]

While being utterly unique, however, the historical moment is also a great political and existential burden. It represents all that remains from the past and it represents all the potential of the future.

The burden of the moment and the task of historical reproduction is too much to bear for many actors in global politics. War is the application of military technology to the manipulation of the historical moment by actors who have no real energy or capacity for the historical reproduction of society in all its complexity and diversity. Through military means, an actor attempts to ease the burden of historical reproduction by preventing a 'troubling' aspect of the past or present appearing in the future. But an actor who resorts to war disrupts the onward flow of time and alters its reality and constitution. International conflict has the potential just to remove great chunks of experience from the flow of history. Indeed, when it occurs, this is its phenomenological impact. As Arendt writes, 'The weirdness of this situation resembles a spiritualistic seance where a number of people gathered around a table might suddenly, through some magic trick, see the table vanish from their midst.'[31]

An inability to cope with the plethora of experience which history has bequeathed is a symptom of political and cultural decline. Within the world, and from an evolutionary point of view, no living thing is stationary. Life is constantly either declining or ascending in power, where 'power' can be defined as the ability to cope with the complexity of environmental stress. Equilibrium is inherently unstable. It is constantly being disrupted by the sheer pressure of events. There are, therefore, no completed states, there is only statecraft. And there are only two directions, growth or decay.[32] In this context, applying military technology to the task of historical reproduction is equivalent to admitting an inability to cope with the abundance and complexity of political life.

At a time of international crisis, mediation serves the task of cultural and historical reproduction. It rescues the historical moment from the threat of destruction at the hands of a failing political order. Mediation procedures are part of a mature international order. The transmission of historical experience depends a great deal on the success of international politics. International politics is part of the great framework of the world, a mechanism which defines how history and identity are transmitted into the future. Like all forms of life, global society needs mechanisms which ensure that history itself survives the passing of time.

Mediation and questions of agency

Successful mediation protects the world. The world, as Arendt writes, is that which lies 'between people'.[33] It includes material infrastructure and institutions of politics, law, economics and culture. Arendt writes that, 'To live together in the world means essentially that a world of things is between those who have it in common, as a table is located between those who sit around it; the world, like every in-between, relates and separates men at the same time.'[34] In protecting the world, actors affirm their agency and identity on the international stage. As Arendt puts it, 'With word and deed we insert ourselves into the human world, and this assertion is like a second birth, in which we confirm and take upon ourselves the naked fact of our original physical appearance.'[35] Successful international action depends on the development of effective international identity. It is necessary for all international actors to avoid Nietzsche's retort: '"I know not which way to turn; I am everything that knows not which way to turn" – sighs modern man ... Formula of our happiness: a Yes, a No, a straight line, a *goal*.'[36]

The problem is that the philosophical foundations of modern political identities are unsure of themselves. What Nietzsche wrote one hundred years ago is still relevant today: 'The entire West has lost those instincts out of which institutions grow, out of which the future grows.'[37] The project of the European Enlightenment is corrupted with the problems of imperialism, racism, colonialism and the fact that Europe dragged the world into two world wars within the space of fifty years. The great political projects of the Enlightenment, centring around the spheres of religious, political and economic rights, have proven hard enough to enforce within the nation-state, leaving aside the international dimension. Nation-states have enough trouble managing the global economy, without adding international conflict resolution to the burden of responsibilities. It is perfectly possible that the world has outgrown a political capacity to cope, despite the self-confidence manifested in the growth of modern science and technology. And, of course, the great counter-currents of the Enlightenment, specifically the various strands of Marxism, are moribund as political forces and are highly unlikely to revive. Thus, what identities can be developed in the pursuit of effective international agency?

Effective international agency has to be able to accommodate plurality. Plurality refers 'to the fact that men, not Man, live on the earth and inhabit the world'.[38] Through a universalist, abstract and procedural framework, the cosmopolitan tradition seeks to unify diversity and difference within common political traditions. In a later chapter, therefore, we will examine this account of international agency. This ethic may appear to be idealistic. However, in many situations, as we shall see with the case of the Middle East, implementing a cosmopolitan ethic is a profound problem which will require sophisticated political manoeuvring. Invoking the importance of a cosmopolitan ethic is not a woolly exercise in wishful thinking. It is a challenging task for our national and international authorities, a task which will tax the minds of the most adept strategists and tacticians of contemporary diplomacy.

NOTES

1 J. Rothman, *From Confrontation to Cooperation* (London: Sage Publications, 1992), p. 39.
2 J. Habermas, *Legitimation Crisis* (Cambridge: Polity Press, 1992), p. 2.
3 *Ibid.*, p. 3.
4 Rothman, *From Confrontation*, p. 39.
5 Habermas, *Legitimation Crisis*, p. 2.
6 A. Camus, *The Rebel* (London: Penguin, 1971), p. 62.
7 J. Burton, *Violence Explained* (Manchester: Manchester University Press, 1997), p. 114.
8 Rothman, *From Confrontation*, p. 38.
9 I. Clark, *Globalization and Fragmentation: International Relations in the Twentieth Century* (Oxford: Oxford University Press, 1997).
10 A. Linklater and J. Macmillan (eds), *Boundaries in Question: New Directions in International Relations* (London: Pinter Publishers, 1995), p. 12.
11 Clark, *Globalization and Fragmentation*, p. 17.
12 *Ibid.*, p. 4
13 *Ibid.*, p. 66
14 A. G. A. Valladao, *The Twenty-First Century Will be American* (London: Verso, 1996), p. 185.
15 H. Arendt, 'Karl Jaspers: Citizen of the World', in *Men in Dark Times* (New York: Harcourt, Brace and Co., 1968), p. 83.
16 F. Nietzsche, *The Gay Science* (New York: Random House, 1974), section 356.
17 A. Linklater, *The Transformation of Political Community* (Cambridge: Polity Press, 1998), p. 85.
18 H. D. Crone, *Banning Chemical Weapons* (Cambridge: Cambridge University Press, 1992), p. 13.
19 M. Kidron and R. Segal, *The State of the World Atlas* (London: Penguin, 1995), p. 97.
20 E. Hobsbawm, *The Age of Extremes* (London: Abacus, 1994), p. 561.
21 F. Heisbourg, *The Future of Warfare* (London: Phoenix, 1997).
22 Other gases used in WW1 include hydrogen cyanide, phosgene and mustard – which is not a gas but a liquid which disperses vapour. Unlike the other gases, which attack the lungs, mustard destroys any living tissue it touches. Crone points out that it is important to remember that chemical warfare is actually liquid/vapour warfare – see *Banning Chemical Weapons*.
23 *Ibid.*, pp. 22–3.
24 *Ibid.*, p. 74.
25 'The Gulf War Jigsaw', shown on BBC1's *Horizon*, 14 June 98.
26 H. Arendt, *The Human Condition* (Chicago: University of Chicago Press, 1958), p. 6.
27 Arendt, 'The Concept of History', in *Between Past and Future* (London: Penguin, 1977), p. 57.
28 *Ibid.*, p. 62.
29 Hobsbawm, *Age of Extremes*, p. 545
30 Arendt, *The Human Condition*, p. 176.
31 *Ibid.*, p. 53.
32 The distinction between state and uncompleted statecraft is discussed in Richard Devetak,

'Incomplete States: Theories and Practices of Statecraft', in Linklater and MacMillan (eds), *Boundaries in Question*, pp. 19–39.
33 Arendt, 'On Humanity in Dark Times: Thoughts About Lessing', in *Men in Dark Times*, p. 4.
34 Arendt, *The Human Condition*, p. 52.
35 *Ibid.*, p. 176.
36 F. Nietzsche, *The Anti-Christ* (London: Penguin Books, 1990).
37 F. Nietzsche, *Twilight of the Idols* (London: Penguin Books, 1990), section 38.
38 Arendt, *The Human Condition*, p. 24.

3

Geostrategic mediation

THE GEOSTRATEGIC APPROACH to international mediation is the most prominent form of third-party intervention in the recent history of the international world. We can associate this approach with the international activities of the United States in the world order since 1945. Projections of US power across the globe, in the Middle East, South-East Asia and Latin America, are testimony to the existence of a political and economic structure with global reach. This structure exerts huge influence over global economy, trade, communications and culture. This structure has also political mechanisms designed to deal with conflicts which threaten its internal functioning. The US Secretary of State, for example, is a figure who projects American 'muscle' into conflict situations and attempts to manipulate them to suit whatever the current policy in Washington demands.

Mediation, here, is not necessarily an impartial attempt at resolving conflict, although it may have a variety of effects – both negative and positive. Primarily, geostrategic mediation pursues the perceived interest of a global structure of power. In a sense, to use Wallerstein's formulation, mediation is management of the 'periphery' in the interests of the 'core'.[1]

This chapter will analyse the geostrategic view. Often it rests on a belief that the international world is necessarily an unceasing competition for global mastery and power. The argument is that all states are caught in the struggle for power, given that the international system lacks proper government. It follows automatically from this world-view that regional dynamics are the tool of a much greater struggle for survival.

We shall examine the argument that these neo-Darwinist beliefs stem from an intellectual construction rather than from an acute perception of an underlying global reality – that is, geostrategic approaches rest on ideology rather than history. There is scanty evidence for the geostrategic thesis. It is possible to state that neo-realism rests on hunches dressed up as science.

Geostrategic analyses also reify the state and the existing realities and facts of global power. Cultural and historical reproduction in a time of crisis must, however, concern themselves with issues of change at the level of society. Historical and cultural reproduction at a time of crisis should penetrate the 'hard shell' of the state and work with a more diverse social reality, which includes, as Habermas has argued, cultural knowledge, questions of social integration and the socialisation of individual actors. As it never peers beyond the 'hard shell' of sovereignty, geostrategic analysis never really grasps the complex social context in which it works.

The first section of the chapter will deal with the structuralist arguments. The second section will confront the reification of the state and the positivist attention to the existing facts of power. Finally, in the closing section of the chapter, a brief case study will demonstrate geostrategic mediation in action by examining Henry Kissinger's disengagement policy towards Egypt in the 1970s. Kissinger primed a regional conflict with all the tensions of a global Cold War, thus exacerbating a regional conflict which, as a result, remains unresolved to this day.

The critique of the immutability thesis

The subsumption of regional dynamics in favour of a geostrategic struggle for power receives support from the structuralist idea that international politics is a fixed system of power relationships which is incapable of being changed in its fundamental aspects. This argument is admirably summarised by Frost. He writes:

> On this view, the system determines the ideas (including the normative/ethical ones) which people have. Normative theorising can thus not be of any importance; the system operates independently of such theories and itself determines whatever operative normative notions arise.[2]

Kenneth Waltz is the realist thinker most obviously associated with this position. As Waltz puts it:

> Structural constraints cannot be wished away, although many fail to understand this. In every age and place, the units of self-help systems – nations, corporations, or whatever – are told that the greater good, along with their own, requires them to act for the sake of the system and not for their own narrowly defined advantage ... The very problem, however, is that rational behaviour, given structural constraints, does not lead to the wanted results. With each country constrained to take care of itself, no one can take care of the system.[3]

Instability, war and competition do seem to be endemic to international politics. Also, international politics deals with problems on a global scale which, as Waltz argues, seem to defy the efforts to solve them pursued by individual states or actors. And coalitions of states and actors are difficult to build given the free-rider problems involved in the organisation of common endeavour. However, when the arguments are examined, the role of agency in the construction of geostrategic identity is stronger than geostrategic analysis contends. Structures constrain, but they do not determine.

Kenneth Waltz is most obviously associated with the argument for geostrategic international identity. In *The Theory of International Politics* he argues that the global system of competition and power politics is exogenously given by the structure of the international world.[4] According to Waltz, the 'organizing principle' of the global system is anarchy. Change can occur within the international system; the character of the units within the system may change, as may the distribution of capabilities. Fundamentally, however, and as a matter of structural logic and historical fact, no change of the principle of anarchic organisation has ever occurred, nor is it likely to occur in the foreseeable future. The organising principle of the international system forces individual units (states) into a perpetual mode of 'self-help' and will continue to do so. With its opposition of the domestic and the international, fact vs. value, progress vs. *stasis* and so on, structuralism articulates a tragic view of international politics. For Waltz, 'the framework of world politics' is a never-ceasing struggle for global power, mastery and survival.[5]

Geostrategists find confirmation for their ideas in history. While admitting that 'history is considerably more diverse than many realists suppose', Buzan, for example, writes of the 'timeless wisdom of realism'.[6] Buzan peers into history and he also highlights the wars and instability which have followed the end of the Cold War. There he finds correlations between structure and anarchy and argues that they are evidence for the 'timeless' character of realism. Waltz adopts a similar view. He writes:

> Although changes abound, continuities are impressive . . . One who reads the apocryphal book of First Maccabees with events in and after World War I in mind will gain a sense of the continuity that characterizes international politics. Whether in the second century before Christ or in the twentieth century after, Arabs and Jews fought among themselves . . . while states outside of the arena warily watched or actively intervened.[7]

Waltz then goes on to 'cite the famous case of Hobbes experiencing the contemporaneity of Thucydides'.[8]

There are problems with the inductive appeal to history, which attempts to support the 'timeless wisdom' and 'striking sameness' of geostrategic insights. To put the point simply, the basic problem is that there is an almost complete lack of evidence.

The construction of a causal pattern relies on uncovering and documenting a series of confirming instances in discrete aspects of experience.[9] Consider the example of Charles Darwin and how his efforts to prove evolutionary theory took him on HMS *Beagle* to all sorts of exotic locations around the world.[10] There must be some doubt as to whether the geostrategic appeal to patterns in history has cast its 'evidential net' wide enough to document the variety of cases needed to satisfy the inductive canons of evidence, which are needed, in turn, to support a strong causal hypothesis. As Halliday writes of Waltz's arguments, '... it is a-historical, in the sense that it takes as transhistorical, or permanent, features of the system that are the product of, and hence specific to, distinct phases of international relations.'[11]

The fact that geostrategic approaches refer to an enduring and monolithic international structure undermines the appeal to inductive standards of evidence. The latter rely on documenting a variety of observations across time and space and under different evidential conditions. Geostrategic thinking has made it quite clear that history has given us only one form of international relations. But if this is the case, then inductive methods of collecting evidence are undermined. The fact that history may afford only one experience of international relations is a problem for geostrategic identity, not a vindication of it.

The existence of geostrategic competition in the global economic marketplace, or the reality of war in different epochs within international history, may be offered as examples of different sets of circumstances which can be used to support or falsify the hypothesis that there exists some correlational link between an anarchical international structure and geostrategic behaviour.[12] However, the now full-blooded pursuit of the structuralist causal law within existing historical knowledge opens up a whole can of 'philosophy of science' worms.

First, geostrategic analysis would have to account for historical change – the reason why one state of affairs is different from another.[13] This is problematic, as (a) it would contradict the emphasis on stability and uniformity in international history and (b) it opens the door to questions of political agency. To what extent is historical change a result of intentional political change or conscious revolutionary activity, for example?

Second, in approaching historical study with questions of change in mind, the geostrategist confronts problems surrounding the status of his or her own knowledge. How does the geostrategist determine what is to count as a 'similar structure' or 'a different set of circumstances'? The problems stem from the fact that the application of any denotative term is constrained, as philosophers of language have long argued, by intersubjective and not 'monological' criteria.[14] That is to say, an individual consciousness alone does not determine the meaning of a word which is part of a language that he or she has inherited from the past and which is shared with many others. It is a presupposition of meaningful speech that a term, argument or proposition can be warranted and given validity only by appeal to a set of publicly available socially constituted criteria which can be used to assess the argument.[15] Once the intersubjective character of language and consciousness is recognised, however, then the role of human agency in the construction of knowledge and social enquiry moves to the forefront of analysis.

In reply, the structuralist might admit that knowledge of the causal law is always saturated with social and intersubjective values. However, the structuralist might claim that it does not follow that 'real' and determining structures do not actually exist. Waltz believes, as we shall see below, that theory contains an element of 'creativity' and that the 'scientific community' acts as the standard-bearer of acceptable knowledge. Waltz is still a geostrategist, nevertheless. Here, the argument is that knowledge of the structures may well be socially constructed but structures themselves still have an objective existence and continue to determine geostrategic identity behind, as it were, the back of agency.

The structuralist might argue that a similar intellectual process occurs in natural scientific enquiry. The physicist believes in the existence of 'quarks' even though the evidence determining a belief in their existence is inconclusive. The tentative and socially constructed nature of belief does not imply, however, the absence of genuine science.

There is some truth in this line of argument. Scientific knowledge may well be tainted with all sorts of prejudice and still be able to grasp some independent objectivity. As Neufeld writes, 'an interpretive approach does not imply idealism because such an approach recognizes that the process of self-reflection and self-interpretation always takes place *in relation to* a concrete historical context (- material and social).'[16]

The crucial point to be made is that in these circumstances the construction of knowledge ought to be infused with a fallibilistic consciousness. And as we have no definitive proof that structures determine international identity, we cannot, and ought not, rule out the possibility that the geostrategic world-view is just one possible interpretation of the world among many others. The central problem arises – and herein lies the central difference between social and natural science – given the potential effects of structuralist belief on the practice of international politics. The danger is that structuralism will become a self-fulfilling prophecy. Despite a lack of conclusive evidence ruling out the possibility of human agency, an actor has a basic faith in the existence of underlying structures. This faith then shapes his or her perceptions of the international world and the actor then acts in the world as though his or her beliefs are in fact true. At this point structures might as well exist, because social life is determined by them whether they exist or not. This is the strange paradox of reflexivity which effects beliefs about the social world. Critics of geostrategic analysis have long pointed out that neo-realism has always been in danger of becoming an ideology, an article of faith and not knowledge. As Richard Ashley argued, neo-realism always runs the risk of becoming 'an apologia for the status quo'.[17] Conclusive proof pointing to the noumenal existence of anarchical structures is not forthcoming; nor, for that matter, is it ever likely to be.

A second possible relationship between international structure and geostrategic identity relies on the method of meaningful implication. Here the logic of anarchy is a construction of particular meanings and social practices. 'Self-help' is a practice rightly associated with anarchy and self-interested conceptions of 'unit security' are constitutive of the meaning of the term 'anarchy'. 'Self-help' behaviours are the meaningful practices of an anarchical world.

Waltz comes close to articulating this view when he argues that structure causes anarchy through 'socialisation'. Waltz writes:

> A group's opinion controls its members. Heroes and leaders emerge and are emulated. Praise for behaviour that conforms to group norms reinforces them. Socialisation brings members of a group into conformity with its norms... The first way in which structures work their effects is through a process of socialisation that limits and moulds behaviour.[18]

Waltz is on a very 'sticky wicket' when he appeals to socialisation as a force shaping geostrategic identity. If 'socialisation' creates 'self-help', then, as Alex Wendt puts its, 'self-interested conceptions of security are not a constitutive property of anarchy'.[19] In his paper, 'Anarchy is what states make of it', Wendt argues that many different types of social institution and many different types of intersubjectivity could be grafted onto the condition of structural anarchy. A variety of meanings and practices could flourish in an anarchical structure and remain, as it were, meaningful. As Wendt puts it, 'To assume otherwise is to attribute to states in the state of nature qualities that they can only possess in society. Self-help is an institution not a constitutive feature of society.'[20]

Of course, the structuralist might modify the claim and argue that while 'self-help' is not the only meaningful behaviour in the condition of structural anarchy, it is the only behaviour that makes sense. In the absence of government, and in a situation of chronic insecurity, only self-interested behaviour is prudential, although other behaviours may well be meaningful. Thus Waltz uses the metaphor of a 'game', implying that 'self-help' is the right move to make.[21] However, the notion that an actor is playing a 'game', that he or she is being socialised by rules and norms, does imply strong notions of autonomy and responsibility in the generation of international identity.

A final version of the strong relationship between anarchy and self-help is termed the permissive cause. Here, if (a) occurs, then (b) is permitted to happen. This relationship between structure and geostrategic behaviour and practices is put forward by Waltz. As Waltz put it in his earlier work, 'wars occur because there is nothing there to prevent them'.[22] The argument is put forward in another form when Waltz argues that structures act as 'selectors'.[23] Structure allows anarchy and 'self-help' to develop and flourish as it permits/selects this type of behaviour.

This argument makes some sense. The lack of international government or international governance would seem to allow the logic of anarchy to emerge. However, the conditions of geostrategic identity are not determined by this theory. The argument is too weak to rule out a role for differences in agency and identity. If something is permitted to occur by a structure, it does not follow that it will or has to occur. The explanatory leap to 'self-help' behaviours and practices would have to rely on non-structural factors: such as, for example, the foreign policies of particular units within the system or the general understanding of the nature of appropriate international practice prevalent at any one time.

It is still an open question as to whether or not international structures exist. I can find no conclusive evidence that they do in the geostrategic analysis of Kenneth Waltz, the world's sharpest exponent of structuralism in international politics. The argument that individual international actors must adopt geostrategic identities to survive is, therefore, and despite structuralist protestations to the contrary, a moral and existential choice – a intellectual construction resting on autonomy and responsibility. Geostrategists are not forced to sacrifice regional dynamics in favour of a global pursuit of power by the structure of the international system. Rather, this is a foreign policy which they choose to adopt.

History, states and facts

Habermas argues that the historical and cultural reproduction of society takes place across three domains: the store of cultural knowledge, social integration and individual identity. Habermas writes: 'the individual reproduction processes can be evaluated according to standards of the rationality of knowledge, the solidarity of members, and the responsibility of the adult personality.'[24] In a time of crisis, where the reproduction of society breaks down or is threatened, there occurs, correspondingly, a loss of meaning, widespread anomie and a crisis in individual orientation and identity. In this section, the central theme to note is the following: at a time of crisis, historical reproduction via mediation should not focus solely on the 'well-being' of states; rather, mediation has to focus on the transformation of the *society* in question. In its confrontation with the historical moment, in a time of crisis, geostrategic approaches adopt a narrow perspective defined by states and the facts of power. This perspective is then reified into a 'reality' of international life. However, given that the existing state structures may be in question, and that it is the reproduction of society which is at stake, geostrategic models are a symptom of cultural and historical decline. There is no automatic relationship between the reproduction of state structures and the reproduction of society. A critical account of international mediation is needed to determine the relevance of the state.

The geostrategic approach deliberately skirts around the deeper questions of context, justice and identity, which inevitably surround a situation of social, economic and political conflict. As it is forced to subsume regional dynamics under the global view, the geostrategic mediation is necessarily limited in its outlook and scope. A global view is possible only if 'shreds' of regional history are perceived. For example, in its confrontation with the historical moment, the geostrategic view concentrates on the physical manifestations of conflict and tries, in Touval and Zartman's own words, to 'manage' and 'dampen' them by removing 'its violent means and manifestations and by arranging trade-offs among its immediate causes and issues'.[25] The relevant historical 'facts' in the geostrategic analysis are states, manifestations of power and the relations and hierarchies within a competitive political structure. This is the history of international relations and the future of international relations, its 'timeless wisdom' – the very stuff of international history.

But too much history and society is missing from this analysis. If the institutional role of mediation is the historical reproduction of society, geostrategic mediation may leave too much in the past.

Underlying the power-political mediation is an instrumental approach to the social world. Such an approach, as Habermas writes, has 'deeply marked the self-understanding of the modern era'. We see this philosophy of action embodied in the analysis of the great political philosopher of modernity, Thomas Hobbes; we see it in the philosophies of utilitarianism, micro-economic analysis, game theory and neo-realist approaches to international relations. Here, as Habermas writes:

> The realist can confine himself to analyzing the conditions that an acting subject must satisfy in order to set and realise ends. On this model rational actions basically have the character of goal-directed, feedback-controlled interventions in the world of existing states of affairs.[26]

The problem with this approach to the social world is that it ignores what Habermas calls the 'phenomenology of the moral'.[27] The cognitive-instrumental approach to the social world, as Habermas puts it, 'annuls the communicative roles of I and thou, the first and second persons, and neutralizes the realm of moral phenomena. The third-person attitude causes this realm of phenomena to vanish.'[28] Here, political practice becomes 'cut off from the intuitions of everyday life', which draw upon all the symbolic structures of the lifeworld.[29] We might say that politics is depoliticised, except that this depoliticisation is only an illusion.

Geostrategic analyses never peer beyond the boundaries of the state. All the actors in Touval and Zartman's analyses of mediation, for example, are states.[30] The geostrategic approach works with the state-as-actor model. As Richard Ashley writes:

> [n]eorealism is bound to the state. At a minimum, this means that for purposes of theory, one must view the state as an entity capable of having certain objectives or interests and of deciding among them and deploying alternative means in this

service. Thus for the purposes of theory, the state must be treated as an unproblematic unity: an entity whose existence, boundaries, identifying structures, constituencies, legitimations, interests, and capacities to make self-regarding decisions can be treated as a given, independent of transnational class and human interests.[31]

The geostrategist theorist takes the speech and action of the state to be 'sovereign' and bases any subsequent analysis on the clash of sovereign wills. A boundary is drawn around discrete sovereign entities. That which lies inside the boundary is international politics – the proper domain of international theory and practice. That which lies inside the outside is of little or no relevance. The geostrategic approach stops at the boundaries of the state and 'digs' no further in either thought or action. It does not attempt to penetrate what John Herz called the 'hard shell' of the nation-state.[32]

However, conflict is often about the nature and scope of sovereignty; it is not based on a secure and rock-solid sovereignty.[33] To paraphrase Ashley, the state is a 'problematic unity', as conflict often exists, as it were, in an international political no man's land. International theory should not take the sovereign will as the starting point for the theory and practice of conflict resolution where the sovereign will is the point in question in the conflict. Here, there is no sovereign will, it remains to be constructed – and possibly by the mediation itself.

Where there exists a question of sovereignty, the theory and practice of mediation has to move into the contested space with a broader approach to politics and history in mind. Where sovereignty is contested, the theory and practice of mediation has to use a more contextual standpoint to adjudicate between the competing claims in the conflict. Here, conflict resolution is not a matter of instrumentally arranging existing sovereign wills so that they form some kind of balance of power. Conflict resolution is about constructing a sovereign will that is seen to be legitimate in the protagonist's eyes. Unless some kind of legitimacy is restored, conflict will just continue. Legitimacy, however weak and tenuous, is the *sine qua non* of conflict resolution, which recognises the central importance of extending analysis beyond the level of the state.

The fact that geostrategic analysis centres on the state leads Jay Rothman to contend that the geostrategic approach must fail to come to terms with the 'human dimension' of international conflict. Rothman argues for an approach to conflict management that is sensitive to the reality of human purpose and need. Following John Burton, Rothman argues that:

> The roots of most if not all international conflict can be traced to circumstances where the needs of individuals, who have banded together in groups (ethnic, religious, national ideological), are threatened or frustrated. These include needs for dignity, expression, and development of distinctive identity, meaning and purpose, safety control over destiny, and justice, all of which are irreducible and very difficult, if not impossible, for parties to compromise.[34]

Geostrategic mediation

In a geostrategic analysis, history is frozen in a narrow and distorted state. Edward Said, in *The Question of Palestine*, discusses the 1980 Israeli–Egyptian Camp David agreements in these terms. He writes how the agreement reified a contingent set of historical dynamics:

> [t]he essence of this trend has been to shrink the unit of political attention and importance; instead of seeing things in their dynamics wholeness, regimes in the region were encouraged by the United States to see them frozen in their present discreteness. The continuity between things, and the coherence of human life, has been abruptly ruptured as a result.[35]

Said highlights a certain methodological approach to the study of international politics, which 'has rightly been called the ideological bent of social science work that pretends to scientific objectivity, particularly since the advent of the Cold War'. This approach dismisses 'as ahistorical anything that cannot be easily made to fit a particular telos or a particular methodology whose goals are "rational", "empirical" and "pragmatic"'.[36] As Said notes, this literature cheerfully announces its attention to the 'realities' of national security in a global context.

In its confrontation with the historical moment, geostrategic analysis reifies the facts of existing international history. Thus, an already narrow focus on states and the facts of power is transformed into an immutable reality and the power of criticism and change is truncated.

In keeping with much social science that has a relationship to empiricism, and its more ideological offshoot, logical positivism, the geostrategic analysis is dominated by an attempt to impose and operate within a fact/value distinction.[37] According to this view, the ideal theory records the world where the act of recording is devoid of normative concepts. For the geostrategic approach, theory is a relationship between mind and reality, where the former passively observes and records the events and processes of the latter.[38] This empiricist approach to meaning shapes the conduct and scope of enquiry into international mediation. According to the empiricism of geostrategic theory only factual and empirical analysis is meaningful. Value-rational analysis is largely meaningless and mediation theory ought to concentrate on the collection and analysis of the mediation facts.[39]

Touval and Zartman write of the 'empirical base' for their 'theoretical formulations' and of case studies based on 'a context of power politics and cost-benefit calculations'.[40] Mediation theory is properly directed according to the geostrategic view to the identification and analysis of the facts of international political life, which are seen to have the status of objective and independent realities awaiting to be discovered by the neutral, passive and morally disinterested observer.

The problem of assuming too strict a distinction between facts and values has been recognised in the philosophy of science for a number of years.[41]

Recently, critical thinking in the theory of international relations has acknowledged the difficulties. Mark Neufeld writes that the strict fact/value distinction ignores a number of questions: 'They include questions of the historical origin and nature of the community based standards which define what counts as reliable knowledge as well as the question of the meaning of those standards in the light of possible alternatives.'[42]

The ways in which 'facts' can be interwoven with a broader moral and cultural consciousness can be seen if we take an example from the natural sciences. Note that generations of people forgot Aristarchus of Samos and his ancient notion that the earth revolved around the sun.[43] Throughout the Dark and Middle Ages, when classical learning was forgotten in the West, the reality of an earth-centred universe had the status of a fact, or something equivalent, in medieval cosmology. Following Copernicus and Galileo, we now know that heliocentrism is true. Nevertheless, the belief in an earth-centred universe must have appeared unshakeable during those hundreds of intervening years between Aristarchus, Copernicus and Galileo.

The moral of the tale for social enquiry is twofold: first, beliefs about states of affairs which are considered to be true for even hundreds of years – supposed immutable facts which can simply be passively observed – can turn out to be 'true' only because those beliefs are laid down and sanctified by the sediments of preceding social life; second, enquiry into objective realities, though supposedly neutral and disinterested, is necessarily politically, socially and culturally controversial.

The embeddedness of factual enquiry in broader social and moral consciousness means that, often, facts have a politically charged status. Galileo was brought before the inquisition in the 1630s because his scientific opinions contradicted Holy Scripture and undermined the political, religious and cultural authority of the Catholic Church.[44] Of course, disputes about the nature of mediation are unlikely to be of such world-shattering importance. Nevertheless, it is important to remember that supposedly disinterested factual enquiry can be laced with normative and ideological meanings which are open to fierce criticism.

Fred Halliday writes that empiricism needs to be rethought as '[t]he facts are myriad and do not speak for themselves'.[45] The point is that the meaning of enquiry is a question that goes beyond the act of enquiry itself. We may wonder what the role and place of factual enquiry is in the context in which it is embedded. Critical approaches in the theory of international relations recognise that self-reflection is needed to uncover the political status of knowledge. Andrew Linklater writes that, 'critical theory collapses the subject/object distinction and emphasises the human needs and purposes which determine what counts as valuable knowledge'.[46] Valuable theory attempts to make explicit the often deep-rooted moral and analytical assumptions on which it is based. Mark Neufeld writes that 'answering the question "what do the facts mean?" requires a move to a higher [and deeper] level of abstraction'.[47]

Kenneth Waltz – our archetypal geostrategist – is aware that 'the facts are myriad and do not speak for themselves'. He argues, echoing Halliday, that:

> facts do not speak for themselves, because associations never contain or conclusively suggest their own explanation. The idea of 'knowledge for the sake of knowledge' loses its charm and indeed its meaning, once one realizes that the possible objects of knowledge are infinite.[48]

Despite the acknowledgement of the problems of fact and value, Waltz's understanding of the significance of facts is not as developed as that articulated by a more critical understanding.

First, Waltz judges the significance of 'normal science' using utilitarian standards of prediction and control. He writes, 'the question, as ever with theories, is not whether the isolation of a realm [of reality] is realistic, but whether it is useful. And usefulness is judged by the explanatory and predictive power of the theory that may be fashioned.'[49] There is a basic problem with this argument. The criterion of 'usefulness', measured in terms of predictive and explanatory power, ignores the critical-cognitive interest in freedom and emancipation. This, too, can be used to assess the validity and significance of a claim to understanding.

Second, Waltz's analysis does not emphasise the social and intersubjective character of the judgements which determine the significance of theories. Casting doubt on the method which emphasises the inductive collection of facts, Waltz asks himself how theories are made: he answers; '[t]he best, but unhelpful answer is this: creatively... The longest process of painful trial and error will not lead to the construction of a theory unless at some point a brilliant intuition flashes.'[50] Here, the creative and interpretive elements of theoretical understanding are explained in a highly individualistic manner and acts of interpretation appear as bolts from the blue. The influence of the sediment of understanding laid down by previous generations or by the prevailing cultural climate on the process of 'normal science' is obscured in this analysis. Every act of interpretation becomes, implausibly, a transcendence, an act of genius. Waltz's understanding would obscure the way in which international politics is formed as an idea in the minds of social movements: for example, nationalism or Marxism.

Third, where Waltz does recognise the importance of the prevailing cultural values embedded in the understanding of a community, he relies on the judgements of experts. He writes that 'some part of the scientific community has to decide whether enough of an empirical warrant exists to give a theory credibility'.[51] The problem with this view in terms of international politics is twofold. First, judgements about the latter ought to be part of the public domain. Thus, whether an understanding is significant or not does not depend solely on the judgement of the 'scientific community' – whatever this might mean in the case of international relations theory. Second, and to repeat a point, interpretations about international politics are not generated only by the scientific community. More plausibly, the 'scientific community' is influenced by a wider social and cultural consciousness. The idea of a nation-state, for example, was not formed in the minds of contemporary theorists of international relations.

Waltz acknowledges the problems associated with the fact/value distinction and the way in which deeper forces operate to shape enquiry. However, his understanding of the way in which reality is interpreted and constructed is deeply flawed.

Writing about peace processes needs a good dose of theoretical self-consciousness. Explicit value judgements can often masquerade as the facts of a 'problem-solving' 'normal science' thus lending illegitimate support to contentious beliefs about the essence of history. Here, the fact/value distinction becomes dangerous, as it merges with the realms of intentional or unintentional political ideology. In the case of Touval and Zartman, we can see that this danger is a real one.[52] They write of US mediation in the politics of the Middle East. However, the supposedly neutral or factual case study – the US has 'mediated' between Israel and the Palestinians and it 'mediated' in Lebanon in the 1980s – is, as we shall see, a highly contestable, historical value judgement. There is considerable evidence that US policy is deliberately skewed in particular directions in the Middle East and that the USA is a key player with strong interests of its own.[53] If this is the case, are we talking about genuine mediation?

Waltz attempts to rebut the charge that geostrategy could reify a state of affairs and become mere ideology. He writes:

> [h]ow can theory have these effects? A theory applies only so long as the conditions it contemplates endure in their essentials. If the anarchy of international politics were to give way to a world hierarchy, a theory of international politics would become a theory about the past.[54]

Waltz's rebuttal is flawed. If theory becomes sufficiently rooted in society then it can influence wider society, and become an ideology. There is an example of a theory which endured despite the fact that the 'conditions it contemplated' contradicted it. This theory was the belief in an earth-centred universe. Waltz should say that a theory is supposed to apply 'so long as the conditions it contemplates ensures their essentials', not that it does.

While the difficulties surrounding the notion of factuality have to be recognised, it is important to be aware of one crucial qualification to the general argument: recognising the importance of interpretation and opinion in the generation of social enquiry is not the same as denying the existence of facts altogether. Facts do have a certain status. We would not, as the political philosopher Hannah Arendt once argued, wish to deny that Germany invaded Belgium in

1914.[55] Such an argument would be absurd. More dangerously, it would be an attempt to change the face of history. Facts are important in all sorts of ways. Without facts, how would a court of law or a jury ever decide the rights or wrongs of a legal case? How, as a society, could we ever administer justice?[56] There is such a thing as factual reality – that which is obvious and cannot be reasonably denied. The problem is to balance this type of concern with a recognition of the value-laden character of much social enquiry.

Perhaps we should say, along with Habermas, that in the course of factual enquiry we make a claim which, referring to an external world, aspires to descriptive validity or truth.[57] With the concept of 'descriptive validity claims' three things become possible: facts maintain their status as 'accurate descriptions of an external world', all descriptions are fallible and are open to revision, and the meaning of factual enquiry can be determined by a philosophical self-consciousness which views that enquiry in the light of broader human interests.

In the preceding two sections we have reached three important conclusions. First, geostrategic identity is a moral and political commitment not a natural response to an underlying reality of anarchy in international relations. Second, the process of historical and cultural reproduction at the international level has to look further than the state. The reproduction of *society*, not states, is the task of international politics. States only exist to serve the societies they control, they are not ends in themselves. There is no automatic relationship between the reproduction of state structures and the reproduction of society. Criticism is needed to link the former to the latter. Third, geostrategic analyses reify the existing facts of power and do not attempt critically to reproduce society in the act of historical reproduction. In geostrategic analysis, an already narrow perspective is reified into an immutable reality. If the purpose of international mediation is the historical reproduction of a society in crisis, geostrategic approaches, by sacrificing or ignoring regional dynamics and by reifying existing power relations, leave too much behind.

We can see the problems caused by geostrategic analysis and its effect on regional conflict when we turn to US mediation in the Middle East in the 1970s.

Geostrategy in the Middle East

In the modern period, the Middle East has been the focus of geostrategic rivalry since 1786, when Napoleon's revolutionary army invaded Egypt only to be evicted by the British a few years later. Historically, much of the Middle East is in the path of giants. A US geographer Colbert C. Held puts it like this:

> Located at the tricontinental hub of Europe, Asia, and Africa, the Middle East possesses unique geopolitical significance. It is the cradle of civilization, birth place of the three great monotheistic religions, crossroads of movement and trade, base of extensive empires, resource area for 67 percent of the world's petroleum, home to

241.5 million people in sixteen countries, fountain of political and ideological ferment, and locus of some of the most persistently explosive conflicts since World War II.[58]

Analysis disagrees as to whether all the significant international events in the region are determined completely from the outside. Historian Bernard Lewis, for example, argues that Napoleon's invasion of Egypt:

> began a period during which ultimate power, and with it responsibility, for what happened in this region resided elsewhere; when the basic theme of international relations and of much else in the Middle East was shaped by the rivalries of non-Middle Eastern states.[59]

Similarly, Chomsky would claim that superpower involvement in the region was, and remains, determinative. For Chomsky, the principles governing 'world orders, old and new' in many parts of the globe remain essentially the same: 'the rule of law for the weak, the rule of force for the strong; the principles of "economic rationality" for the weak, state power and intervention for the strong.'[60]

Other writers claim a greater degree of autonomy for the regional dynamic. Sayigh and Shlaim write, for example, that 'Middle East specialists . . . tend to assign much weight to local forces'.[61] In favour of this view, one could point to the fact that neither Egypt nor Syria seems to have informed the Soviet Union about the October 1973 attack on Israel,[62] – and this, despite the likely global repercussions of a military defeat for Israel. Thus, for Sayigh and Shlaim, local powers 'are at least as likely to manipulate outside powers as they are to be manipulated by them'.[63] Determining the exact autonomy of regional powers is beyond the scope of the present enquiry. Whatever the balance between regional and global factors, the following analysis should prove that geostrategic considerations are frequently the driving force behind events.

Consider the geostrategic mediation conducted by Henry Kissinger in the Middle East in the early 1970s. By viewing conflict in the Middle East through the lens of superpower rivalry, Kissinger, elevated Israel to the position of strategic asset to America. As a result, all the tension, conflict and friction of the global Cold War became concentrated on the conflicting politics of a region.

At a theoretical level, Kissinger argues that diplomacy is the manipulation of a hostile international environment. As an academic, he sought to portray the virtues of the Austrian Foreign Minister Prince Metternich, architect of the Congress of Vienna and restorer of the conservative values of the *ancien régime*. For Kissinger, 'diplomacy can achieve a great deal through the proper evaluation of the forces of international realities and their skilful utilisation'.[64] In his memoirs, Shimon Peres writes that Kissinger's conversation comprised 'predictions of imminent or global catastrophe coupled with accounts of his own virtuoso diplomacy'.[65] Kissinger maintains that international security is achieved through a concert of Great Powers, which can create regional power balances in unstable regions across the globe.[66]

The 1967 war rendered Israel a strategic asset to the United States in the Middle East. Under pressure from events in Vietnam, the 'Nixon Doctrine' recognised that the United States would have to call on the help of regional allies to protect perceived US geostrategic interests.[67] Valladao describes the substance of this idea: 'The nascent world democratic empire requires all the states within it to make a large contribution to the organisation of collective defence, with the American president as the legitimate commander in chief.'[68] By defeating Egypt and Syria in the Six-Day War, Israel weakened Soviet influence in the region, revealed the weakness of the nationalist Arab states and demonstrated to a potential superpower patron how a regional power could defend US interests without actually risking American lives.

The first test of Israel's new role came during 'Black September' (1970). When Russian-built Syrian tanks crossed the border to aid Palestinians being massacred by King Hussein's Jordanian army, Hussein requested help from he USA. Kissinger convinced Nixon that direct US intervention would be 'difficult to manage' and so he called upon Israel to deal with the regional operation on behalf of the superpower. A 'quart' of Israeli jets flew over the Syrian tanks causing them to retreat rapidly. As Efraim Karsh writes, 'Nixon was elated. Without firing a shot the US had helped defeat two Soviet allies – Syria and the PLO – and underscored the merits of association with the West.'[69]

Kissinger's aim following the Arab defeat in 1967 was to prise Soviet communism and Arab nationalism apart by demonstrating to the Arab states that peace and the return of captured territory could only be achieved with the help of Washington. Kissinger described the plan like this: 'we are trying to get a Middle East settlement in such a way that the moderate regimes are strengthened and not the radical regimes. We are trying to expel the Soviet military presence.'[70] In a report to a Senate Foreign Relations Committee in the late 1970s, Kissinger described his thinking in the following terms: 'The geopolitical equilibrium must be maintained lest radical forces hostile to the West gain such momentum that they appear the irresistible wave of the future.'[71]

The geostrategic approach demanded that stalemate and procrastination in negotiations following the Six-Day War would continue until, as Kissinger put it, 'some Arab state showed a willingness to separate from the Soviets'. Thus Bailey, in a detailed diplomatic history of the time, records Kissinger's attempts to prevent diplomatic momentum in the two years immediately following the Six-Day War.[72] For example, Kissinger stalled a US State Department initiative which aimed to construct a political settlement between Israel and the Arab states based on the concept of land for peace embodied in UN Security Council Resolution 242. What eventually became the Rogers Plan was delayed by Kissinger for ten months, to be finally published in December 1969. Heikel writes:

Cosmopolitan mediation?

Rogers strongly believed that peace in the Middle East was essential to American interests, and wanted to seek a comprehensive Arab–Israeli agreement. Another group of officials saw the conflict as an aspect of superpower relations, and wanted that perspective to dictate US policy. Henry Kissinger was the leading perspective of the second group.[73]

At this time, Egypt was engaged in the War of Attrition with Israel and had called upon Soviet technical and military assistance to prevent Israeli air raids deep into Egyptian territory, raids which threatened civilian populations and the Soviet-built Aswan dam. These developments lifted the tension from the regional to the superpower level, thus aiding Kissinger's attempts to control Middle East policy at the expense of Rogers and the State Department.

In 1971, the Americans received various peace offers from President Sadat, offering, for example, to reopen the Suez canal in return for a partial Israeli withdrawal eastward across the Sinai. The Israeli Premier, Golda Meir, blocked Defence Minister Moshe Dayan's wish to respond positively to such proposals. Meir intended to hold on to all the territory captured during the 1967 war.

Kissinger informed Sadat that he could gain more leverage against Israel in the context of an international crisis.[74] Sadat had to act to regain the Sinai; the status quo was an intolerable position for a leader whose power was legitimated through nationalism. Accordingly, Sadat planned, with Syria, to attack Israel. As the War of Attrition escalated into the Yom Kippur War of October 1973, Kissinger had the opportunity to pursue his geopolitical policy and remove Egypt from Soviet influence and Arab nationalism for good.

Bailey writes that Kissinger saw his task after October 1973 as twofold: to stop the fighting before either side gained a decisive advantage, and to use the upheaval to get the diplomacy started.[75] The aim was to ensure that the necessary diplomacy would move via Kissinger's mediation. Kissinger feared that events would prompt a greater role for the UN. Abba Eban and the US Ambassador Jo Scali were told to procrastinate at the UN, and Kissinger became angry when Israeli propaganda claimed that Israeli forces were heading towards Damascus, as he believed that this would create greater international interest in the post-war diplomacy.[76] Kissinger managed the military situation in order to keep control of events. He delayed shipments of arms and supplies to Israel in order to prevent a decisive victory. And when a proposal for ceasefire and standfast was rejected by Egypt, Kissinger urged Israel to step up its military offensive and the US airlift to Israel was accelerated. On the 31 October 1973, the Israeli cabinet agreed to General Ariel Sharon's plan to cross the Suez canal and encircle the Egyptian Third Army. With Israel's troops only hours from Cairo, and in the face of yet another military defeat for Egypt, Sadat, via the Soviets and Kissinger, sued for peace.

In the negotiations which followed the end of the war, Kissinger was successful in wooing Sadat into the peace process sponsored by the US. As Adel Safty has documented, Sadat believed that Washington alone could bring the Sinai back under Egyptian control. This tactical belief was supplemented by a broader strategic vision. Karsh writes that, '[t]he two [Sadat and Kissinger] shared a strategic vision predicated on weakening the influence of, and ideally the exclusion of, the Soviet Union from Middle Eastern affairs'.[77] The cornerstone of this policy was the disengagement agreements of 1974 and 1975 – Sinai I and II. It is at this point that the long-term consequences of Kissinger's frantic Middle East mission of the early 1970s emerge into the light.

Sinai II (September 1975) is interesting, as it contains a specific set of 'United States–Israeli Assurances' which solidified Israel's role as a strategic asset to the global superpower. The USA agreed to be 'fully responsive' to Israel's military and defence needs. It also agreed to vote against any Security Council Resolution which, in its judgement, adversely affected the agreement – thus lifting, in a sense, the US–Israeli relationship above the concerns of international law. The US also agreed, rather vaguely, 'to seek to prevent efforts by others to bring about considerations of proposals which it and Israel agree are detrimental to the interests of Israel'. Finally, the USA agreed not to recognise the PLO as long as the latter did not recognise either Israel's right to exist or UN Security Council Resolution 242. This being the case, despite the fact that Resolution 242 does not actually refer to Palestinians, Israel has no internationally recognised borders and Golda Meir informed Kissinger in 1973 that Resolution 242 was irrelevant.[78]

Sinai I and II laid the foundations for the Camp David Accords of September 1978, which effected the final removal of Egypt from the wider Arab–Israeli equation. In a sense, the Camp David order, with its provisions for Palestinian 'autonomous zones' in the West Bank and Gaza, exists to this date. Sinai I and II, plus Camp David and now the Oslo Accords, define the broad contours of the negotiated settlement of the Israeli–Palestinian conflict.

In 1974, Nixon ordered $4.4 billion worth of military support to be given to Israel as part of the post-war settlement. As Karsh notes, in the following decades US support for Israel stabilized at around $3 billion per annum.[79] Around half of this sum is spent on the military. Said claims that the total in aid given to Israel between 1967 and 1991 was $77 billion.[80] This financial support and the cementing of the US–Israeli strategic alliance came at a time when Israeli politics took a dramatic turn to the right. May 1977 saw the rise of Likud to power in Israel. Led by Menachim Begin, Likud referred (and refer) to the West Bank by the biblical names Judea and Samaria or 'liberated territories'. This government was also responsible for the terrorist war in Lebanon in 1982. As Said notes, Carter, who came to power in January 1977, 'was the first president to have spoken seriously, albeit rather distractedly, of the Palestinian people'.[81] However, Carter was frustrated by the Likud government and did not support Egyptian proposals for a Palestinian state at Camp

David.[82] Any further progress on this issue became highly unlikely as the 1970s drew to a close. The Islamic revolution in Iran (February 1979), coupled with the Soviet invasion of Afghanistan (December 1979), led to a second Cold War. The Reagan administration, which defined the whole crusading tenor of western international politics in the 1980s, adopted, as Karsh writes, an 'even more Soviet-centric approach'.[83] Again, from the point of view of the mediating power, the regional dynamics became sacrificed in favour of a global vision. The groundwork laid down by Kissinger's Cold War policy proved to be the cornerstone of a long-term policy commitment. Karsh continues:

> A circle had been closed. Within less than two decades, Israel had managed to transform herself from an embarrassing political and strategic liability into a prominent ally of the US in the Middle East, enjoying a multifaceted and institutionalized relationship.[84]

But this geostrategic mediation causes problems at the regional level. By elevating Israel to the position of strategic asset, and by removing Egypt from the balance of power in the wider Israeli–Arab conflict, Kissinger's geostrategic foreign policy encouraged those forces in the region that were opposed to national rights for the Palestinian people. Chomsky claims that this was the direct intention of the policy.[85] It is hard to say whether this is true. However, with hindsight, interpreting the Israeli–Palestinian issue in geostrategic terms meant that questions of global security became focused on the activities of relatively powerless regional actors such as the PLO. Concessions to the PLO were perceived as having adverse impacts on global security. This macro-perception makes political progress at the regional level infinitely more difficult and challenging.

Furthermore, within the Sinai framework and the Camp David Accords, a partial withdrawal from territory which Israel conquered in 1967 was legitimized, enabling Israeli politicians to claim, to this day, that the provisions of UN Security Council Resolution 242 have been fulfilled.[86] Although Kissinger's policy 'ate away' only at the often illusory structures of Arab unity, the balance of power in the region tilted decisively in Israel's favour with the removal of Egyptian power and the continued and massive economic and military support granted to Israel by its geostrategic patron. The possibility of a broader equality of power is replaced by a complex and intricate network of elite agreements representing narrow interests and held in check by the military balance. As Said writes:

> In the Middle East today, common interests have come therefore to be perceived as part not of a larger integrated picture, but of a narrow bilateralism allying minorities – minority governments and small communities of minorities – with one another, for their own preservation.[87]

Where societies fragment, there is a crisis in historical reproduction. War, instability and conflict have the potential simply to remove great chunks of experience from the flow of history. Parts of the past are prevented from appearing in the future. In this context, mediation serves the task of historical reproduction. In a globalised world, where the forces of fragmentation can travel down networks of power and communication, it is likely that outside powers will be drawn into regional conflicts.

However, these powers must place the regional dynamics first and not see the conflict as a tool of wider geopolitical strategy. By viewing regional conflict as part of a wider geopolitical battle, regional tensions are exacerbated and not relieved. This proposition is proven when Kissinger's policies towards Israel in the early 1970s are examined. All the tensions associated with the great ideological battle of modern history were 'pumped' into a regional conflict.

There is no real evidence to support the view that the structure and nature of international politics forces a geostrategic identity. History is reduced to a set of simple axioms and this undermines the diversity needed to satisfy inductive canons of evidence. Geostrategic identity is a social and intellectual construction as much as it is a rational response to a so-called underlying reality of global structural instability. A gap opens up, therefore, for a form of mediation which does not just reify existing realities, powers and states. There is room for an approach to mediation which aims critically to transform historical experience. In the next chapter, we shall examine one such approach – the facilitative approach to international mediation. While this approach prides itself on its regional and contextual focus, we shall see that the problem of historical and cultural reproduction at a time of crisis remains.

NOTES

1 See, for example, I. Wallerstein *The Modern World System, I: Capitalist Agriculture and the Origins of the European World-Economy in the Sixteenth Century* (New York: Academic Press, 1974).
2 M. Frost, *Ethics in International Relations* (Cambridge: Cambridge University Press, 1996) p. 54.
3 K. Waltz, 'Anarchic Orders and Balances of Power', in R. Keohane, *Neorealism and its Critics* (New York: Columbia University Press, 1986) p. 106.
4 K. Waltz, *The Theory of International Politics* (Reading, Mass.: Addison Wesley, 1979).
5 K. Waltz, 'Man, the State and War', excerpts reprinted in H. Williams, M. Wright and T. Evans (eds), *A Reader in International Relations and Political Theory* (Buckingham: Open University Press, 1993), p. 220.
6 B. Buzan, 'The timeless wisdom of realism?', in S. Smith, K. Booth and M. Zalewski (eds), *International Theory: Positivism and Beyond* (Cambridge: Cambridge University Press, 1996), p. 60.
7 Waltz, 'Reductionist and Systemic Theories', in Keohane (ed.), *Neorealism*, p. 53.
8 *Ibid.*

9 For a discussion of basic issues in the philosophy of science, see A. F. Chalmers, *What is this Thing Called Science?* (Buckingham: Open University Press, 1980).
10 As the editor's Introduction to *The Origin of Species* puts it, '[t]he Origin has a scope and sweep which an age of specialists can scarcely hope to recapture; it is a vast panorama of the natural world written by a polymath in the biological sciences: geologist, zoologist, palaeotologist, botanist and pigeon fancier' (Penguin edition, 1985).
11 F. Halliday, *Rethinking International Relations* (London: Macmillan, 1994), p. 33.
12 Waltz, for example, often uses the example of the firm in the economic marketplace. He writes, '[j]ust as economists define markets in terms of firms, so I define international-political structures in terms of states' ('Political Structures', in Keohane (ed.), *Neorealism*, p. 88.
13 See, J. G. Ruggie, 'Continuity and Transformation in the World Polity: Towards a Neorealist Synthesis', in Keohane (ed.), *Neorealism*.
14 L. Wittgenstein, *Philosophical Investigations* (Oxford: Blackwell, 1953). Wittgenstein follows the logic of Descartes's *cogito* and argues that there cannot be a radically private experience. Of course, the arguments are complicated. However, the basic idea is that there must be an external 'thing' to which mind, when thinking or speaking, refers. And if thought of language necessarily refers to something external to itself, then the act of reference can be checked for its veracity. Although Descartes can doubt the existence of many things external to thought the existence of trees, for example – he cannot doubt the existence of mind itself. From this foundation, Descartes constructs a rationalist, mathematically based knowledge, which, being external to thought, can be used to assess the truth of thought. Wittgenstein argues, in his refutation of solipsism, that speech must presuppose the independent existence of that to which it refers. Meaning would break down if there was no difference between using a term correctly and incorrectly.
15 Habermas articulates these arguments. He writes of uncovering 'the general presuppositions of communication'. Habermas writes, 'anyone acting communicatively must, in performing any speech action, raise universal validity claims and suppose that they can be vindicated. At the very least, a speaker must accept the following: (a) that he/she is uttering something understandable; (b) that he/she is giving the hearer something to understand; (c) that he/she is making her- or himself understandable; and (d) that he/she is aiming to come to an understanding with another person'. ('What is Universal Pragmatics?' in *Communication and the Evolution of Society* (London: Heinemann, 1979), p. 2.) We shall examine the political significance of these arguments in chapter five.
16 M. Neufeld, *The Restructuring of International Relations Theory* (Cambridge: Cambridge University Press, 1995), p. 80. My emphasis.
17 R. K. Ashley, 'The Poverty of Neorealism', *International Organization*, 38 (1984), p. 257.
18 Waltz, 'Reductionist and Systemic Theories', p. 65.
19 A. Wendt, 'Anarchy is what States Make of it: The Social Construction of Power Politics', *International Organisation*, 46:2 (1992) p. 396.
20 *Ibid.*, p. 402.
21 In Keohane (ed.), *Neorealism*, p. 64.
22 K. Waltz, *Man, the State and War* (New York: Columbia University Press, 1959), p. 232.
23 Waltz, 'Reductionist and Systemic Theories', p. 62.
24 J. Habermas, *The Theory of Communicative Action, Vol. 2: The Critique of Functionalist Reason* (Cambridge: Polity Press, 1989), p. 141.
25 S. Touval and W. I. Zartman, 'International Mediation: Conflict Resolution and Power Politics', *Journal of Social Issues*, 41:2 (1985), p. 44.
26 J. Habermas, *The Theory of Communicative Action Vol. 1* (Cambridge: Polity Press, 1991), pp. 11–12.

27 J. Habermas, 'Discourse Ethics', in *Moral Consciousness and Communicative Action*, (Cambridge: Polity Press, 1990), p. 45.
28 Ibid., p. 47.
29 Ibid., p. 48.
30 The main players in the case studies analysed by Touval and Zartman being the USSR, India, Pakistan, Algeria, Iran, Iraq, America, Great Britain and Rhodesia.
31 R. K. Ashley, 'The Poverty of Neorealism', in Keohane (ed.), *Neorealism*, p. 268.
32 J. H. Herz, 'The Rise and Demise of the Territorial State', *World Politics*, 9:4 (1958) pp. 473–93.
33 For example, Touval and Zartman look at the India–Pakistan conflict over the Kashmir province. The writers admit that '[b]oth sides regarded Kashmir as an issue touching upon the legitimising principle of their statehood' ('International Mediation', p. 28). However, they fail to see that this admission undermines their realist analysis. The dispute is not based on conflicting sovereign wills, it is about the construction of legitimate sovereignty. If sovereignty does not yet exist, then the opposition of the international and domestic breaks down. The mediator is not interfering in the sovereign domain of another state by getting involved in the conflict. In theory and practice, there is space and room to dig deeper than the power-political idea of 'immediacy' would allow.
34 J. Rothman, *From Confrontation to Cooperation* (London: Sage Publications, 1992), p. 46.
35 E. Said, *The Question of Palestine* (London: Vintage, 1979) p. 171.
36 Ibid., p. xxxxiii.
37 Michael Nicholson, a defender of positivism in international relations, writes: '[p]ositivism provides a demarcation between what is scientific and what is not. Of particular concern is morality. In itself, positivism concerns what is, not what ought to be, and, furthermore, it is argued that it is important to distinguish between the two . . . A positivist argues that empirical statements are value-neutral, certainly in the sense of moral values.' Nicholson is keen to stress that positivists are not amoral. They may have moral motivations that prompt them towards their empirical enquiries. Despite this, positivism asserts that moral considerations ought not to interfere with the process of judging and interpreting the world ('The Continued Significance of Positivism', in Smith et al. (eds), *Positivism and Beyond*, pp. 140–1).
38 A classic articulation of this view can be found in the writing of John Locke. Locke believed that all our ideas, including space, time, number, infinity and causality, are built upon the simple ideas obtained through perception. He writes: 'the Materials of all our Knowledge, are suggested and furnished to the Mind, only by those two ways above mentioned, *viz. Sensation and Reflection*. When the Understanding is once stored with these simple Ideas, it has the Power to repeat, compare, and unite them even to an almost infinite Variety, and so can make at Pleasure new complex *Ideas*. But it is not in the Power of the most exalted Wit, or enlarged Understanding, by any quickness or variety of Thought, *to invent or frame one new simple* Idea in the mind'. (*An Essay Concerning Human Understanding* (Oxford University Press, 1975), Book II, Chapter II, section 2).
39 The view that morality should stay out of the judgement of the social world is parodied in the speech of James Harthouse in Dickens's *Hard Times*. Harthouse says: '[t]he only difference between us and the professors of virtue or benevolence, or philanthropy – never mind the name – is, that we know it is all meaningless, and say so; while they know it equally and will never say so.' Of course, the truth is not much stranger than fiction. A. J. Ayer's *Language, Truth and Logic*, the foundation of modern logical positivism, expresses similar ideas. Ayer believes that 'one never does really dispute about questions of value'. He adds, echoing Harthouse's remarks, that 'it is because argument fails us when we come to deal with pure questions of value, as distinct from questions of fact, that we finally resort

to mere abuse' (*Language, Truth and Logic* (London: Penguin, 1990), pp. 114–15. First published in 1936 by Victor Gollanz).
40 Touval and Zartman, 'International Mediation', pp. 27–45. As Michael Nicholson writes, 'there are a host of papers in the Journal of Conflict Resolution . . . where formal models are analysed, or quantified relationships studied, and where the whole ethos is one of firm positivism' ('The Continued Significance of Positivism', p 128). I aim to cast doubt on the ethos of 'firm positivism' in the study of conflict resolution.
41 See, for example, Thomas Kuhn's *The Structure of Scientific Revolutions* (Chicago: University of Chicago Press, 1962). Kuhn criticises the idea that scientific development proceeds through the accumulation of facts, techniques and knowledge. For Kuhn, the interpretive judgements, even the faith, of the scientific community are interwoven and constitute judgements about reality. These serve to create 'normal science' over a period of time. Periods of 'normal science' are transformed in revolutionary situations where old and anomalous paradigms are replaced. There are those who stand outside the new paradigms. As Kuhn writes, though, 'the man who continues to resist after his whole profession has been converted has *ipso facto* ceased to be a scientist' (p. 159).
42 Neufeld, *Restructuring*, p. 42.
43 Aristarchus of Samos was born in 310 BC. The treatise in which Aristarchus proclaimed that the sun not the earth was the centre of the universe is now lost. 'The fact that Aristarchus taught the heliocentric system is unanimously accepted by the ancient sources and modern scholars' (A. Koestler, *The Sleepwalkers* (London: Penguin, 1988), p 51. The book was first published by Hutchinson in 1959).
44 Koestler's book, *The Sleepwalkers* (London: Penguin, 1988), attacks the distinction between the sciences and the humanities. He writes, for example, in the preface, how the men of modern science in 'their cosmic quest destroyed the medieval vision of an immutable social order in a walled-in universe together with its fixed hierarchy of moral values, and transformed the European landscape, society, culture, habits, and general outlook, as thoroughly as if a new species had arisen on this planet' (p. 9).
45 Halliday, *Rethinking*, p. 25.
46 A. Linklater, 'The achievements of critical theory', in Smith et al. (eds), *Positivism and Beyond*, p. 281.
47 Neufeld, *Restructuring*, p. 2.
48 Waltz, 'Laws and Theories', in Keohane (ed.), *Neorealism*, p. 31.
49 Ibid., p. 36.
50 Ibid., pp. 36–7.
51 Waltz, 'A Response to My Critics', in Keohane (ed.), *Neorealism*, p. 336.
52 Touval and Zartman, 'International Mediation'.
53 See, for example, N. Chomsky, *The Fateful Triangle* (Boston: South End Press, 1983).
54 Waltz, 'A reply to my critics', in Keohane (ed.), *Neorealism*, p. 340.
55 H. Arendt, 'Truth and Politics', in *Between Past and Future* (London: Faber and Faber, 1961).
56 This argument is made by Norman Geras in the paper entitled 'Language, Truth and Justice' published in the book *Solidarity in the Conversation of Mankind* (London: Verso, 1995).
57 Habermas, *The Theory of Communicative Action, Vol. 1*.
58 Colbert C. Held, *Middle East Patters: Places, Peoples, and Politics* (Boulder: Westview, 1994), p. 3.
59 B. Williams, *The Future of the Middle East* (London: Pheonix, 1997), p. 1.
60 N. Chomsky, *World Orders, Old and New* (London: Pluto Press, 1994), p. 271.
61 Y. Sayigh and A. Shlaim, *The Cold War and the Middle East* (Oxford: Clarendon Press, 1997), p. 3.

62 S. D. Bailey, *Four Arab–Israeli Wars and the Peace Process* (London: Macmillan, 1990), p. 310.
63 Sayigh and Shlaim, *The Cold War*, p. 3.
64 Henry Kissinger, *World Restored* (New York:, Grosset and Dunlapy, 1964), p. 322.
65 S. Peres, *Battling for Peace* (London: Orion, 1995) p. 189.
66 H. Kissinger 'Balance of Power Sustained', in G. Allison and G. Treverton (eds), *Rethinking America's Security: Beyond Cold War to New World Order* (New York: W. W. Norton, 1992).
67 Chomsky, *World Orders*, p. 204.
68 A. G. A. Valladao, *The Twenty-First Century Will Be American* (London: Verso, 1986), p. 183.
69 E. Karsh, 'Israel', in Sayigh and Schlaim (eds), *The Cold War*, p. 166.
70 Cited in A. Safty, *From Camp David to the Gulf* (Montreal: Black Rose Books, 1992), p. 46.
71 Cited in J. Z. Rubin (ed.), *Dynamics of Third Party Intervention: Kissinger in the Middle East* (New York: Praeger, 1981), p. 96.
72 Bailey, *Four Arab–Israeli Wars*, p. 287.
73 M. Heikel, *Secret Channels* (London: Harper Collins, 1996), p. 150.
74 *Israel and the Arabs: The Fifty Years War*, BBC2, April 1998.
75 Bailey, *Four Arab–Israel Wars*, p. 310.
76 *Ibid.* pp. 319–20.
77 Karsh, 'Israel', p. 178.
78 Bailey, *Four Arab–Israeli Wars*, p. 285.
79 Karsh, 'Israel', p. 166.
80 Said, *The Question of Palestine*, p. xvii.
81 *Ibid.*, p. 198. Also see Safty, *From Camp David*, p. 62.
82 Heikel writes that 'The new prime minister lost no time in making clear his dislike of Carter's peace initiative, and especially the emphasis on an overall solution on the basis of pre-agreed principles and in the context of a Geneva conference' (*Secret Channels*, p. 251). For further details see Safty, *From Camp David*, pp. 61–4.
83 Karsh, 'Israel', p. 167.
84 *Ibid.*, p. 168.
85 Chomsky, *The Fateful Triangle*, p. 67.
86 Netanyahu writes about Resolution 242 in this way: 'The Sinai peninsula, returned in the context of Israel's peace treaty with Egypt is on the Israeli scale a very substantial piece of property' (*A Place Among the Nations* (New York: Bantam Books, 1993), p. 290).
87 Said, *The Question of Palestine*, p. 170.

4

Facilitation, problem-solving and mediation

THE PROBLEM OF how to construct a form of third-party intervention which will transform a situation of conflict in an emancipatory direction has exercised the minds of researchers into international conflict for more than three decades. In particular, and in the mid-1960s, the Centre for the Analysis of Conflict at University College London brought together a number of now well-known scholars who aimed to apply social scientific techniques and knowledge to real cases of conflict in, for example, Cyprus, Northern Ireland and Sri Lanka. With some reluctance, this group has acknowledged that their 'analytical seminars came to be called "problem-solving workshops", while the modified form of mediation that we employed became the "facilitation" of conflict resolution'.[1] It is this approach to third-party intervention that we shall examine in this chapter.

Thinking critically about this tradition of theory and practice is difficult. Unlike the various forms of power politics, the theory and practice of facilitation does not neglect serious normative considerations altogether. Facilitation rests upon a belief that international politics can be made to resemble the politics of normal democratic states, or the political relations between normal democratic states. Banks and Mitchell, for example, write that their enterprise is informed by the ideals of 'stability, peace, justice, progress and legitimized authority'. In more recent times, the approach has attempted to legitimate its intellectual credentials through alliance with the themes of a philosophically sophisticated form of social research known as 'critical theory'. Researchers in the 'facilitative' tradition now draw upon the work of critical theorists such as Jürgen Habermas, and a tradition of thought and practice emanating from German philosophy and sociology becomes part of the theoretical tool-kit. However, despite the links with, for example, Habermas's version of a 'communicative politics', I wish to maintain the critical pressure on the facilitative approach.

Facilitation theorists concede that facilitation cannot stand on its own in a process of conflict resolution. Mark Hoffman, for example, writes that facilitation is a 'contingent step which is potentially complementary to other third party initiatives'.[2] If this is the case, then this chapter aims to circumscribe the limits of facilitation. Facilitation has to understand its significant and numerous limitations. We shall see the faults of facilitation being reproduced in the Oslo process which led to the Oslo Accords negotiated between the PLO and the Israeli Labour government in 1993. Many of the problems associated with the Oslo Accords occurred because a powerless facilitation process carried the entire burden of a conflict resolution designed to solve one of the twentieth century's most intractable and potentially deadly international conflicts.

There are a number of problems facing the facilitative approach. First, the distinction between understanding and critique means that emancipatory strategies of conflict resolution cannot remain at the level of hermeneutics. Second, the Burtonian focus on need-fulfilment fails to provide an adequate normative or critical standpoint. Third, the appeal to a Habermasean-style 'communicative politics' means that facilitation has to submit to external authority for its validation as a form of emancipatory politics. Fourth, the distinction between interim and final status means that an abstract model of political justice is needed to supplement the facilitative emphasis on incremental, contextual considerations. Fifth, the metaphor of textual understanding does not capture the strategic and instrumental relationships which dominate international negotiations. Sixth, the problem of power asymmetry means that facilitation risks exacerbating or reproducing conflict-causing inequality. In the following sections, we discuss each of these issues in turn.

The argument concludes with a recognition that emancipatory approaches to the topic of third-party intervention, as interpreted through the cosmopolitan idea of a 'dialogic community', are not reducible to the problem-solving workshop. Many facilitation theorists see a link between the problem-solving workshop and cosmopolitan political ideals, such as the notion of a 'dialogic community'.[3] However, given the problems facing the facilitative tradition, there is room, in both theory and practice, for an approach to international mediation, derived from a cosmopolitan political ethic, which transcends both power politics *and* facilitation. To put the point more sharply, from the moral point of view, there may be no difference between the political consequences of facilitation and the political consequences of power politics.

Conflict and the hermeneutic dimension

In his 1995 *Paradigms* paper, 'Defining and Evaluating Success', Mark Hoffman argues that a great deal of contemporary international conflict is defined by one central feature: 'an existential threat by one group or community towards the identity and security of another group'.[4] Here, as Hoffman writes:

> The rising consciousness of ethnic, racial or linguistic identities poses a major challenge to existing social formations. These often legitimate concerns about identity can generate, reinforce and intensify images of 'otherness' which find their expression in self-perpetuating cycles of violent conflict, creating near insurmountable barriers to efforts at fostering a mutually acceptable means of mediating such differences.[5]

Here, as conflict exists in the realm of intersubjective meaning and understanding, so conflict resolution must also exist in this realm. Hoffman writes: '[g]iven the existential features of identity-driven conflicts, successful third party intervention cannot focus simply on the manipulation of power-political interests but most focus on the social-psychological dimension.'[6]

Similarly, Vivienne Jabri writes: 'advocates of facilitated or problem-solving processes suggest that outcomes based on coercive intervention preclude the possibility of long-lasting resolutions to the underlying causes of conflict.'[7] Geostrategic approaches, as we have seen, never really come to grip with the contextual dynamics which fuel protracted social conflicts.

Facilitation theory argues that power-political bargaining takes place in a context of rational instrumental and strategic action, which, despite being governed by atomistic instrumental relationships, is, nevertheless, a shared intersubjective context – a set of common social experiences and expectations. As Mark Neufeld writes:

> What interpretive theorists stress is that those behavioural regularities and those diverging 'subjective meanings' are dependent upon the existence of negotiation as a social practice for their very possibility. Moreover, negotiation, as a social practice, is itself constituted by a specific set of 'intersubjective meanings'.[8]

Even the limited relationships embodied in power politics break down where enhanced group loyalty, selective perceptions of mutual histories and the dehumanisation of the enemy effect the context of rational choice. Where social and symbolic orders stand in the way of a reconstitution of intersubjectivity, the primary ingredient of the mediation process, according to the facilitative approach, is the promotion of relations of empathy and mutual understanding. The intersubjective fabric of the social world needs to be rebuilt before any rational assessment of a political process can take place. Empathy is designed to overcome existential barriers to the reconstitution of intersubjectivity – for example, the demonisation of the other. Understanding is necessary to overcome cognitive barriers. Competing actors learning to reconstitute mutual social practices must respect the identities and social practices of other groups and develop certain carefully refined relationships and political/psychological attitudes towards each other. As Jay Rothman puts it, 'the problem is defined in terms of troubled relationships'.[9] Hoffman writes of the importance of re-creating shattered intersubjectivity through the development of:

relational and analytic empathy, a common identity based on shared experiences; the development of cooperative social interaction; the development and maintenance of positive attitudes [of] fostering communication. [Here] [t]he goal would be to create conditions for the development of effective communication, including the overcoming of rigid stereotyping and a mutual recognition of each party's identity.[10]

Similarly, Rothman writes of the importance of 'analytic empathy'. Here:

parties may come to understand the power and depth of their adversary's motivations, hurts, hopes, and fears and the way their actions are conditioned by them, even if they do not necessarily believe that the other side's feelings and motivations are rational or correct.[11]

Through developing relationships of understanding and empathy, the facilitative approach emphasises that competing actors can take an initial step towards rebuilding shattered intersubjectivity.

As noted above, the facilitative approach to conflict has much in common with the approach to social science rooted in the German interpretive tradition. This approach emphasises understanding and empathy in its approach to the social world, not positivist prediction and control. As Terence E. Cook writes:

Perhaps it is significant that the German word for 'to intend' (*meinen*) has the same root as the German word for meaning (*meinung*). If it is true that intentionality and meaningfulness are inevitable concomitants of human action, or rather alone make 'action' of what otherwise would be mere movements or motions (i.e. behaviour), our subjectivity has to be understood as well as morally guided.[12]

Where meaning cannot be separated from intentionality, intersubjective interpretation and mutual recognition become something like, to use Gadamer's phrase, 'a fusion of horizons'.[13] A number of points are made. First, the infusion of knowledge by context, tradition and history is not a barrier to understanding, but is, on the contrary, a prerequisite to it. Second, understanding cannot escape the historical weight of tradition. Third, since individuals are constituted by history and tradition, the act of understanding is also a process of self-development and formation. Fourth, the act of understanding moves history forward. Fifth, the contingent character of knowledge and interpretation is recognised – here we see that the process of understanding is never fully complete, as it can always be revised in the light of new social experiences. Finally, understanding is not construed solely as a method of approaching a social subject but it is also construed as a way, or prerequisite, of being in the world.[14]

Hoffman echoes these views in his analysis of the basis of facilitation. He writes of the facilitative view that '[i]t takes as its starting point a recognition that our identities are socially and historically constructed and that such identity-frames are central to the causes and dynamics of conflicts'.[15] Here, the interpretive process is seen to be ongoing, constantly evolving and never finalised or closed. As Hoffman puts it, in facilitation, '[s]uccess is no longer defined in terms of a set on unchanging "objective" categories'.[16] Rothman also notes the influence of hermeneutics where 'the researcher reflexively places him- or herself right in the middle of the subject and, acknowledging personal biases, even employing them, seeks to uncover how actors interpret various events and meanings'.[17] Vayrynen creates an approach to third-party facilitation based on the phenomenology of Alfred Shultz.[18]

Given the links between facilitation and the interpretive approach to social science, the problems and dilemmas faced by the latter must throw light on the nature of the former. Jürgen Habermas, as a representative of critical theory, puts forward a significant criticism of the interpretive tradition. He argues that the tradition, context and history which constitute and inform the act of interpretation can be infused with relations of power, exclusion and domination. These types of relation stand opposed to reason and distort or make opaque an understanding of the social world. Beliefs can be revealed to be ideological because they are in some sense, and in some way, mistaken.[19] Interpretivism argues that empiricist approaches to the social world based on prediction and control can distort social interaction. However, critical theory argues that the recognition of the operation of historical context in both subject and object is, in equal measures, insufficient to allow the formation of genuine understanding, as social context can also be infused with relations of power, exclusion, domination and control. As Habermas puts it:

> Authority and knowledge do not converge. Certainly, knowledge is rooted in actual tradition; it remains bound to contingent conditions. But reflection does not wear itself out on the facticity of traditional norms without leaving a trace. It is condemned to operate after the fact; but, operating in retrospect, it unleashes retroactive power. Authority can be stripped of that in which was mere domination and dissolved into the less coercive force of insight and rational decision.[20]

Mervyn Frost puts the point in another way and argues that interpretivism remains 'descriptivist' in using something akin to the fact/value distinctions of positivism. He writes:

> A correct understanding depends on a positivist match between the understandings of the investigator and the self-understanding of the parties. The positive match does not require any series theorising about matters of value on the part of the theorist.[21]

The 'positivist', though interpretivist, leanings of facilitation researchers are revealed in certain comments articulated by Banks and Mitchell. They write, for example, that 'problem solvers must try to eliminate completely the effects of their own previous assumptions and values'.[22] They add, 'the conflict situation defines its own parties and issues'.[23] Third parties may make comments on the progress of a peace process, 'though the comments should be about processes, not about norms or values'.[24] Banks and Mitchell argue that social scientists make better facilitators than area or regional specialists, as the former deal in 'dispassionate theories' and 'formal techniques', while the latter are too involved with the political issues.[25] Perhaps paradoxically, Banks and Mitchell state that 'positivism is a delusion'.[26] They recognise that the third-party facilitator is bound to intervene substantively at some point in the process. However, this conclusion leads Banks and Mitchell to conclude that the third party 'must not act'. Or rather, action should be confined to procedural and not substantive issues. They continue: 'he should avoid making any substantive comment or, particularly, moral judgement upon the characteristics of the parties'.[27] In a similar vein, Vayrynen describes what we might call the retreat of the facilitator. 'In the situation of participant observation', she writes, 'the status of the ... facilitator ... is consciously reduced to a minimum.'[28]

Given these comments, the following question arises: if the facilitator is prohibited from approaching the conflict situation with explicit political commitment or substantial goals in mind, how can the facilitation workshop produce an emancipated world? Is it possible to construct 'stability, peace, justice, progress and legitimized authority' while the practice of facilitation remains, in a sense, amoral – in the realm of 'dispassionate theory' and 'formal technique', where intervention is 'consciously reduced to a minimum'? Mitchell and Banks are keen to suggest that facilitation theory is not merely about intersubjective understanding. It aims at substantial political reconstruction.[29] However, how are the normative commitments going to be realised while the facilitator is a limited actor, a practitioner in the art of 'dispassionate theory' or symbolic intergroup understanding? Without normative political theory guiding and structuring an intervention, how can the goal of substantial political reconstruction become a reality?

The facilitation of human need

Within facilitation theory as a whole, one answer to this question is provided in the work of John Burton. Burton argues that formal facilitation can help construct a normative order based on human need. Through promoting dialogue, in a formal manner, facilitation creates a form of politics which gets to the roots of conflict and can reconstruct society from the 'bottom up'. The belief is that human nature, needs and purposes are somehow thwarted by the international system and that the process of conflict resolution is merely, or mainly, one of adjusting the surface superstructure of the system to ease and facilitate into the system what is, basically, an underlying harmony of human purposes and needs. We might call this the 'volcano' model of social change.[30] The exact nature of this philosophy is hard to capture, but it has much in common with the 'world society' approach developed over the years by John Burton. Burton, as Halliday describes, 'developed a theory of international relations based upon individual needs and the system of issue-related linkages established by such needs'.[31] In this model, facilitation processes are applied to crisis points in the world system and, on a piecemeal basis, the international system is gradually changed to suit the requirements of the underlying human form. Rothman acknowledges his debt to Burton, as does Herbert C. Kelman, another prominent facilitation theorist.[32] Hoffman, too, draws heavily on the work of Burton, Rothman and Kelman, while acknowledging some difficulties.

In the work of Burton, dialogue and facilitation are conceived as instruments of social engineering, which are used to ease, facilitate and bring into being a normatively legitimate international order described as the fulfilment of human needs for security – in both a physical and existential sense. In an article which outlines his ideas Burton refers to the 'inadequacies of the power frame', which ignoring 'human attributes', have 'led to dysfunctional policies'. Burton argues for a shift in thinking towards a needs approach. 'There are needs of individual development and control', he writes, 'that will be pursued, regardless of consequences.'[33] The central premise is the one of 'dysfunction' and adjustment of the structure or system to the underlying needs whose requirements it ought to serve. Burton argues that, '[n]eeds theory directs attention to the need to *adjust* systems to people, rather than the other way round'.[34] And facilitation processes – the problem-solving workshop – is one way of bringing the system into line with the frustrated, underlying human form.

Rothman echoes the basic thrust of this analysis. For Rothman, the Israeli–Palestinian conflict is 'an example of a conflict in which the human dimension can be seen so clearly in the faces, hopes, and fears of the peoples in dispute, each side threatens the other's existential requirements of recognition, safety, and full expression of identity'.[35] According to Rothman, these existential needs fuel or power the conflict situation and will continue to do so until they are satisfied. In this context, Rothman applies his 'conflict management framework' to facilitate the emergence of mutual recognition through satisfying needs for both existential and physical security.

While he does not explicitly refer to needs, Hoffman also writes of 'existential threats' to 'security and 'identity'. For Hoffman, conflict arises as 'legitimate concerns about identity can generate, reinforce and intensify images of "otherness" which find their expression in self-perpetuating cycles of violent conflict'.[36] Hoffman hints at the metaphorical strategies of the 'volcano' model – the tension between underlying forces and surface structure. He writes, for example, referring to the Cold War, that 'ethnic conflict' had been 'submerged beneath the contours of a militarised bipolar system' and how violence has 'returned with a vengeance'.[37] Hoffman, too, emphasises facilitation as technique. He writes of 'techniques', 'interconnected strategies', 'methods' and 'the manner in which they are employed'.[38] Facilitation is applied to the crisis point of conflict to ease underlying, 'intensified', dynamics into the structure of the system and to accommodate the latter to the demands of the former.

The role of the facilitator on this model is one akin to the role assigned to the social critic in Habermas's *early* conceptions of critical theory. In an article called 'Systematically Distorted Communication', Habermas looked to psychoanalysis to model the role of critical social theory.[39] Here, insight and reflection are brought to bear on hitherto repressed experiences, as the patient (or society) achieves a new-found autonomy and emancipation – an enlarged measure of rational control over his or her actions. In Freudian terms, the *ego* is adjusted to meet the demands of the *id* – the inner world of drives and motivations; similarly with the facilitative problem-solving workshop. Here, insight and reflection are brought to bear on troubled relationships (systematic distortions) in order to understand the nature of the underlying motivations – drives resulting from frustrated human need. Underlying motivations and drives are then facilitated or eased into the system and, simultaneously, the system is adjusted to accommodate them. As Hoffman writes, 'violent conflict [is] an indication that the assumptions underpinning the character, nature and structure of social relations are in need of redefinition and rearticulation.'[40] The facilitator in this situation plays a similar role to the psychoanalyst or therapist. Like the psychoanalyst, as Kelman writes, 'we do not propose (and certainly do not impose solutions). Rather, we try to encourage a process whereby solutions will emerge out of the interaction between the parties themselves.'[41]

There are problems with the view that conflict is the expression of a frustrated dynamic of human need.

The use of terms such as 'frustrate', 'emerge', 'generate', 'intensify', 'expression', pressure' and 'self-perpetuating' by facilitation theory all point to the idea of needs as 'drives'. As Doyal and Gough write, with reference to the concept of needs as drives, '[h]ere "need" refers to a motivational force instigated by a state of disequilibrium or tension set up in an organism because of a particular lack.'[42] The socio-biological view of needs as drives underlying this aspect of facilitative theory is problematic in that it divorces the concept of need and any resulting political action from the concept of normative justification. As Tamari writes about this analysis of the Palestinian intifada, if needs are drives then violence becomes a 'mindless eruption' not 'a politically motivated act'.[43] Action becomes an 'expression' of an underlying force or drive which has a quasi-natural nature. The problem, as Doyal and Gough write, is that:

> one can have a drive to consume something, like lots of alcohol, which one does not need and at the same time have a need for something, like exercise of to diet, which one is in no way driven to seek ... To have an urge to act in a particular way must not be confused with an empirical or normative justification for doing so.[44]

To identify needs with drives means that there is no way to criticise or gain rational control over drives that are obviously destructive. As Jabri writes, 'to suggest that the individual is driven by needs the violation of which could lead to violent conflict is to remove moral agency from the individual.'[45] Action in pursuit of need needs to be rationally redeemed. Habermasean critical theory is thus largely hostile to the idea that human nature, needs or drives can provide some kind of absolute fulcrum for critical enquiry. As Stephen White remarks, 'Habermas usually does not refer simply to "needs" but, rather, to "need interpretations," a locution which expresses their cultural variability.'[46] Given a strict identification of needs with drives, facilitation theory becomes just another form of social science orientated towards prediction and control. If needs are not understood as drives, or if need claims, as a subset of political claims generally, have to be subject to critical scrutiny and be rationally redeemed, then dialogue, facilitation and third-party intervention in general cannot merely be an *instrument* used to '*handle* deep-rooted conflicts'.[47] Rather, the dialogic situation created in a facilitation workshop, or more generally in a peace process, has two different characteristics. First, dialogue and language are the ways in which we discharge our moral responsibility to evaluate critically claims made by particular parties that a particular state of affairs is a normatively legitimate one. Second, the practice of dialogue in conflict resolution is constitutive of moral identity. Dialogue is not an instrument but, rather, it is a method or way, from the moral point of view, of being in the world. Facilitation theory should 'free itself' from the socio-biological or socio-psychological discourse.[48]

Communicative ethics and the practice of facilitation

In an attempt to remedy the normative deficit bequeathed by earlier formulations of facilitation theory, scholars have tried to anchor the practice of facilitation in the political philosophy of Jürgen Habermas. Hoffman argues that facilitation 'emphasises the centrality of an analytic and relational empathy, a shared sense of "otherness", which becomes discernible through something like a process of Habermasean "communicative discourse".'[49] Rothman argues that Habermasean critical theory is one of the 'deep conceptual structures' which underlies the ARI (adversarial, reflexive and integrative) conflict framework.[50] Jabri's *Discourses on Violence* is perhaps the most sustained attempt to date to analyse a peace process on Habermasean lines. Jabri suggests that we consider the concept 'peace' as a form of communication free from power and deception.

Through the link with Habermas, the hope is that facilitation can remain in the realm of 'dispassionate theory' and 'formal technique', while also promoting 'stability, peace, justice, progress and legitimized authority'. Habermas's political ethics have the virtue of being formal and neutral, while also aiming to deliver substantive political goals. Habermas offers a procedural account of justice. Thus the facilitator may remain a neutral practitioner of social science through empowering a formal framework of negotiation, while substantive political goals are delivered by the parties themselves. Though Banks and Mitchell do not draw upon Habermas themselves, they capture the flavour of the idea of formal dialogue as the goal of third-party intervention quite neatly. 'Scholars may be able to illuminate a conflict', they write, 'but only the parties could finally resolve it.'[51]

Furthermore, it is possible to argue that the theory and practice of facilitation overcomes and supplements certain defects in traditional Habermasean political theory. Commentators sympathetic to contextualist themes in political thought have always doubted whether Habermas has completely succeeded in escaping the problems of abstract universalism which have faced a more traditional Kantian moral theory. As one writer argues:

> Communicative ethics demands from its participants a willingness and ability to consider normative questions from a universalist standpoint and to regard every being as an equal regardless of the actual constellation of relations in real life.[52]

The problem facing Habermasean discourse ethics stems from the fact that, as Seyla Benhabib puts it, '[d]iscourses arise when the intersubjectivity of ethical life is endangered; *but the very project of discursive argumentation presupposes the ongoing validity of reconciled subjectivity.*'[53] Here, facilitation can help manoeuvre disputants into a position whereby they are actually capable of engaging in discourse. From a philosophical viewpoint, facilitation would move in two stages. First, there is an attempt to bring parties to the negotiating table by overcoming a basic unwillingness to recognise the other as a legitimate partner in dialogue. Second, an attempt is then made to institute a dialogue governed by the formal, abstract and therefore neutral rules of Habermasean 'dialogic ethics'.

There are strong links between a Habermasean-inspired political theory and the theory and practice of facilitation as a form of international conflict resolution. Both centre on the intersubjective negotiation of difference. However, in seeking to unite procedure and substance through an appeal to Habermasean political ethics, facilitation theory must pay a rather heavy price.

It must accept that, in both theory and practice, it is linked to a wider political tradition, which transcends the more narrow theory and practice of the problem-solving workshop. What this means in practice is that whether substantial goals are actually achieved in a facilitation process is a question which can only be answered *outside* the problem-solving workshop. Criticism is needed to unite the problem-solving workshop to a set of normative goals. Consequently, in appealing to the theory of communicative action to unite procedure and substance, facilitative approaches make way for an analysis of mediation which transcends both geostrategic approaches *and* facilitative approaches as the theory of mediation merges with the wider trends in the theory of international politics.

For all its emphasis on dialogue and communication, for example, Habermas's political theory offers a theory of *justice*, not an unambiguous model of political practice which can simply be equated with some vague notion of a politics of dialogue or communication. 'Discourse ethics' is a theory of *the right*.[54] It attempts to establish the argument for an abstract Kantian ethic in philosophical terms. Just as Kant's categorical imperative cannot be translated into a simple 'duty ethic', the ideas set forward in 'discourse ethics' are not reducible to a form of politics which simply promotes 'dialogue'. 'Discourse ethics' is a philosophical theory of the right in a post-Kantian setting, not a blueprint for political action.

Thus, while facilitation theory's critical power seems limited to analysing and promoting the micro-dynamics of the problem-solving workshop, a critical theory will take a broader historical view of an emancipatory political process. Applied to a process of conflict resolution, critical mediation theory wishes to know whether, overall, a peace process respects, as Habermas puts it, the principle of universalisation (U). As Habermas writes (U) states that:

> All affected can accept the consequences and the side effects its general observance can be anticipated to have for the satisfaction of everyone's interests (and these consequences are preferred to those of known alternative possibilities for regulation).[55]

Normative validity depends on a general 'acceptance' that a particular state of affairs is right. Habermas argues that he wishes to rule out the 'monological' application of this principle. Knowledge of what the principle entails must be generated discursively. However, it does not follow from the argument against monologicality that the advent of a facilitative problem-solving exercise is either necessary or sufficient to secure either (a) the general acceptance of an norm or (b) theoretical knowledge that a particular norm is, in fact, accepted and therefore valid. Habermas claims that: 'Only those norms can claim to be valid that meet (*or could meet*) with the approval of all affected in their capacity as participants in a practical discourse.'[56]

Note two points. First, Habermas leaves the nature of a 'practical discourse' largely unspecified, and deliberately so. Practical discourses may manifest themselves in different and as yet unspecified ways. Habermas writes that 'a discourse of application' is needed to determine how 'discourse ethics' refers to a particular context. However, there is no implication that practical discourse is equivalent to a facilitation exercise.

Second, Habermas states that a valid norm is one which could meet the approval of all those affected if a practical discourse were actually to take place. This second condition leaves open the possibility that an actor could legitimately believe a norm to be valid even though it had never actually been tested by that actor in a practical discourse – face to face with other actors, as it were. Of course, an actor would have to know that a practical discourse, and we leave its nature unspecified, could validate the norm. However, knowledge that a norm could meet with general approval in a practical discourse may legitimately come from other sources. For example, it could stem from any broad dialogical relationship which makes up what Habermas calls, in another context, 'the web of human relationships'.[57] Normative knowledge of international conflict resolution is not necessarily generated via the facilitative problem-solving workshop.

It is not possible to separate the cognitive question of what norms are just from the organisational problem of creating democratic procedures. This position would rightly be accused of falling into the problems associated with the monological application of the Kantian will.[58] However, critical theory operates at a higher level of abstraction than the theory and practice of facilitation. Facilitation theory may try and unite procedure and substance through communicative ethics, but, in doing so, it admits that the problem-solving workshop is only one potential political strategy among many and that there is a contingent relationship between the problem-solving workshop and the generation of 'the right' in politics.

This separation of facilitation theory and practice from Habermasean political theory, and the distinct concerns of the latter, can be seen from a rather simple logical point of view. Facilitation is neither necessary nor sufficient to fulfil the conditions specified in (U). However, as Habermas's political theory and (U) are one and the same, it follows that (U) is a necessary and sufficient condition of reality to fulfil the conditions specified by what is, in effect, itself. The conclusion is plain: as facilitation theory and Habermasean political theory are not reducible to each other, there is room to develop an approach to third-party intervention which transcends both power politics and facilitation – an approach which subjects both aspects of the tradition to external critical standards. The shape of a critical approach to international mediation will be discussed in the next chapter. For now, just note that an approach derived from a critical theory, such as the one specified by Habermas, is potentially much wider in its application and scope than the problem-solving workshop and that the latter can only contingently rely on the former to redeem its normative ambitions. It is important to realise that facilitative and critical approaches may move in separate political directions. And that, from the perspective of the latter, there may be, in certain cases, no moral distinction between facilitation and the practice of power politics. The analysis of Oslo conducted in the following chapters will, in a sense, support this conclusion.

The contingent character of the relationship between problem-solving and a normative legitimate outcome means that criticism is absolutely necessary. Only criticism can link the former to the latter. There is, therefore, room for a distinct, critical theory of international mediation. Facilitation has its place, but it must be situated in a broader framework if it is to redeem its normative ambitions. Without being attached to this framework, it is possible that, from the moral point of view, and despite facilitation theory's good intentions, there is no difference between the outcomes of power politics and the outcomes of facilitation.

Questions of action and practice

Problems with the facilitative model stem from the identification of reflection with practical engagement. As Rick Roderick writes, echoing a critical theoretic point:

> Reflection, in the philosophical sense, as a thorough examination of all claims to truth or rightness may be said to pursue an interest in emancipation from dogmatism in all its forms. But this interest . . . cannot be confused with that interest Marx pursued in claiming (against philosophy) that the world was not merely to be interpreted but changed. This interest involves specific (and sometimes dangerous) political and practical engagement.[59]

Reflection releases a normatively legitimate order, as, for the facilitative approach, it is 'legitimate concerns' and not sheer 'lawlessness' which underlay a situation of conflict. Here, systems need to be 'adjusted' through facilitation to allow 'legitimate concerns about identity' and 'frustrated human needs' to be integrated into a renewed international order. If we remove the assumption that it is only 'legitimate concerns' and 'frustrated human needs' which underlay conflict, and replace it with a view of conflict conceived as the expression of 'desires', 'illegitimate concerns' or 'lawlessness', however, then the act of reflection in a facilitated problem-solving workshop becomes more problematic.

Said writes that the problem-solving workshop has to work with 'reasonable people, with reasonable goals such as peaceful coexistence'.[60] As Rothman writes, 'participants [are] relatively moderate in their attitudes towards the other side . . . [O]ur goal . . . is to build upon a greater will for dialogue and foster an much greater skill in dialogue.'[61] Take away the assumption that 'reasonableness' is hidden but nevertheless there and the point of reflection in a problem-solving workshop is hard to identify. If you scratch the surface and find 'lawlessness' and 'illegitimate concerns', instead of their opposites, then facilitation as the act of reflection will not serve to generate a legitimate international order on its own.

The identification of action with reflection creates two further difficulties. The first problem concerns the distinction between interim and final status. The second problem concerns structural inequality and power asymmetry.

According to Vayrynen, '[t]he culturally sensitive facilitator does not ground his or her conduct on rules, rather he or she grounds his or her legitimacy on situational ethics.'[62] Vayrynen argues that facilitation is suspicious of abstract procedural interpretations of a dialogic ethic. Universal conceptions of justice or procedure are replaced by more interpretive or contextual considerations. Thus, in practical terms, it might be argued that one of the advantages of the facilitative approach is that it works with an incremental approach. Not all the issues are on the negotiating table from day one. Peripheral issues are dealt with initially, and once a momentum for change has been created disputants move on to the more intractable debates.

This idea underlies the Oslo process, as we shall examine in more detail later. Agreement on peripheral issues – the status of Gaza, for example – was to predate debate on the more intractable issues – the status of Jerusalem or Palestinian national self-determination. The interim phase is a time when parties learn to cooperate and overcome the dynamics of mutual suspicion and hostility in preparation for the full political settlement which is to be created once the parties have learned to interact.

It is important to remember that critical theory recognises the need to compromise and is sympathetic, for example, to ideas of 'interim periods', which are divided from 'final status' solutions. The 'ideal speech situation', for example, is approximated in a process of moral development. Thus, a more robust cosmopolitan ethic can combine both interim and final stage considerations. The idea of moral development is central to the critical or cosmopolitan program.[63]

However, while a critical or cosmopolitan perspective combines sensitivity to both interim and final status, it is not clear that facilitation theory can adequately grasp the notion of a final status without relying on a broader critical vision. Thus the Norwegian-facilitated Oslo Accords, for example, have been criticised, as the principles setting out the basic framework of the facilitated peace process have been too weak to stop Israel from exploiting the weakness of the Palestinians and the peace agreement during the interim stage.[64] (Arguably, the weak notion of final status will prove to be the ultimate cause of Oslo's failure.) In this situation, agreement over final status was not sufficiently strong to support the 'process' and the latter has collapsed as a result. The process model of facilitation theory, with its concepts of compromise, 'interim' and 'final status', has to rely on an understanding supplied by a more uncompromising and 'abstract' model if it is to translate the concept of 'process' into the concept of 'progress'.

Thus Jan Egeland and Geir Pederson, who both played a part in the Oslo facilitation exercise, stated their belief that Oslo would deliver what the international community said was just or right – national rights for both Palestine and Israel. This claim by Egeland and Pederson is not anything to do with the theory and practice of facilitation as such. Rather, they articulate a claim about the ultimate normative foundations of their activities – i.e., a belief that 'unrestrained communication', could it be achieved, would result in a bi-national agreement.[65]

An interim stage requires agreement about final status before it can be implemented. The contextual and interpretive understanding supplied by the theory and practice of facilitation has to rely on a more abstract and robust cosmopolitan or universalistic understanding. Rouhana and Korper make a similar point when they argue that facilitation needs to move beyond vague phrases about final status, such as 'changing the conflict relationship'. Instead, more open commitments to the concrete nature of final status need to be built into the process itself. 'The third party', they write, 'needs to be prepared for "truth in advertising" with the participants.'[66]

The second reason for developing a broader understanding of political practice becomes apparent when we examine questions of structural power asymmetry. Put simply, the relationship of facilitation to the interpretive tradition of social science means that, as a form of practice, the problems of power asymmetry become fairly acute. As Rouhana and Korper write, in a highly perceptive critique of the problem-solving workshop, 'few have examined how power asymmetry influences the objectives of third parties and the dynamics of their interventions'.[67]

Doubts produced by the facilitative attitude to 'final status' and the need to embed facilitative practices in a wider political setting have led Palestinian lawyer, Jonathan Kuttab, to describe the facilitative model of conflict resolution as a potential 'false dialogue'.[68] For Kuttab, dialogue can be a meaningful form of political action but only if it is linked to wider struggles. The facilitative, problem-solving workshop tends to abstract itself from the wider political, economic, social and cultural setting. The facilitation exercise is often about wider considerations. However, the quality and analysis of the facilitation workshop is determined by events which are wholly internal to the dialogue. As a result, a false impression about the quality of political interaction can result. Rothman, for example, bases his analysis on what he calls negotiation 'scripts'. These 'scripts' detail the micro-dynamics of particular dialogues and only this is the focus of attention.[69] But these micro-dynamics may be isolated instances of a dialogic politics in a broader context of structural inequality.

The concentration on the micro-dynamics of particular facilitation exercises can create an illusion of genuine communication. In the workshop there is, as Kuttab writes, the danger of assuming 'a false symmetry between the oppressor and the oppressed; between the occupier and the occupied; between the powerful and the weak'. Kuttab continues:

> It is a false symmetry because different groups are made to brand the meeting of individuals as being more or less an open and free meeting between individuals. Yet the reality of the situation mandates major differences in terms of the freedom of expression granted to members of each group, their immunity from retaliation, options other than dialogue available and the resources and general interests that each group has in the furtherance of dialogue.[70]

Although sympathetic to the facilitative approach, Vivienne Jabri echoes the point made by Kuttab:

Facilitation and problem-solving

[w]hile coercive mediation may be criticized for failing to change its power political base, the facilitative approach may also be criticized for negating power asymmetry in its discourse. Such negation can be instrumental in creating a myth of equality between the parties involved in unobstructed dialogue.[71]

Relations of power, domination, exclusion and control could permeate the dialogic situation, from the outside, in many different ways: freedom of expression could be curtailed for some groups outside the facilitation exercise, immunity from retaliation could be distributed unequally, one group may have other political options aside from the facilitation, resources may be distributed unevenly, the place of dialogue may suit certain groups more than others, certain groups may be better organised and have greater legal or technical knowledge, one group may have more to learn than another about the nature, plans and intentions of the other group. More importantly, the wider context may be one of continuing military oppression and economic, political and cultural structural inequality. In this type of circumstance, the neutrality and quality of any 'dialogue' is undoubtedly compromised. Edward Said writes, for example, of the Palestinian experience:

> There is still a military occupation, people are still being killed, imprisoned and denied their rights on a daily basis. The main prerogatives for us as Arabs and Palestinians are therefore clear. One: we must struggle to end the occupation, two: we must struggle even harder to develop our own independent institutions and organizations until we are on a relatively equal footing with the Israelis. *Then we can begin to talk seriously about cooperation.* In the meantime cooperation can all too easily shade into collaboration with Israeli policy.[72]

Whether or not one agrees with Said's particular analysis, the wider point that he makes is a valid one. Dialogue could never be a neutral and disinterested search for analytical empathy when couched in a broader situation racked by massive structural inequalities.

Related to this point is the fact that the problem-solving workshop approach can appear to pacify the reality of the conflict. Years of struggle against oppression and injustice can be put to one side in favour of, to put it bluntly, a cosy fireside chat. Edward Said is therefore correct to point out the virtues of the intifada as opposed to the problem-solving workshop. He calls this 'an authentic intellectual idiom' and not a mere 'discourse of politics'. As Said writes of the problem-solving workshop, '[c]an one imagine endorsing similar discussions between a few well-intentioned German and French intellectuals during the occupation of France?'[73] He continues: 'I am for dialogue between cultures and coexistence between people . . . But I think real principle and real justice have to be implemented before there can be true dialogue.'[74] Kuttab also makes this point. Dialogue must go hand in hand with political action:

Individuals who are engaged in dialogue must do so with the full knowledge that dialogue must only be a first and preliminary step towards action . . . Keeping action in mind means that through the process of dialogue individuals can remain rooted in reality and think about useful strategies, tactics, and modalities for furthering the constructive process.[75]

Both Said and Kuttab point to the fact that speech and action must never part company. To paraphrase Kant, speech without action is empty while action without speech is blind.

But action is restricted to 'facilitation' in the tradition we are describing. Here, the presence of the facilitator is 'consciously reduced to a minimum'. Banks and Mitchell write that '[a]n ideal panellist should have a comprehensive grasp of conflict theory in addition to substantial experience of its application.'[76] Here, 'the common theme is that all are behavioural scientists, scholars with an interest in how people respond to their environment.'[77] With these remarks, Banks and Mitchell convey the idea that the causes of conflict are an inscrutable part of social reality which can only be uncovered with the aid of social scientific expertise. They write of the importance of observers 'who can note unexpected statements or reactions, subtle shifts of position, nuanced comments or coded messages'.[78] Such observers record, 'the "detailed" flow of interactions'.

A further manifestation of this rather weak interpretation of political action is the analogy or metaphor of textual understanding which is used to illuminate the process of conflict resolution in a facilitation exercise. Vayrynen draws on the example of textual understanding at the root of hermeneutic approaches to the social world. Vivienne Jabri, similarly, writes of 'textualising the self' in a process of 'intercultural discourse'.[79] One need not be a realist to understand that international negation is not best understood along the rather relaxed lines of trying to understand new meanings in a book. The 'textual' metaphor obscures the intense pressures faced by negotiators who operate in a hostile environment, where questions of life and death are frequently at stake. Later chapters will describe the geostrategic pressures which gave rise to the Oslo channel. Strategic and instrumental action capture the nature of the relationships in the Oslo process, not hermeneutic understanding. This claim does not rely on a realist philosophy of international relations with its commitment to the immutable structures of international life. Rather, it is a commonplace observation about how international politics tends to manifest itself.

But if conflict exists in a wider social, political and economic context, it is difficult to understand what the facilitator hopes to discover or bring into being with his or her expertise in intergroup interaction. How will noting down 'nuanced comments or coded messages' change the wider reality if the conflict is not about a misunderstanding? Imagine the conflict in South Africa or, as we shall see in later chapters, the conflict in the Middle East between Israel and the Palestinians. In the former case, the conflict was about human rights, democracy and so forth. In the latter, the conflict, among other things, is about land and national rights. The basic issues in the dispute are clear to the actors involved; there is no need to note the micro-dynamics of the problem-solving workshop to grasp the causes of the dispute. Here, conflict resolution is not to be acquired or realised through the application of formal, abstract, behavioural theory. Conflict resolution depends on rebalancing the scales of justice in a way which satisfies all parties interests. And this is part of a much wider political project. Banks and Mitchell write that 'a thorough knowledge of the area its history, economy, politics and culture could actually be harmful'.[80] But it is difficult to see how the scales of justice can be righted if this type of knowledge is excluded from the mediation process.

There is strong empirical evidence that facilitation exercises fail to deal adequately with the problems of structural power asymmetry. Rouhana and Korper surveyed a series of problem-solving workshops which brought together Palestinian and Jewish citizens of Israel:

> This structural asymmetry is manifested, for example in officially defining Israel as a Jewish state, delineating immigration policies, regulating use of state-owned land, restricting public transportation for observance of Jewish religious holidays, and determining eligibility of a party to run for the Parliament.[81]

Rouhana and Korper conclude that structural asymmetry and the lack of substantial political engagement in a problem-solving workshop has a number of adverse implications. First, the focus on 'knowing the other', which is so central to facilitation theory, itself becomes politically charged. As Rouhana and Korper write, referring to the minority Arab experience, 'the lower-power groups must know about the other's institutions in order to function adequately in the society'.[82] Thus the agenda of the problem-solving workshop may prove irrelevant to the lower-power group, which, owing to the relationship of dependence, may already have intimate knowledge of the higher-power group's society and institutions. Second, the high-power group wishes to use the problem-solving workshop to decrease the intensity of the conflict, while the lower-power group wishes to use the workshop to discuss the power asymmetry itself, and sees the conflict and its intensity as a inevitable function of inequality. Third, the higher-power group uses the workshop to focus on issues of identity, while the lower-power group wishes to focus on the substantive issues. Fourth, for the higher-power group the facilitation exercise is an opportunity to 'relieve feelings of ambivalence, anxiety, and threat'.[83] For the lower-power group, these are 'goods' which cannot be granted to the higher-power group while the inequality persists. As we shall see, many of these points are confirmed when we come to examine the Oslo process and Accords in later chapters.

The presence of underlying structural inequalities leads Vivienne Jabri to call for a 'structuration theory' of international mediation. This approach recognises the interaction between social and symbolic orders and underlying structural and material forces. As Jabri writes:

> This form of analysis is critical in orientation in its recognition that the specific instance of a conflict is always a manifestation of deeply embedded social processes which situate conflict within a complex network of symbolic orders, interpretative schemes, and normative expectations reinforced through differential access to resources.[84]

Hoffman writes of:

> the need to view all third party initiatives within the context of a much wider process. They need to be understood and assessed as part of an interconnected third party process in which each is viewed as an contingent step which is potentially complementary to other third party initiatives'.[85]

Hoffman's opinion as to the ultimate efficacy of the problem-solving workshop is, on balance, probably the most sensible one. Facilitation may well play a role in an 'interconnected context'. Despite this, doubts about the political capacities of the problem-solving workshop must remain. For example, facilitative exercises may be redundant as a form of conflict resolution in the Israel–Palestine dispute. The main obstacles standing in the way of conflict resolution are intransigent political forces which have to be marginalised if progress is to be made.

The theory of international mediation needs to turn towards international political theory. Criticism is needed to redeem the theory and practice of facilitation in the problem-solving workshop. Geostrategic approaches reduce the production of international history to the reproduction of the state, yet criticism is needed to redeem the power of states. The theory and practice of third-party facilitation claims to realise certain normative goals. Again, the theory of mediation, breaks into the realm of international theory.

NOTES

1 M. Banks and C. Mitchell, *Handbook of Conflict Resolution. The Analytical Problem-Solving Approach* (London: Pinter, 1996), p. viii.
2 M. Hoffman, 'Defining and Evaluating Success: Facilitative Problem-Solving Workshops in an Interconnected Context', *Paradigms*, 9:2 (1995), p. 5.
3 The concept of the 'dialogic community' and its relationship to critical theory and cosmopolitan political thought is discussed in great detail in A. Linklater, *The Transformation of Political Community* (Cambridge: Polity Press, 1997). The attempt to link the concept of a dialogic community to the problem-solving workshop is made in Tarja Vayrynen, 'Ethnic Communality and Conflict Resolution', *Cooperation and Conflict*, 33:1 (1998) and in Mark Hoffman, 'Defining and Evaluating Success'.
4 Hoffman, 'Defining and Evaluating Success', p. 1.
5 *Ibid.*
6 *Ibid.*, p. 7.
7 V. Jabri, 'Agency, Structure and the Question of Power in Conflict Resolution', *Paradigms*, 9:2 (1995) p. 3.

8 M. Neufeld, *The Restructuring of International Relations Theory* (Cambridge: Cambridge University Press, 1995), p. 78.
9 J. Rothman, *From Confrontation to Cooperation* (London: Sage, 1992), p. 56.
10 Hoffman, 'Defining and Evaluating Success', p. 7.
11 Rothman, *From Confrontation*, p. 33.
12 T. E. Cook, *Criteria of Social Scientific Knowledge: Interpretation, Prediction, Praxis* (London: Rowman and Littlefield Publishers, 1994), p. 16. Key figures in this approach to the social world include, among others: Max Weber, Heidegger, Leo Strauss and Hans-George Gadamer (see W. G. Runciman (ed.), *Weber: Selections in Translation* (Cambridge: Cambridge University Press, 1978); L. Straus, *Persecution and the Art of Writing* (Glencoe, Ill.: Free Press, 1954); M. Heidegger, *Being and Time* (Oxford: Oxford University Press, 1976); H. G. Gadamer, *Truth and Method* (London: Sheed and Ward, 1975)). Note, in addition, as Giddens writes, that 'contemporary German philosophers and social thinkers influenced by hermeneutics, such as Apel and Habermas, have acknowledged a convergence of thought between contemporary trends in hermeneutic philosophy and the break with logical empiricism signalled by Anglo-Saxon ... "post-Wittgensteinian" philosophy'. (*New rules of Sociological Method* (Cambridge: Polity Press, 1992), pp. 60–1.) The influence of hermeneutics has spread far and wide.
13 Gadamer, *Truth and Method*, p. 273.
14 D. Held, *Introduction to Critical Theory* (Cambridge: Polity Press, 1980) pp. 313–14.
15 Hoffman, 'Defining and Evaluating Success', p. 9.
16 *Ibid*.
17 Rothman, *From Confrontation*, p. 71.
18 Vayrynen, 'Ethnic Communality'.
19 Raymond Geuss describes the critique of ideology as 'a program of criticism of the beliefs, attitudes, and wants of the agents in a particular society. This research program is initiated by the observation that agents in the society are deluded about themselves their position, their society, or their interests' (*The Idea of a Critical Theory* (Cambridge: Cambridge University Press, 1981), p. 12.
20 J. Habermas, *On the Logic of the Social Sciences* (Cambridge: Polity Press, 1988), p. 170. The work originally appeared in German in 1967.
21 M. Frost, *Ethics in International Relations* (Cambridge: Cambridge University Press, 1996), p. 29.
22 Banks and Mitchell, *A Handbook*, p. 32.
23 *Ibid*., p. 33.
24 *Ibid*., p. ix.
25 *Ibid*., p. ix.
26 *Ibid*., p. 116.
27 *Ibid*., p. 117.
28 Vayrynen, 'Ethnic Communality', p. 74.
29 Banks and Mitchell, *A Handbook*, p. x.
30 While there are several different variants of this model, in general it attributes episodes of collective violence to 'period eruption of social-psychological tensions that boil up in human groups like lava under the earth's crust' (R. Aya, 'Theories of Revolution Reconsidered: Contrasting Models of Collective Violence', in *Theory and Society* 8 (1979), p. 49). I reject this understanding of action for the reasons put forward by Salim Tamari. Tamari writes, with regard to the Palestinian intifada, that, '[t]he word frustration obfuscates the relationship between Israel and the occupied territories. One, because it obscures the hierarchical form of control. Two, because it misconstrues the nature of the response, which is not a mindless eruption but a politically motivated act, spontaneous,

but with clear objectives.' ('What the Uprising Means', *Middle East Report*, 15:28 (1988)).
31 F. Halliday, *Rethinking International Relations* (London: The Macmillan Press, 1994), p 17. Halliday writes, '[w]ith a special emphasis on the resolution of conflict through small-group and individual mediation, Burton's work broke flamboyantly with the state-centric view of international relations by introducing not only an alternative analysis but also an alternative approach to policy.' (See J. Burton, *World Society* (Cambridge: Cambridge University Press, 1972)).
32 Referring to Burton, Rothman writes, '[t]he roots of most if not all international conflict can be traced to circumstances where these needs of individuals, who have banded together in groups are threatened or frustrated', *From Confrontation*, p. 46. (H. C. Kelman, referring to the problem-solving workshop, writes that 'this approach derives from the work of John Burton and follows the general principles that he has laid out', 'Applying a Human Needs Perspective to the Practice of Conflict Resolution: The Israeli–Palestinian Case', in J. Burton, *Conflict: Human Needs Theory* (London: The Macmillan Press, 1990), p. 283).
33 J. Burton and T. Vayrynen, 'The end of international relations', in A. J. R. Groom and M. Light (eds), *Contemporary International Relations: A Guide to Theory* (London: Pinter, 1994), p. 74. The emphasis is mine.
34 *Ibid.*, p. 75.
35 Rothman, *From Confrontation*, p. 55.
36 Hoffman, 'Defining and Evaluating Success', p. 1.
37 *Ibid.*
38 *Ibid.*, p. 2.
39 J. Habermas,, 'Systematically Distorted Communication', *Inquiry*, 13 (1970).
40 Hoffman, 'Defining and Evaluating Success', p. 1.
41 Kelman, 'Applying a Human Needs Perspective', p. 285.
42 L. Doyal and I. Gough, *A Theory of Human Need* (Basingstoke: Macmillan, 1991), p. 35.
43 Tamari, 'What the Uprising Means'.
44 *Ibid.*, p. 36.
45 In the Foreword to John Burton's, *Violence Explained* (Manchester: Manchester University Press), xiii.
46 S. White, *The Recent Work of Jürgen Habermas: Reason, Justice and Modernity* (Cambridge: Cambridge University Press, 1988), p. 70.
47 Hoffman, 'Defining and Evaluating Success', p. 2.
48 Vayrynen, 'Ethnic Communality', p. 74.
49 Hoffman, 'Defining and Evaluating Success', p. 10.
50 Rothman, *From Confrontation*, p. 72.
51 Banks and Mitchell, *A Handbook*, p. viii.
52 J. Mendelson, 'The Habermas-Gadamer Debate', *New German Critique*, 18 (1979), pp. 44–73.
53 S. Benhabib, *Critique, Norm and Utopia* (New York, 1986), p. 321.
54 'Discourse Ethics' is Habermas's model of political engagement. We will discuss what it means and how it is translated in the theory of international relations in the following chapter.
55 J. Habermas, 'Discourse ethics', in *Moral Consciousness and Communicative Action* (Cambridge: Polity Press, 1992), p. 65.
56 *Ibid.* (my emphasis).
57 J. Habermas, 'Hannah Arendt's Communications Concept of Power' in S. Lukes (ed.), *Power* (New York: New York University Press, 1986).
58 As Stephen K. White remarks, 'it is not difficult to see a 19th-century American father forbidding his adolescent daughter from studying to be a doctor on the grounds that it is not

proper for woman, given their "nature", to enter professions. That father could, in good conscience, will his proscription as a universal law' (*The Recent Work*, p. 82).
59 R. Roderick, *Habermas and the Foundations of Critical Theory* (London: Macmillan, 1986), p. 63.
60 E. Said, *Peace and its Discontents* (London: Vintage, 1995), pp. 32 and 33.
61 Rothman, *From Confrontation*, pp. 91 and 92.
62 Vayrynen, 'Ethnic Communality', p. 75.
63 Habermas's 'ideal speech situation' allows for the formation of compromises provided that two conditions are met. First, where generalisable interests are at stake in conflicts about fundamental moral issues an effort has to be made to produce an agreement based on generalisable interests, thus keeping within the overall rationale of communicative action. Habermas is rightly suspicious of agreements which neglect generalisable interests, as they are often based on relations of force. Second, Habermas permits compromise agreements provided that the resort to compromise is not imposed by the stronger party. See J. Habermas, *Legitimation Crisis* (Cambridge: Polity Press, 1988).
64 The final status negotiations between Israel and the PLO were supposed to reflect the provisions of UN Security Council Resolution 242. However, it can be argued that Resolution 242 is too weak to serve as an underlying set of principles guaranteeing the legitimacy of introducing an interim stage. Netanyahu, for example, has long made clear his belief that Resolution 242 was respected with the Israeli withdrawal from Sinai under the Camp David Accords. See B. Netanyahu, *A Place Among the Nations* (New York: Bantom Books, 1993), p. 290.
65 Interviews with Jan Egeland and Geir Pederson at the Norwegian Foreign Ministry August 1996.
66 N. N. Rouhana and S. Korper, 'Dealing with the Dilemmas Posed by Power Asymmetry in Intergroup Conflict', *Negotiation Journal*, 12:4 (1996) p. 363.
67 Ibid., p. 353.
68 J. Kuttab, 'The Pitfalls of Dialogue', *Journal of Palestine Studies*, XVII:2 (1988).
69 Jane Corbin describes Terje Rod Larsen, the Norwegian facilitator of the Oslo Accords, as 'a keen amateur psychologist'. She continues, '[h]e believed in the sociological approach when dealing with small groups. He was convinced that, if he could encourage them to form a tight-knit group by discussing and sharing their feelings and their emotions, they would be able to build trust, and even intimacy on a personal level.' (*Gaza First* (London: Bloomsbury, 1994), p. 87).
70 Kuttab, 'The Pitfalls', p. 85.
71 Jabri, 'Agency, Structure', p. 8.
72 Said, *Peace and its Discontents*, p. 37. My emphasis.
73 Ibid., p. 35.
74 Ibid., p. 36.
75 Kuttab, 'The Pitfalls', p. 91.
76 Banks and Mitchell, *A Handbook*, p. 93.
77 Ibid., p. 96.
78 Ibid.
79 V. Jabri, 'Textualising the Self: Moral Agency in Inter-Cultural Discourse', *Global Society*, 10 (1996).
80 Banks and Mitchell, *A Handbook*, p. 97.
81 Rouhana and Korper, 'Dealing with the Dilemmas', p. 354.
82 Ibid., p. 356.
83 Ibid., p. 358.
84 Jabri, 'Agency, Structure', p. 1.
85 Hoffman, 'Defining and Evaluating Success', p. 5.

5

Cosmopolitan mediation

NORMATIVE INTERNATIONAL RELATIONS theory has increased its power and scope in recent years. The uncertainty surrounding the end of the Cold War prompted a re-evaluation of the state of international relations as its theorists envisaged new possibilities for agency emerging from the frozen bipolar structures which had dominated most of the second half of the twentieth century. As Mark Hoffman writes:

> The late 20th century poses considerable challenges of an intellectual and practical nature which reflect the state of flux which has come to characterize the post-Cold War environment. Within this environment, normative concerns have come to occupy a central place. Questions about the moral standing of states, and the nature and extent of our obligations and responsibilities within, between and beyond individual states have taken on a new immediacy.[1]

The theory and practice of international mediation does not escape the state of 'flux' alluded to by Hoffman. In the Middle East, for example, the onset of the post-Cold War period was accompanied by two great international events which were both associated with mediation efforts: the Gulf War and the resulting attempt to institute a 'new order' in the Middle East through the Madrid and Washington process, and the Oslo agreement initialled between the Israeli government and the PLO in 1993. Mediation has thus been used to manage a changed and fluctuating post-Cold War international environment and, accordingly, its profile has been raised.

In addition, and as we have seen, the theory of international mediation can no longer resist the arguments of normative international relations theory. The theory of international mediation has reached a conceptual impasse. Mediation theory has to develop if it is to respond to the theoretical problems besetting its intellectual traditions. Both the theory and practice of mediation are in a state of flux.

The normative stance developed in this chapter stems from the critical-theoretic and cosmopolitan stream of the theory of international relations. Accordingly, we will examine the work of thinkers such as Jürgen Habermas, David Held and Andrew Linklater.[2] Despite the broad theoretical efficacy of these latter approaches, they are not to be applied to the theory of international mediation without any consideration as to their merits or demerits.

There are three basic problems to be addressed. First, the critical theory of international relations does not yet appreciate the place of historical and contextual knowledge in the course of intellectual enquiry. This last statement can be qualified, given Andrew Linklater's more sociological cast of mind and his recognition that historical, contextual and postmodern themes are important to international relations theory.[3] However, the neglect of history within the critical theory of international relations continues to manifest itself. Unlike Foucault's detailed examinations of the asylum and the clinic, as Linklater puts it, '[f]or the most part, critical theorists have failed to develop empirical investigations of the constraining role of micro- and macro-social and political structures'.[4] To remedy this problem, future approaches to international relations must recognise the importance of what Edward Said calls the 'committed engagement' of 'secular and affiliated criticism'.[5] If critical theory is to avoid the charges articulated by postmodernism – of presuming to speak with a 'sovereign voice, a voice beyond politics and beyond doubt' – it has to be able to justify its normative stance with reference to the historical detail embedded in the politics of particular contexts.[6] We shall see in the chapters on the Oslo Accords that cosmopolitan or critical themes can shed some light on an aspect of contemporary international politics.

A second problem concerns the public nature of the type of diplomacy associated with the application of what David Held calls 'democratic public law' at the international level.[7] A mediator who attempts to apply 'democratic public law' to a particular conflict may be immediately disqualified by one or more of the parties to the dispute as being biased, with the result that the mediation effort collapses before it even begins. One of the strengths of facilitation theory, it might be argued, is that not all issues can be on the table from day one of the negotiations.

The third problem is the fact that any cosmopolitan political project of the present day would undoubtedly be compromised by its association with the unjust and massively unequal distribution of military, economic, cultural and political resources which exists in the world. Given the end of the Cold War and the collapse of the Soviet Union, as Danilo Zolo writes, 'at the centre of the planetary system of the Cosmopolis there now shines no more than a single star'.[8] We will see in a subsequent chapter how the 'imperial presidency' of George Bush referred back to the ancient idea of a civilising world mission to justify its interventions in the regional politics of the Middle East. There is a danger that the ideals of cosmopolitanism will just mask some underlying political reality, which is, from the moral point of view, completely arbitrary. This is linked to the argument that cosmopolitan international political theory seriously underestimates the Nietzschean point that there is no moral world order. Neither Nature, God, Reason, Language or History guarantee the cosmopolitan project in international history.

It is necessary to provide a rough working definition of the approach to international mediation which is derived from international political theory before we embark on the detailed discussion. Such a definition would proceed as follows: genuine international mediation is the application of a cosmopolitan democratic public law based on dialogue and mutual recognition to a situation of international conflict. This ambition towards a cosmopolitan political order is tempered by a recognition of the arbitrary and contingent nature of much international practice and a knowledge of the basic inefficacy of reason and rationality in changing the world. Accordingly, international mediation is inevitably an agonistic arena of politics, where actors will struggle to project their identities across the globe.

Habermas and the roots of critical international relations

Habermas has a conception of rationality which aims to overcome more problematic forms of modern reason: Marxism, Kantianism, postmodernism and instrumentalism. We will examine Habermas's criticisms of these philosophical positions and detail Habermas's own approach. In the next section we shall see how these ideas have been translated into a cosmopolitan international political theory.

Marxism is problematic for Habermas, as it fails adequately to distinguish economic, technical and scientific progress from progress in the moral-political sphere. At the very least, Marxism concentrates its theoretical energies on the former sort of historical progress, and neglects the latter. Conceiving man as a toolmaker, and history as the advancement of man's technical mastery over nature, Marx (and classical Marxism) placed too much confidence in the emancipatory power of technical and economic progress – the goals of the modern Prometheus. By the same token, classical Marxism failed to notice forms of oppression that are not reducible to class relations. National, ethnic, racial and gender dominations are given as examples of forms of oppression not reducible to class analysis.[9] Critical theory aims to remedy the defects of traditional Marxism. As Linklater writes:

> Post-Marxist critical theory extends conventional Marxist analysis by considering axes of exclusion other than class . . . Particular emphasis is placed upon the forms of social learning. Recent analyses stress how human beings learn to include some within, and exclude others from, their bounded communities and also how they can develop their capacity to engage all others in open and potentially universal discourse.[10]

These issues are too wide and deep in their scope to be discussed properly in the present context. For example, I agree with Norman Geras, discussing the issue of Marx and justice, when he writes:

> [a]ll parties to this dispute agree ... that there is some such normative dimension to his [Marx's] thought, and frankly, I do not think the denial of it worth taking seriously any longer. The question is the more specific one; does Marx condemn capitalism in the light of any *principle* of justice?[11]

Marx lived with a normative consciousness. The central question concerns the *type* of moral theory to be expected from Marxism and whether or not its standards are adequate to assess central international political problems of modern times.

Note a few points which cast doubt on the critical potential of Marxist international political philosophy. First, what could Marxism tell us about the politics of conflict resolution between, for example, Israel and Palestine, the subject of our case study in the following chapters. Of course, it may be able to highlight issues of economic exploitation and the fact that the conflict is bound up with western control over Middle East oil markets. However, take some of the key normative issues in the dispute: the issue of Jerusalem, for example. How does a Marxist theory help decide the competing normative claims which have little to do with economic relations? Second, we can ask ourselves whether a Marxist revolution on a world scale, supposing that it could be imagined, would abolish the relations between separate communities? It is hard to conceive that it would. Critical theory is right to suppose that identities, meanings and contexts, which are interwoven within particular and unique communities, would survive a communist revolution in the economic sphere. Finally, note that Marx believed that capitalist society was most developed in British society and that communist revolution could be expected to happen in Britain. This analysis obscures the imperialist position of the working class in Britain's nineteenth-century imperial role – a role based on powerful cultural assumptions as well as economic and military power.[12] The mills of Lancashire were successful on the basis of Britain's imperial position in the world. Marx imbibed the imperialist prejudices of his day. In *The Communist Manifesto*, for example, he writes how the bourgeoisie has drawn even the most 'barbarian nations into civilisation'.[13] Habermas is right to insist that critical theory must take another look at the tradition.

Habermas turns Marxist sociology back towards its Enlightenment roots. Fundamentally, Habermas's normative understanding is Kantian in character. The mark of moral consciousness in 'discourse ethics' – Habermas's boldest statement of moral theory – is deontological (concerned with duty), cognitivist (aiming to deliver moral knowledge), formal (it does not prescribe substantive injunctions), and universalist (the moral point of view is deemed to apply across time and space).[14] However, according to Habermas, 'discourse ethics' improves, in part, on the Kantian ethical tradition. Rather than relying on abstract standards of right, which are applied by individuals in isolation from one another, 'discourse ethics' is rooted, instead, in the structures of intersubjective consciousness embedded in the modern lifeworld. 'Discourse ethics' connects Kantianism with real social processes and is better placed to overcome Hegel's seminal critique of Kantian abstraction. The dialogic shift enables 'discourse ethics' to avoid the problems associated with the monological application of the universal Kantian will. As Stephen White remarks in *The Recent Work of Jürgen Habermas* 'the core ideas of intersubjective recognition and equal accountability make the universalism of communicative ethics one which is not "imperialistic" in the sense of always threatening to smother the "other".'[15]

Habermas resists the claim, put forward by postmodernism, that reason is inevitably caught up in relations of power and domination. Postmodernism's suspicion of reason has led it to reformulate the 'critical question'. Instead of attempting to uncover transcendental grounds of analytic and normative knowledge, postmodernism is defined by what is called a 'permanent withholding operation'.[16] This ongoing scepticism, while totally justified *in itself*, wrongly resists the articulation of positive moral and political goals. Recognising the fundamental role of contingency in all aspects of life, postmodernism constantly probes political discourses for evidence of the suppression of marginal voices. Postmodernism asks the following question: 'in what is given to us as universal, necessary, obligatory, what place is occupied by whatever is singular, contingent, and the product of arbitrary constraints?'[17] Seeing the history of reason as the history of distortion and oppression, postmodernism argues that our most important duty is not a 'responsibility to act', but a 'responsibility to otherness'.[18] This is a responsibility which can make us humble before what one writer calls 'the generations of the oppressed'.[19]

Habermas acknowledges the postmodernist critique of modern rationality. However, he also claims that postmodernism remains bound to the 'paradigm of the philosophy of consciousness'.[20] Through being based on the 'philosophy of consciousness', postmodernism is a form of reason that has many problems and contradictions of its own.

First, it blurs the distinction between art, literature, science and philosophy. The world-disclosing functions of language embedded in aesthetic consciousness and the consequent romantic disruption of reason are privileged, and the action-coordinating or problem-solving functions of language are neglected.[21] Although aesthetic consciousness has a role in world disclosure, there is still a need to preserve abstract standards of truth and morality. Claims to truth and claims to moral validity cannot be redeemed through aesthetic criteria. A theory may be aesthetically pleasing and misrepresent the world. Ptolemaic astronomy, with its complex system of circular motion, may be described as a false theory which was maintained for aesthetic reasons.

Second, the 'totalizing critique of reason' involves the postmodernist critic in what Habermas calls a 'performative contradiction'. In a 'performative contradiction', the presuppositions of the act of criticism contradict the propositional content embodied in the content of the criticism.[22] Postmodernism, in rejecting the role and place of reason altogether, cannot, at the same time, reasonably defend its position.

Third, postmodernism appeals to a 'crypto normativity'. It fails to articulate the implied normative standards involved in its critique of reason. Postmodernism would reject concepts of a flourishing human life as essentialist. However, there must be some positive normative ideas motivating the postmodern critique. Distortions of reason can be perceived only if more emancipatory forms of reason are simultaneously conceived.

Fourth, as Habermas puts it, in postmodernist thought '[t]he essentially ambiguous phenomena of modern culture are flattened down onto the plane of power'.[23] Modernity is an historical epoch that has produced both gains and losses. Distortion and oppression do not accompany all forms of modern reason.

Finally, postmodernism ignores the 'everyday' and 'problem-solving' characteristics of language.[24] However, the forms of reason that enable, for example, a newborn child to learn how to speak and write cannot be completely condemned as oppressive and distorting. And Habermas retains some faith in the moral abilities of the western democracies. Modern reason is not uniformly unredeemable. There are twists and turns in the character of modern reason which postmodernism does not recognise.

Against the dominant modes of instrumental rationality, Habermas's writings point to the importance of communication in the reproduction of society. Habermas writes:

> [u]nder the functional aspect of mutual understanding, communicative action serves to transmit and renew cultural knowledge; under the aspect of coordinating action, it serves social integration and the establishment of solidarity; finally, under the aspect of socialization, communicative action serves the formation of personal identities. The symbolic structures of the lifeworld are reproduced by way of the continuation of valid knowledge, stabilization of group solidarity, and socialization of responsible actors. . . . Corresponding to these processes of cultural reproduction, social integration and socialization are the structural components of the lifeworld: culture, society, person.[25]

When communicative action is distorted, culture, society and the person suffer. The store of cultural knowledge is not transmitted, political relationships are no longer connected to questions of legitimacy and the individual suffers anxiety and alienation from the context in which he or she finds him- or herself. In one sense, as Habermas puts it, 'I never say that people *want* to act communicatively but that they *have* to.'[26]

It is a central component of the concept of 'communicative action' that the claim or claims to 'comprehensibility', 'truth', 'rightness' or 'truthfulness' can be validated only on the basis of reason or argumentation. Validity claims require the 'force of the better argument' for justification. As Habermas writes:

> [o]wing to its linguistic structure, it [the validity of the claim] cannot be induced through outside influence... A communicatively achieved agreement has a rational basis; it cannot be imposed by either party, whether instrumentally through intervention in the situation directly or strategically through influencing the decisions of opponents.[27]

From the necessary fact that 'communicative reason' involves the rational redemption of validity claims, Habermas deduces a number of norms that are designed to govern political/moral interaction. At this point, a philosophy of language merges into a moral, political and legal theory – the 'discourse ethics' discussed briefly in the previous chapter. To uphold the norms of authentic and rational public discourse, Habermas insists on a number of points: communicative action should be free from deception, self-deception and the exercise of power and domination; all participants should be allowed to express their views, opinions, interests and needs; and any actor who wishes to introduce a political proposal defensible on the basis of universalisation may do so.

In more recent writings, Habermas has argued that the necessary structure of argumentation, embedded in the assessment of validity claims in communicative action, also rests on, and generates, a set of legal rights which guarantee both private and public autonomy.[28] Here, as Kenneth Baynes puts it, it is correct to speak of the '"interpenetration" of the legal form and the "quasi-transcendental" discourse principle'.[29]

Habermas is aware that real-life political interaction fails to live up to the stringent normative requirements laid down in the concept of 'discourse ethics'. There are, however, a number of caveats to the argument.

First, Habermas allows for the formation of compromise agreements, providing that two conditions are met. Under the first condition, compromises are acceptable. However, a genuine commitment must first be made to address and test arguments and to reach rational consensus if possible. Under the second condition, a compromise is acceptable but it must be struck under the condition of a roughly equal balance of power. This latter condition ensures that the resort to compromise is not strategically imposed by any one party involved in the political process.[30] Generally, Habermas is suspicious of compromise formulations where 'generalisable interests' are at stake. 'Generalisable interests', by their nature, admit of consensus and rational will-formation and compromises over them hint at relations of domination, power, exclusion and control.

The second response recognises that the norms of communicative action are equivalent to what Kant called 'regulative ideals'.[31] Considered thus, even though they may be rarely manifested in political reality, they remain a source of knowledge not illusion.[32] As Habermas notes, the 'regulative ideals' of 'communicative reason' can give us knowledge of the 'suppression of generalizable interests'.[33] Here, the norms of communicative action serve as critical standards which allow the identification of justified and justifiable political and moral norms. Conversely, the norms of communicative action can aid the identification of, as Habermas writes, 'norms that merely stabilize relations of force'.[34]

Third, Habermas draws an important distinction between moral discourses and other types of discourse – ethical or pragmatic discourses, for example. The strong universalising logic of discourse applies only in the case of moral discourses where the basic, fundamental and 'generalisable interests' of actors are affected. As Ciaran P. Cronin writes in the introduction to *Justification and Application*, 'not all practical questions admit of resolution in this manner since they do not necessarily involve potentially common interests'.[35] Habermas puts it this way:

> A mode of examining maxims or a heuristic for generating maxims guided by the question of how I want to live involves a different exercise of practical reason from reflection on whether from my perspective a generally observed maxim is suitable to regulate our communal existence. In the first case, what is being asked is whether a maxim is good for me and is appropriate in the given situation, and in the second, whether I can will that a maxim should be followed by everyone as a general law.[36]

Importantly, the fairness of the various negotiations and compromises which surround the various exercises of practical reason *is* a moral question, as it concerns an actor's autonomy. An actor who is illegitimately excluded from a practical discourse is one whose democratic rights are being curtailed. As William Outhwaite writes, '[t]he complex relations between these various discourses includes at least a process model of rational will formation'.[37]

Habermas's writings introduce a number of themes which find their way into cosmopolitan international political theory: a reformulation of the critical-philosophical tradition, a continuing faith in modern reason and rationality and its potential, the importance of communication and dialogue, and a democratic political theory designed to support a concept of legitimacy.

Contemporary cosmopolitanism

To be a cosmopolitan is to see the entire world as a political community. Or rather, to be a member of a cosmopolitan community is to seek to extend the political influence of the cosmopolitan community and state across as much of the universe as possible whenever this is deemed necessary by reason or virtue of cosmopolitan morality. Cosmopolitan international morality can be the most active form of international ethics, as it may involve the power of everyone. If mass space travel, life in space for increasing numbers of people or alien encounters ever become a reality, the cosmopolis could include it all. A cosmopolis is the largest political community of which we can conceive given that all we can conceive of has the potential to be part of it. In theory, particular members of a cosmopolis may never be related by substantial political relations, even for periods lasting a thousand years. Cosmopolitanism merely desires the possibility of substantial political relations involving all, should they ever be required.

What characteristics constitute contemporary cosmopolitanism? Both Held and Linklater make use of Habermas's analysis of 'communicative action', where the legitimacy of a political order rests on the rational consent of those who are subject to it.

Held writes that Habermas's 'discourse ethics', a normative off-shoot of the more sociological theory of 'communicative action', can help 'disclose the constitutive basis of democratic public law'.[38] Here, 'the goal is to elucidate those conditions of autonomy capable of defence on the ground that they are in principle equally acceptable to all parties or social groups.'[39] Thus, as Held puts it, 'the creation of a cosmopolitan democracy requires the active consent of peoples and nations . . . It would be a contradiction of the very idea of democracy itself if a cosmopolitan democratic order were created non-voluntarily.'[40]

Linklater bases his cosmopolitan theory on Habermasean 'discourse ethics', a perspective which combines 'justification' and 'application' in a universalism mediated through real social processes. Linklater writes that 'a post-Westphalian order has to honour various obligations to other societies who do not share its principles of association'.[41] Here, '[c]osmopolitan citizenship refers to the commitment to perfecting these mechanisms for wooing the consent of others.'[42] In addition, Linklater writes, 'the principles of international order will lack legitimacy unless they command the consent of the world's peoples'.[43]

Held and Linklater base their argument for the cosmopolitan ethic on the failures of the Westphalian order. They point to the growth of a world economy, the growth of transnational linkages with new sites of decision-making, the growth in international communications, the proliferation of military technologies and the global nature of environmental problems.[44] On top of these pressures from above, the state is also facing the forces of 'fragmentation' as sub-national groups challenge the rights of others to incorporate them into a dominant national culture. Fragmentation is a reaction to globalisation as well as nationalist pressures. Indeed, as Linklater argues, 'with its homogenizing tendencies, globalisation fuels the politics of identity and community'.[45]

With the power of the state on the wane, Held writes of a 'new fluidity' in international affairs which can help push democratic thinking and institutions into the central sites of power in international politics.[46] Contemporary political theory and action can break through impotent and illegitimate state structures and establish new forms of power on the global stage.

Cosmopolitan analysis does not reject the state altogether. Rather, the state can be expected to 'wither away' under new forms of political arrangement, or become instead 'but one focus for legal development, political reflection and mobilization'.[47] Citizens of the cosmopolis will have legal and political affiliations with a variety of institutions existing at different levels of governance. Understanding the 'cosmopolitan order' involves understanding the 'arrangements underpinning autonomy for all in the political community'.[48] Here, 'the effective entrenchment of democratic law' takes place in 'sites of power' that are 'national, transnational and international' in character. Furthermore, 'sovereignty is an attribute of the basic democratic law, but it could be entrenched and drawn upon in diverse self-regulating associations, from states to cities and corporations.'[49]

As theory and practice move beyond the nation-state, cosmopolitanism involves a strong sense of active duty where each individual is bound by a moral law, given concrete expression in a set of legal and political obligations, to project and protect autonomy in the primary sites of global power, which include the welfare, culture, civic association, the economy, the organisation of violence and legal institutions.[50]

Linklater argues that 'modern conditions require more radical remedies' than the admirable, though politically quiet, Kantian respect for international law. The duties defined by the modern cosmopolitan moral law cannot be willed in isolation. They are known only through active democratic procedures and they take on a social, economic and cultural dimension. Cosmopolitanism:

> requires international joint action to ameliorate the condition of the most vulnerable groups in world society and to ensure that they can defend their legitimate interests by participating in effective universal communicative frameworks.[51]

Cosmopolitanism promotes an active form of political agency. As Held writes: 'a democracy would be fully worth its name only if citizens had the actual power to be active as citizens.'[52]

For Held, cosmopolitan commitments take on a largely legal and institutional character. He proposes to 'restrict the meaning of cosmopolitanism to a form of law, and to a form of political community which might create and sustain this law'.[53] He calls this law 'cosmopolitan democratic public law'. The law states that individuals 'should be free and equal in the determination of the conditions of their own lives, so long as they do not deploy this framework to negate the right of others'.[54] Enforcing this law involves the creation of 'an expanding framework of democratic institutions and procedures', which exist at the sub-national, national and supra-national levels across key sites of social power.[55] This cosmopolitan legal and political structure differs from a Westphalian and a 'UN' model. The state is only one form of legitimate institution among many, whose decision-making power is granted by a pragmatic principle of appropriateness rather than a metaphysical neo-realism.[56] And the cosmopolitan order is not subject to the stringent interpretations of sovereignty which underpin the UN system.

For Linklater, cosmopolitanism is defined by the need to engage the 'systematically excluded' through 'enlarging the moral boundaries of the political community'.[57] The moral resources of democracy and public law which have evolved in the struggle against 'wrongful exclusion' at the level of the nation-state can be used to promote inclusiveness at a global level. Like Habermas, Linklater believes that modernity is an unfinished rather than a bankrupt project. 'Realizing the promise of the post-Westphalian era is', as Linklater writes, 'the essence of the unfinished project of modernity.'[58]

Linklater's account of cosmopolitanism is philosophically attuned to disagreements with postmodernism and communitarianism. Taking inspiration from Habermas, Linklater moves beyond both Kant and Marx and envisages a situation where 'dialogic communities' and 'domination-free communication' can combine both universality and difference. Linklater is sensitive to the postmodern criticism that cosmopolitanism has 'the potential for domination'.[59] However, as postmodernism's political stance has 'a certain resonance with the Kantian principle of respect for persons', it can be coupled with a 'thin' cosmopolitanism, which rejects transcendent modes of justification in favour of a 'dialogic community', which combines a responsibility to otherness with a desire to include the 'systematically excluded' in a 'higher level of universality and difference'.[60] The task of 'praxeological' analysis is to 'assist the development of new forms of political authority and novel conceptions of citizenship which strike a balance between universality and difference'.[61] Linklater marries postmodernism and critical theory in a non-foundationalist dialogical ethic, the rationale of which is to include the systematically excluded through the extension of moral community.

The versions of cosmopolitanism described by Held and Linklater are in a sense complementary. While Held concentrates more on institutional questions, Linklater provides a philosophical analysis. This is an oversimplification. Held refers to Habermasean discourse ethics in a 'democratic thought experiment', designed to 'disclose the fundamental enabling conditions for possible political participation'.[62] Linklater investigates Hedley Bull's analysis of 'the feasibility of a neo-medieval political framework' and 'new relationships between sub-state, national and transnational authorities'.[63] Taken together, however, Held and Linklater provide an almost exhaustive account of contemporary cosmopolitanism's institutional nature and philosophical foundations.

The application to international mediation

In an article entitled 'Incomplete States: Theories and Practices of Statecraft', Richard Devetak says that 'there is statecraft, but there is no completed state'.[64]

Devetak analyses statecraft as an ongoing, ceaseless activity aimed at the 'inscription of boundaries' which mark outside from in, self from other, domestic from international, order from anarchy and so on. In this conception of statecraft, the state is not a fixed entity from which statecraft proceeds – as if the state exists prior to and independently from statecraft. On the contrary, as threats to the boundaries of the state are ceaseless, state identity can never be complete. Consequently, statecraft is a term given to those activities which 'produce the *effect* of a completed state'.[65]

We can talk about mediation in similar terms. Mediation is an activity in which a third party attempts to keep up a momentum of negotiation between disputing parties. Like those who practise statecraft, the mediator tries to inscribe, maintain and enhance a boundary. At a basic level, the boundaries involved in a mediation process separate dialogue and conflict, resolution and stalemate, peace and war and so on. Conflict, stalemate and war are to be kept on the outside. Dialogue, resolution and peace are to be kept on the inside.

Mediation is a practice which attempts to enhance dialogue through the inscription of borders which divide conflict from negotiation. The mediator is locked in a constant battle to keep disputing actors inside and within the borders of negotiation. But with Habermas's 'discourse ethics', Held's 'democratic public law' and Linklater's 'dialogical community' in mind, this border takes on a particular normative or 'communicative' quality. Dialogue and negotiation governed by cosmopolitan principles are to be inside the border, and dialogue whose end point is what Habermas once called the 'suppression of generalizable interests' or the negation of 'rational will formation' ought to lie outside that border.[66] Thus the practice of mediation can be assessed with reference to the extent to which it manages to uphold the borders of a cosmopolitan communicative ethic capable of disclosing and realising Held's 'democratic public law' or Linklater's 'dialogic community', which derive their ultimate authority from the principles of 'discourse ethics'. Mediation which manages to introduce, maintain and even enhance the strength and quality of the cosmopolitan communicative ethic ought to be deemed better than mediation practice which fails to introduce, maintain and enhance such an ethic. In essence, this is the critical theory of international mediation at an abstract level.

The critical approach also embodies certain sociological and praxeological considerations. In the postscript to the 1990 edition of *Men and Citizens*, and in a 1992 article entitled 'The Question of the Next Stage' published in *Millennium*, Linklater, recognising 'the lack of significant progress in developing a critical theory of international relations', moves debate on and urges future critical theory to pursue more empirical and sociological analyses.[67]

A sociological standpoint is a necessary adjunct to the normative approach. Here, analysis focuses on the means by which boundaries, borders and systems of inclusion and exclusion are developed, maintained and enforced. Linklater argues that this sociological approach has three aspects: an epistemic axis, which examines the discursive construction and maintenance of particular identities (the ways in which self and other are understood); an axis, which refers to the character of the moral relationships that are developed between self and other; finally, a praxeological analysis, which examines the ways in which a particular community enforces its borders – in both an ideological and more practical sense. The sociological aspect of enquiry, by examining the practices, institutions and ideas of a particular situation, can also seek to question whether or not 'a political community is likely to expand or contract, remain bound up with the sovereign state or change so that sub-national and transnational loyalties acquire greater importance'.[68]

The praxeological dimension seeks to determine how new and more inclusive political communities can be created. What shifts or realignments of power would be necessary to generate borders and systems of inclusion and exclusion which conform more readily to the conditions of legitimacy specified by cosmopolitan principles? Linklater writes: 'a critical approach to foreign policy analysis can explore the ways in which the potential for internationalism which exists in most modern states can be realized in international conventions which enshrine the moral principles of an alternative world order.'[69]

In the following two chapters we shall put this threefold critical structure to the test in an analysis of the Oslo process and Accords.

Three problems facing cosmopolitan international theory

The first problem concerns the continuing lack of concrete historical analysis in the critical or cosmopolitan tradition. In contrast to Foucault's detailed analysis of the clinic and the asylum, as Linklater writes:

> For the most part, critical theorists have failed to develop empirical investigations of the constraining role of micro- and macro-social and political structures. Inquiries into methodology and the philosophy of the social sciences and more recently, in Habermas's work, studies of communicative action and communicative rationality have outpaced empirical analyses of the contexts in which human beings confront (to use the language of the Frankfurt School) unnecessary social constraints and distorted forms of culture and communication.[70]

That the critical theory of international relations remains empirically underdeveloped is a point also made by the US liberal institutionalists, Judith Goldstein and Robert Keohane. In their book, *Ideas and Foreign Policy*, they write:

> The key issue, however, is not whether identities matter but how they matter, and how their effects can be systematically studied by social scientists. Unfortunately, reflectivist scholars have been slow to articulate or test hypotheses. Without either a

well-defined set of propositions or a rich empirical analysis, the reflectivist critique remains more an expression of understandable frustration than a working research program.[71]

Without historical analysis, political thinking is, to borrow a phrase from Nietzsche, 'anthropomorphic through and through'.[72] As Nietzsche writes, describing the nature of anthropomorphic thought in his essay 'Truth and Falsity in their Extra-Moral Sense':

> [i]f somebody hides a thing behind a bush, seeks it again and finds it in the self same place then there is not so much to boast of respecting this seeking and finding; thus, however, matters stand with the seeking and finding of 'truth' within the realm of reason. If I make the definition of the mammal and then declare after inspecting a camel 'Behold a mammal', then no doubt a truth is brought to light thereby, but it is of very limited value.[73]

The problem of anthropomorphism affected Linklater's earlier approaches to the theme of 'men' and 'citizens'. Linklater admits that *Men and Citizens* is based on a philosophical history that is without historical grounding. He writes:

> [o]ur scale of types of international relations is not drawn directly from historical experience. Although some examples may have a rough correspondence with actual historical forms . . . each is principally a construct. It will be clear that the scale of forms of external relations does not correspond with anything that has ever happened.[74]

In *Men and Citizens*, however, Linklater states that the lack of historical knowledge is not undue cause for alarm, given, as he puts it himself, 'that his argument is an exercise in political theory'.[75] Since when, though, did political theory have nothing to do with history? The lack of attention to history is obviously a problem. For example, Linklater's particular assessment of our modern moral predicament – as a 'bifurcated moral subject' – is developed without any reference to real conditions; this cannot be possible.[76] The lack of reference to particular historical circumstances can result in generalisations which gloss over the detailed nature of historical reality. Linklater writes, for example: 'the challenge to systems of exclusion based on race, nationality and ethnicity, gender and class has been one the distinctive features of Western political theory and practice during the last two hundred years.'[77] Claims like this one are generalisations which universalise particular perspectives: especially if we consider, for example, the victims of the European conquest of the globe. Linklater himself writes that the above claim exists on a 'general level'.[78] The problem with generalisations, however, is that they invariably turn out to be false when they are applied to concrete particular circumstances.

There is a need to develop a body of case-study material within critical approaches. The Oslo Accords and process described in the following two chapters are intended to remedy the lack of case-study material within the critical literature.

A second problem facing a cosmopolitan or critical analysis is, potentially, a more serious one. A discourse theory of morality has a vision of an ideal society in which all parties come to the negotiating table as equals to judge any claim which may be advanced, and they do so without any prior assumption about the nature of the ultimate outcome. In Habermasean terms, cosmopolitan morality presupposes post-conventional reasoning. The problem, however, is that this ideal can only be approximated to in real life. For example, disputing parties may not be able to discuss certain positions in the context of democratic public law without losing political office. The application of democratic public law to a particular situation of conflict may immediately result in a hopeless antagonism between the mediator and one or more of the disputants, with the result that the mediator is immediately disqualified as an impartial intervenor. The strength of facilitation theory, it might be argued, is that it works with a concept of dialogue more attuned to the problems inherent in protracted social conflict. A cosmopolitan approach might result in paralysis.

While recognising some truth in this argument, there are a number of potential cosmopolitan responses. First, a critical or cosmopolitan approach can still work with a strong and abstract sense of justice if it is willing to conceive its political model only as a Kantian 'regulative ideal'. Here, the theory is still a source of knowledge and not illusion. And, as noted in the previous chapter, the cosmopolitan theory can act as an ultimate, abstract theoretical authority to which facilitation must turn when it wishes to redeem its normative ambitions. In addition, as we shall see in the analysis of Oslo, facilitation works with the distinction between interim and final status. Here, facilitation can be the form of interim practice which aspires to a final status, which is conceived using a more abstract cosmopolitan approach.

While this approach has much to recommend it from a purely theoretical point of view, it is unsatisfactory considered on its own. It leaves the field of practice to other approaches, and there seems to be no way to develop a critical or cosmopolitan form of policy. Without some idea of policy, however, cosmopolitan or critical approaches would work largely at the level of theory and would leave all non-realist forms of third-party practice to facilitation. Is it possible to conceive of an emancipatory form of practice which is not reducible to facilitative methods?

A critical or cosmopolitan approach can seek to overcome obstacles to dialogue through *strengthening the forces of democracy in the region of conflict*. This approach is derived from a basic assumption: namely, that dialogue arises out of necessity and that where power operates to shape a political context dialogue is rendered redundant. Through strengthening the forces of democracy, the intervening power can hope to alter the future course of negotiations without becoming 'facilitative'. A critical or cosmopolitan approach seeks to strengthen the weaker forces of democracy in order that stronger or more intransigent parties will gain more of an incentive to talk.

This approach is similar to what one writer has recently called a 'governance-based approach' to international mediation. As Hampson writes:

> governance-based approaches see the challenge of peacebuilding and third party involvement largely in terms of the creation of participatory governance structures, the development of new social norms, and the establishment of the rule of law and democracy.[79]

Governance-based approaches see power as a force in politics, but this is the form of power that Hannah Arendt described as 'action in concert'.[80] Here, power depends on organisation and is rooted in popular support. Thus, through developing a disputing parties' economy and civil society, the third party helps the parties of democracy and compromise to mobilise themselves more effectively. The long-term goal is to neutralise intransigent opposition to a negotiated agreement. The EU's funding of the Palestinian National Authority in the wake of Oslo is a possible attempt to institute such a policy, despite the failures of Arafat's rather dictatorial regime. The EU hoped that building the Palestinian economy and civil society would lead to a more just and long-term solution as the bargaining strength of the Palestinians would be improved and the forces of democracy strengthened in the region as a whole.

The cosmopolitan focus in empowerment differs from the practice of facilitation. Facilitative approaches apply behavioural science techniques to bring parties to a more inclusive and wide-ranging dialogue. This involves, for example, a high degree of political intimacy. Like the power-political approach, however, the critical or cosmopolitan approach can act from a distance in a situation where political relations are tense. But unlike the power-political approach, the critical or cosmopolitan form of practice does not treat the conflict as an instrument of a wider global struggle for power. Rather, it attempts to empower political forces more likely to negotiate a settlement which approximates to the ideal of cosmopolitan democratic law. The conflict is treated as an end in itself. The critical approach attempts to ensure that those parties that are committed to negotiations receive the diplomatic, technical, economic and political support necessary to defeat, obstruct or weaken the forces of intransigence. The cosmopolitan political goal involves the long-term objective of strengthening forces committed to negotiation.

There are, of course, risks associated with this approach. The intransigent parties are likely to regard the outside power as hostile and will aim to disrupt its plans. And rather than forcing a compromise in the long term, the mobilisation of a democratic power may lead to an escalation of the conflict. As Hampson writes: 'governance-based approaches underestimate the difficulties of democratisation and the unstable political forces that may be unleashed by democratic institutions and processes in societies unaccustomed to democracy the rule of law.'[81] In this sense the facilitators are correct. However, the risks inherent in alienating intransigent forces are unavoidable, given a genuine commitment to solutions based upon cosmopolitan ethics in a situation defined by intransigence.

Furthermore, this type of intervention is expensive and difficult to manage. It involves long-term commitment and expense in political, economic and diplomatic terms. The cosmopolitan mediator may even face threats to its international security. For these reasons, cosmopolitan forms of mediation practice are probably best undertaken by coalitions of states embedded in regional security frameworks, such as, for example, the EU.

Despite the difficulties, the concept of 'governance' creates a critical or cosmopolitan ideal of practice which supplements its normative scope. Such action can be termed mediation. Third external parties aim for an overall settlement based on cosmopolitan political ideals. They seek to do this by mobilising the resources and strengths of democratic parties in order that intransigent parties will see the long-term costs of intransigence. It is, of course, a risky strategy. But the same can be said of nearly all forms of international action.

Facilitation and the cosmopolitan approach may complement each other. The former offers a more nuanced understanding of political context, while the latter stands as a reminder of the political ideals. But this distinction cannot be couched in terms of theory and practice, where facilitation is a form of practice which approximates to the ideals laid down by cosmopolitan theory. It is just as likely that barriers to genuine dialogue exist because more powerful parties do not *need* dialogue to achieve their goals; as it is, that dialogue fails because of mistrust and an inability to recognise the identity of the other. In the former case, the application of facilitative techniques will be insufficient to alter the situation. In which case, a critical form of practice is introduced. This is a genuine critical form of mediation, as it takes the intransigence of the stronger party to task, and seeks to alter the balance of power through a variety of strategic options. A governance-based approach, designed to help weaker democratic parties mobilise their resources more effectively, is a critical form of practice which still warrants the term mediation.

A third and final problem facing cosmopolitanism is its overestimation of the extent to which there exists a moral world order in its favour. Cosmopolitan international political theory rests on a view of the world which contains assumptions about the moral resources available for the forces of cosmopolitan change. Held writes, for example, that the cosmopolitan order will 'be enshrined within the constitutions of parliaments and assemblies at the national and international level'.[82] In addition, the cosmopolitan model would seek the creation of an effective transnational legislative and executive with 'enforcement capabilities'.[83] Held is optimistic that existing institutions could adapt to suit the cosmopolitan goal.

Following Habermas, Linklater draws on the resources of modern western cultural development. Linklater writes, for example, that, 'intimations of the post-Westphalian world are apparent in Western Europe'.[84] He repeats the point: '[a]lternative means of organizing human beings which are already immanent within the modern states seem most likely to appear in Western Europe and in the neighbouring societies which are being drawn inside its orbit.'[85] Furthermore, within the international system as a whole, '[a]n elementary universalism underpins the society of states and contributes the survival of international order.'[86] Within this world order, '[m]odern citizens learn the language of a transcendent moral code which makes the critique of abuses of national power ... possible.'[87]

It must remain an open question as to whether the potentials for cosmopolitan rationality are as deeply embedded in the western tradition as Held and Linklater, following Habermas, would claim. It may be true, as Danilo Zolo writes, that, 'the ordinary morality to which international moralists appeal would appear to be an academic hypothesis rather than a sociological datum to be assumed without further discussion.'[88]

For the great critic of modernity – Nietzsche, for example – the mark of the truly modern individual is that he or she recognises the world to be essentially chaotic, meaningless and arbitrary. Nietzsche describes in *The Gay Science* the lack of any principle ordering the world:

> Let us beware of attributing to it [the world] heartlessness and unreason or their opposites: it is neither perfect nor beautiful nor noble, and has no desire to become any of these; it is by no means striving to imitate mankind! It is quite impervious to all our aesthetic and moral judgements! It has likewise no impulse to self-preservation or impulses of any mind; neither does it know any laws.[89]

The point is put with incredible perception. He writes that, 'life is no argument, among the conditions of life could be error.'[90]

Held is clear that there is no strong teleological vision of history underlying his approach to cosmopolitan morality. He writes that there are no metaphysical, religious or foundational grounds for being a democrat.[91] Similarly, Linklater seeks to transcend the 'thick' universalisms of Kant or Marx, for example. However, both Held and Linklater draw on 'reason' to support their cosmopolitan world-view. For them, strong conceptions of human nature are abandoned, but rationality of some sort remains in place as a moral resource which can direct the future. But, if pushed, scepticism can 'shave' reason 'right to the bone.' And we may legitimately wonder whether the fragments which remain are a sufficient foundation upon which to build.

Habermas, Held and Linklater put forward a variety of arguments to sustain

Cosmopolitan mediation?

the proposition that emancipatory forms of reason exist as moral resources in the contemporary world. But scepticism dogs these arguments all the way. With Habermas, it is possible to state, for example, that:

> I never say that people want to act communicatively, but that they have to . . . Our intersubjectively shared, overlapping lifeworlds lay down a broad background consensus, without which our everyday praxis simply couldn't take place. The Hobbesian state of nature . . . that's the truly artificial construction.[92]

Linklater adopts this stance to some degree. The authority of cosmopolitan ethics is based on practical realities of modern life and the solutions they require. Social coordination in the modern world rests on, and requires, plurality and consensus. As Linklater writes, 'no modern community is immune from international ethical debates', as we are all 'implicated in complex moral questions about the character of modern political community.'[93] Held, too, bases the cosmopolitan edifice on the practical problems in the modern world, global economies, nuclear proliferation and so on, which can only be sorted out with the cooperation of all. A pragmatic form of reason points international policy in the direction of cosmopolitan ethics.

A supplement to this argument is the Habermasean idea that modern decentered structures of society and consciousness embody higher learning potential. The modern separation of science, morality and art from nature or quasi-natural categories means a possible increase in autonomy if the potentials of modern universalist rationality are realised. Thus, although modernity creates problems of a complex global nature, it also provides the solutions. As modernity breaks up traditional modes of thought, which weld society and nature together, it creates a potential for the higher levels of moral learning and development, which are necessary to overcome the complex global problem created by itself.

The problem with the modern pragmatic argument, as Linklater himself notes, is that, 'whether these themes have any claim whatsoever on human beings elsewhere – that is, whether they are obligated to share these ethical sensibilities – is, for many, the central question.'[94] If, as William Rehg writes, the grounds for 'discourse ethics' 'reside in a particular historical experience', then they lose their ultimate moral force.[95] One could equally, and rationally, reject the problems created by modernity and attempt to turn back the clock of history rather than accept the modern cosmopolitan solution to modernity which relies on a synthesis of *de facto* modernism and *de jure* cosmopolitan ethics.

The Habermasean may argue that modern insights and structures of consciousness are not easily forgotten, thus it is not possible to travel back in history to a premodern normative structure. However (a) modernity may embody higher learning potential (b) modernity may simultaneously cause the problems, yet provide the solutions and (c) while modern insights are not easily forgotten, why is higher, universalist learning potential in the realm of morality an ultimate moral good? Habermas is faced with a dilemma. If we only need higher learning potential, given a set of modern contingencies, then modern structures of moral consciousness are only contingently good. If, however, modern structures of moral consciousness are to be preferred as an ultimate moral good independently of modern contingencies, then (a) a defence of their value has to supersede the pragmatic argument and (b) Habermas would need to show why a *discursive* 'communicative reason' has more intrinsic moral worth. The problem with this second argument is that it may rely on a 'thick' conception of human nature and Habermas wants to avoid the charges of foundationalism and cultural relativism which beset all attempts at what he calls 'first philosophy.'

Furthermore, why assume that insights gained can never be lost? An evolutionary approach to human society, one adopted by Habermas and Linklater to a strong degree, can also follow the Nietzschean path, which recognises that what was brought into being can also fade away. As Nietzsche writes, 'onward development is not by any means, by any necessity the same thing as elevation, advance, strengthening.'[96]

An additional cosmopolitan response is to argue that, as the rationalisation of the lifeworld along cosmopolitan lines is something which all cultures could achieve independently of each other, cosmopolitanism is universal in scope without being culturally specific in its nature. Given time, modern cosmopolitan rationality would appear 'naturally' in many parts of the world. Habermas writes:

> Is it the case that universal world religions converge in some core condition of moral intuition according to their own claims, a core that we interpret as equal respect for all, equal respect for the need to promote the integrity of each individual person, and for the damageable intersubjectivity of all forms of human existence?[97]

Here, as there are 'variously routed trips to the telos of rational cooperation', cosmopolitan norms can be said to have a universal status of some description.[98] As Linklater writes, 'critical and dialogic components of culture are evident in different societies and the outlines of a cosmopolitan culture . . . are already apparent.'[99] It is important to note, however, that notions of dialogue, 'may not have exactly the same meaning, and rival understandings deserve due recognition.'[100]

While this argument may buy some time for the cosmopolitan, it is an argument, as Rehg writes, that 'shoulders a large burden of proof.' It has to show that 'social evolution displays structural homologies with individual ontogenesis' across different cultures.[101] In addition, and more importantly, cosmopolitan necessity would have to arise for all societies at the same time and independently of every other society if no imposition of value commitments were to take place and interfere with autonomous moral development towards the 'modern structure.' Some may argue that it is already too late for this to happen. The complex global connections which have existed historically, and the concomitant destruction of many forms of life, entail the proposition that all societies have been shaped by others and power has been a predominant force in this shaping. The test of universal structural homology, if this view is correct, is thus rendered impossible. The evidence has already been corrupted and no future political order will escape the elements of force and chance.

The point I wish to make in these arguments is that reason does not necessarily point in a cosmopolitan direction. Thinking in the vein of post-conventional morality, Habermas, Linklater and Held reject strong conceptions of history or human nature. For these thinkers, reason exists in the world, and it is reason which provides the moral resources of a cosmopolitan future. However, we can recognise, with Nietzsche, that the world contains few, if any, moral qualities and resources upon which the cosmopolitan project can draw.

Of course, critics of the modern world order, such as Habermas, Held and Linklater, agree, in some respect, with this proposition. Critical approaches argue that there is no moral world order and that the world has to be remade. But the sceptical point to be made here is a stronger one. If the world is to be changed, there have to be moral resources upon which the critical project can draw. Thus, Habermas, Held and Linklater rely on certain moral resources in their critical project; admittedly, not a strong teleological conception of history or human nature, but a conception of reason, all the same. However, if we push the sceptical point a little further, even a 'thin' or 'dialogic' reason may take on the quality of a will-o'-the-wisp.

I cannot hope to answer these questions decisively. My purpose is to strike a note of caution or pessimism as we move towards the analysis of the case study. The following chapter examines the push and pull of geostrategic forces which underpinned the Oslo process. The picture which emerges is of a political situation dominated by the forces of randomness, complexity and chaos – the forces of Fortune. The principal protagonists may like to have appeared as though they were directing forces of change. However, the Oslo channel resulted, in many ways, from the sheer pressure of events. It is to a description of these events that we now turn.

NOTES

1 M. Hoffman, 'Normative International Theory: Approaches and Issues' in A. J. R. Groom and M. Light (eds), *Contemporary International Relations Theory* (London: Pinter Publishers, 1994).
2 J. Habermas, *The Theory of Communicative Action* (Cambridge: Polity Press, 1991), first published in German in 1981. For an introductory summary of Habermas's work, see W. Outhwaite, *Habermas* (Cambridge: Polity Press, 1994). Also, see M. Hoffman, 'Critical Theory and the Inter-Paradigm Debate', *Millennium: Journal of International Studies*, 16: 2, pp. 231–49; M. Hoffman, 'Conversations on Critical International Relations Theory', *Millennium: Journal of International Studies*, 17: 1, pp. 91–5; A. Linklater, *Men and Citizens*

in the *Theory of International Relations*, 2nd edition (London: The Macmillan Press, 1990); A. Linklater, *Beyond Realism and Marxism: Critical Theory and International Relations* (Basingstoke: Macmillan, 1990); A. Linklater, 'The Question of the Next Stage in International Relations Theory: A Critical-Theoretic Point of View, *Millennium: Journal of International Studies*, 21: 1, pp. 77–98; A. Linklater, *The Transformation of Political Community* (Cambridge: Polity Press, 1998); D. Held, *Democracy and the Global Order* (Cambridge: Polity Press, 1995).
3 See, for example, the postscript on Habermas and Foucault in the 1990 edition of Linklater, *Men and Citizens*.
4 *Ibid.*, p. 219.
5 E. Said, *Culture and Imperialism* (London: Vintage, 1993), p. 71.
6 The quotation is taken from R. K. Ashley and R. J. B. Walker, 'Reading Dissidence/Writing the Discipline: Crisis and the Question of Sovereignty in International Studies', *International Studies Quarterly*, 34:3 (1990), pp. 367–416.
7 Held, *Democracy*, p. 229.
8 D. Zola, *Cosmopolis: Prospects for World Government* (Cambridge: Polity Press, 1997), p. 22.
9 See, for example, A. Giddens, *The Nation-State and Violence: Volume Two of a Contemporary Critique of Historical Materialism* (London: Polity, 1985).
10 A. Linklater, 'The Achievements of Critical Theory', in S. Smith, K. Booth and M. Zalewski (eds), *International Theory: Positivism and Beyond* (Cambridge: Cambridge University Press, 1996), p. 280.
11 N. Geras, 'The Controversy about Marx and Justice', in *Literature of Revolution: Essays on Marxism* (London: Verso, 1986), p. 3. My emphasis.
12 See, for example, Said., *Culture and Imperialism*. As Said writes, 'Hardly any North American African, European, Latin American, Indian, Caribbean, Australian individual . . . who is alive today has not been touched by the empires of the past' – p. 6. Said argues that the major trends in critical social theory – including Marxism and the Frankfurt School – 'have avoided the major . . . determining political horizon of modern Western culture, namely imperialism' - p. 70. Habermas's critical theory has not directly addressed the issue of imperialism – a fact which Said notes (p. 336). However, the general focus on questions of culture and intersubjectivity inherent in Habermasean critical theory point to the importance of turning criticism towards the construction of oppressive and exclusionary discourses.
13 K. Marx and F. Engels, *The Communist Manifesto* (London: Penguin, 1967).
14 'Discourse Ethics', in J. Habermas, *Moral Consciousness and Communicative Action* (Cambridge: Polity Press, 1990).
15 S. K. White, *The Recent Work of Jürgen Habermas* (Cambridge: Cambridge University Press, 1988), p. 82. White gives the example of a 19th-century Victorian who may forbid his adolescent daughter from studying to become a doctor on the grounds that it is not proper for women. As White writes, '[t]hat father could, in good conscience, will his proscription as a universal law' – p. 82.
16 S. K. White, *Political Theory and Postmodernism* (Cambridge: Cambridge University Press, 1991), p. 16.
17 P. Rabinow (ed.), *The Foucault Reader* (Harmondsworth: Penguin, 1984), p. 45.
18 White, *Postmodernism*, p. 20.
19 G. M. Simpson, 'Theologica Crucis and the Forensically Fraught World: Engaging Helmut Peukert and Jürgen Habermas', in Don S. Browning and Francis Schuster Fionenza (eds), *Habermas, Modernity and Public Theology* (New York: Crossroad, 1992), p. 177.
20 J. Habermas, *The Philosophical Discourse of Modernity* (Cambridge: Polity Press, 1987), p. 310.

21 *Ibid.*, p. 205.
22 *Ibid.*, p xv. Also, see, 'Discourse Ethics.' The idea of a 'performative contradiction' is the philosophy of language's equivalent of Kant's transcendental *a priori*. The idea points to a contradiction which is not merely analytic – i.e. an idea which is self-contradictory, but only in formal terms (for example, 'all brothers are not male'). Like the idea of the synthetic *a priori*, the idea of a 'performative contradiction' tells us something substantial about our place in the world – what can be done, thought, known or said. The concept highlights some existential reality. A 'performative contradiction' points to a 'minimal logic' which grounds ideas of rationality and truth, and it illustrates some antagonistic aspect of thought or action. Descartes's *cogito* can be reconstructed in terms of a 'performative contradiction', as could Bertrand Russell's argument about a theory of types or the classical paradox of the Cretan who argued that all Cretans are liars.

Less formally, and in more social and political terms, the idea of a 'performative contradiction' points to the ways in which language and communication can be misused or abused either intentionally or not. Those who commit 'performative contradictions' *intentionally* – for example, the strategic liar, the propagandist or the purveyor of ideology – free-ride on the *prima facie* commitment to truth and language embodied in acts of everyday communication. They exploit the communal and universal ideas of truth and rationality for their own benefit. They exploit a resource which has evolved for communicative purposes for strategic and self-interested reasons. What Habermas calls linguistically mediated strategic action threatens a 'generalisable interest' in the maintenance of a resource, language, which is vital to the reproduction of society.

23 *Ibid.*, xv.
24 *Ibid.*, p. 399.
25 Habermas, *The Theory of Communicative Action*, vol. II, pp. 137–8.
26 'What Theories Can Accomplish', in *The Past as Future: Jürgen Habermas interviewed by Michael Haller* (Cambridge: Polity Press, 1994), p. 111.
27 Habermas, *The Theory of Communicative Action*, vol. 1, p. 287.
28 K. Baynes, 'Democracy and the *Rechsstaat*: Habermas's *Faktizitat und Geltung'*, in S. K. White (ed.), *The Cambridge Companion to Habermas* (Cambridge: Cambridge University Press, 1995), pp. 201–32.
29 *Ibid.*, p. 211.
30 See J. Habermas, *Legitimation Crisis* (Cambridge: Polity Press, 1988), part 3.
31 I. Kant, *The Critique of Pure Reason*, trans Norman Kemp Smith (London: Macmillan 1929), para A 644/B672.
32 R. Scruton, *Kant* (Oxford: Oxford University Press, 1982), p. 54.
33 Habermas, *Legitimation Crisis*, p. 111.
34 *Ibid*.
35 Translator's Introduction to J. Habermas, *Justification and Application: Remarks on Discourse Ethics* (Cambridge: Polity Press, 1993), p. xvii. Pragmatic discourses, for instance, aim to uncover the appropriate strategies and techniques to be employed in the solution to certain practical problems pertaining to particular situations. The particular policies developed in such discourses are clearly not universalisable in nature (what is pragmatically sensible in one case may not be in another). In addition, actors are not bound to observe the policies developed in pragmatic discourses as if they were fundamental moral duties. The breach of a pragmatic norm of practical discourse is not as morally compromising as a breach of a norm of moral practical discourse.

Ethical discourses concern culturally specific interpretations of the good, a particular group's self-understanding or definition, and are, similarly, not subject to the stringent court of universal appeal which underlies the validity of moral discourse. The product of ethical discourse does not need to command universal validity as it pertains to the identities of particular groups. In addition, claims to ethical validity may well involve an appeal to aesthetic criteria, something which could never happen in a moral discourse. Moral discourse pertains to situations where actions affect fundamental and potentially 'generalisable interests' and there is a corresponding need to adjudicate conflict in an impartial manner; that is, from the moral point of view. Moral discourses are more exacting than ethical ones as they concern fundamental duties.

36 Habermas, *Justification and Application*, p. 7.
37 Outhwaite, *Habermas*, p. 144.
38 Held, *Democracy*, p. 163.
39 Ibid.
40 Ibid., p. 231.
41 Linklater, *Transformation*, p. 207.
42 Ibid., p. 183.
43 Ibid., p. 210.
44 Held, *Democracy*, p. ix
45 Linklater, *Transformation*, p. 32.
46 Held, *Democracy*, p. ix.
47 Ibid., p. 233.
48 Ibid., p. 222.
49 Ibid., p. 227.
50 Ibid., chapter 8.
51 Linklater, *Transformation*, p. 207.
52 Held, *Democracy*, p. 190.
53 Ibid., p. 227, footnote 1.
54 Ibid., p. 147.
55 Ibid., p. 267.
56 Ibid., pp. 77–8, 85–7.
57 Linklater, *Transformation*, p. 7.
58 Ibid., p. 220.
59 Ibid., p. 47.
60 Ibid., p. 74.
61 Ibid., p. 44.
62 Held, *Democracy*, p. 161.
63 Linklater, *Transformation*, see chapter 6.
64 R. Devetak, 'Incomplete States: Theories and Practices of Statecraft', in A. Linklater and J. Macmillan (eds) *Boundaries in Question: New Directions in International Relations* (London, 1995), p. 19.
65 Ibid., p. 31.
66 Habermas, *Legitimation Crisis*.
67 Linklater, 'The Question of the Next Stage', pp. 77–98.
68 Ibid., p. 94.
69 Ibid., p. 97.
70 Ibid., p. 219.
71 J. Goldstein and R. Keohane (eds), *Ideas and Foreign Policy: Beliefs, Institutions and Political Change* (Ithaca and London: Cornell University Press, 1993), p. 6.
72 F. Nietzsche, 'On Truth and Falsity in their Extra-Moral Sense', in Dr Oscar Levy (ed.), *The Complete Works of Friedrich Nietzsche, Vol 2., Early Greek Philosophy* trans. Maximillian A. Mugge (New York: Gordon Press, 1974), p. 187.
73 Ibid.

74 Linklater, *Men and Citizens*, p. 167. My emphasis.
75 *Ibid.*
76 *Ibid.*, p. 208.
77 *Ibid.*, pp. 217–18.
78 *Ibid.*, p. 217.
79 F. O. Hampson, 'Third-Party Roles in the Termination of Intercommunal Conflict', *Millennium: Journal of International Studies*, 26:3 (1997), p. 737.
80 Arendt writes, 'Power is actualized only where word and deed have not parted company, where words are not empty and deeds not brutal, where words are not used to veil intentions but to disclose realities, and deeds are not used to violate and destroy but to establish relations and create new realities,' *The Human Condition* (Chicago: Chicago University Press, 1958), p. 200. Here, power depends on organisation, so 'whoever, for whatever reasons, isolates himself and does not partake in such being together, forfeits power and becomes impotent, no matter how great his strength and how valid his reasons' – (*ibid.*, p. 201).
81 Hampson, 'Third -Party Roles', p. 740.
82 Held, *Democracy*, p. 272.
83 *Ibid.*, pp. 272 and 276.
84 Linklater, *Transformation*, p. 9.
85 *Ibid.*, p. 218.
86 *Ibid.*, p. 24.
87 *Ibid.*, p. 25.
88 Zola, *Cosmopolis*, p. 64.
89 F. Nietzsche, *The Gay Science*, 'Let us Beware!' (New York: Ramdom House, 1974).
90 *Ibid.*
91 Held, *Democracy*, p. 223.
92 Habermas, *The Past as Future*, p. 111.
93 Linklater, *Transformation*, p. 100.
94 *Ibid.*, p. 101.
95 W. Rehg, *Insight and Solidarity: The Discourse Ethics of Jürgen Habermas* (Berkeley: University of California Press, 1997), p. 145.
96 F. Nietzsche, *Twilight of the Idols* (London: Penguin Books, 1990), section 4.
97 Habermas, *The Past and Future*, p. 20.
98 Rehg, *Insight and Solidarity*, p. 148.
99 Linklater, *Transformation*, p. 102.
100 *Ibid.*
101 Rehg, *Insight and Solidarity*, pp. 146 and 148.

6

From Madrid to Oslo: the origins of Norwegian facilitation

> In the wake of the Gulf disaster, Palestinian fortunes touched rock bottom . . . the moment seemed ripe to inflict a fatal wound on hopes for a sovereign Palestinian state. Whence the Oslo initiative.
>
> (Norman Finkelstein – *The Rise and Fall of Palestine*).

THE TERM 'ACCORDS' has connotations of agreement in the sense of harmony. The Greek word *khorde* denoted animal gut, which was used in a musical instrument. To accord with something is to be in harmony in relation to that thing. By the same token, discord implies disagreement, dissonance, quarrel, even contradiction. The critical approach to international mediation is ideally placed to assess whether the term 'Accord' is rightfully applied to the relationship established between Israel and the PLO in Oslo in the Autumn of 1993. A cosmopolitan-inspired political ethic promotes rational agreement: a state of affairs where all concerned parties to a dispute accord with a set of political propositions and acknowledge the validity of the reasons which support those propositions.

The breakdown of common authority existing between Israel and the Palestinian population necessitates a politics based on dialogue and mutual recognition. Given the lack of common political authority, there can be no executive or administrative production of peace in this part of the Middle East. The breakdown of common authority necessitates peace agreement based on the institution of 'generalisable interests.' Peace treaties based on the suppression of 'generalisable interests' will require excessive amounts of force to implement them, they will be unjust and unstable. In any case, implementing 'generalisable interests' is possible in this context. A 'two-state' settlement in the Israeli–Palestinian conflict has been proven to be possible.[1] Suspicion should be directed against settlements which suppress 'generalisable interests' or postpone them to final status talks whose outlines are ill-defined. A cosmopolitan political ethic suspects that agreements which suppress 'generalisable interests' are not based on rational will-formation. Where 'generalisable interests' are at stake, and where there is no need to compromise, there ought not to be compromise. And what compromises there are need to be grounded in consensus and be supported by considerations which compensate the compromised party.

In this chapter we place the Oslo Accords in their historical context. As Fred Halliday puts it, history 'places the present in perspective.' Moreover, as Halliday continues, 'a conception of history involving social and economic, as well as political, change, can address the very question that realism denies, namely the historicity of the international system itself.'[2] The Oslo Accords arose, as we shall see, from the push and pull of geo-international political forces. Nevertheless, to some extent, the Accords also embody conscious political agency. They constitute an idea of legitimate international relations. This idea concentrates, distils and freezes a set of opinions which, placed in the ascendant, then influences the future direction of history. Although we confine the bulk of our analysis in this and the following chapter to the early Oslo period, we shall see that its dynamics continue to the present day.

Accounts of the 'Oslo backchannel' are now numerous. The nature and origins of the channel have been described from Israeli, Palestinian and Norwegian perspectives.[3] In addition, the Oslo Accords have been subjected to fierce criticism (in both theory and practice).[4] In developing the critical normative analysis, this, and the following chapter, will draw upon the existing range of sources. Both chapters also draw upon personal interviews with central Norwegian figures involved in the facilitation.[5] And the chapters will demonstrate how international mediation can be studied in the light of a cosmopolitan theory of international mediation.

This chapter focuses on the history and context of the Oslo Accords. In it, we ask the following questions: how did a small Scandinavian country with a population of only 4.3 million, a budget surplus and a limited presence on the international stage come to be involved in one the deadliest and most intractable conflicts of the twentieth century? What drove Arafat and the PLO to seek a deal with Israel? Why did Peres and Rabin break with Israeli political tradition and recognise the PLO? How did the geopolitical circumstances surrounding the end of the Cold War create an opportunity to refashion a part of international politics previously frozen by Cold War rivalries? I cannot hope to detail all the relevant historical considerations. Nevertheless, and as a result, my analysis places the Gaza Strip, and its wider political repercussions, at the centre. I examine its political influence on Arafat, Rabin and Peres, the Egyptians and the Palestinians themselves. The Oslo Accords promoted 'Gaza First', so our account of their origins will do so also.

The origins of Norwegian facilitation

On 26th of October 1996, Terje Rod Larsen, UN Special Coordinator to the Occupied Territories, left Gaza City to take up the post of Minister for National Reform and Planning in the Norwegian Labour Cabinet.[6] The Norwegian government was not, in public at least, dismayed at the news of Netanyahu's election in May 1996. Geir Pederson, who went to see members of Netanyahu's government in August 1996, argued that the Prime Minister's rhetoric was perhaps less important than his potential deeds. Foreign Affairs Minister Bjorn Tore Godal described the doubts over the future of the peace process as 'exaggerated.' Others, including Labour Party leader Thorbjorn Jagland and Peace Research Institute Oslo (PRIO) researcher Hilde Waag, forecasted that, at the very least, Norway's role would be affected, given that the Norwegian Foreign Office had no contacts in conservative circles in Israel.[7]

Norway's role had continued after the Oslo Accords were signed in September 1993, although in a less intense form. Deputy Foreign Minister in Norway's Labour administration, Jan Egeland, claims that Norway expected their role to be over after September 1993. However, Norway was given, by the United States and the European Union, the task of coordinating international aid to the Palestinians through the Holst fund, named after the Norwegian Foreign Minister, Johan Jürgen Holst, who died shortly after Oslo was signed. Norway was also asked to lead the international presence in Hebron following the massacre at the Ibrahim Mosque in February 1994; this was the case despite the fact that Islamic Jihad warned that their priority will be to kill them (the Norwegians). Also, Rabin, Peres and Arafat accepted the Nobel Peace Prize in Oslo in December 1994. Curiously, Norway abstained from a UN General Assembly Resolution affirming the Palestinian right to self-determination passed in December 1994. In all, there were 147 votes in favour, 2 (Israel and the USA) votes against, and 19 abstentions.

Larsen's departure from Gaza marked the end of this particular Norwegian facilitative role in the Israeli–Palestinian conflict. Although Larsen was only charged with coordinating the educational and relief work of the UN in the region, his job always had a more political edge. UN education and welfare coordination would always lead to political mediation between the conflicting parties, given the torturous political environment of the Israel–Palestinian conflict. As political circumstances changed, with the election of Likud's Netanyahu as Prime Minister of Israel in May 1996, historical and contemporary Norwegian political commitments meant that Larsen could no longer work on his more general UN welfare tasks.

The problem facing Larsen was the fact that, historically, Norway's involvement in the Israel–Palestine conflict was premised on what Jan Egeland calls the 'very close relations' and 'uniquely positive relationship' between the respective Labour movements in Norway and Israel. The Norwegian and Israeli Labour movements were in contact throughout the years following the end of the Second World War. Egeland states that Norway was an actor in the Middle East even before the creation of the state of Israel in 1948. Geir Pederson, another official at the Norwegian foreign ministry, also traces the Norwegian involvement in Israeli politics right back to the Holocaust and the subsequent creation of the Jewish state.

In the mid-40s the Norwegian Labour movement was against the creation of a Jewish state in Palestine. There were, for example, Norwegian proposals to move surviving victims of the Holocaust to parts of Africa and South America. However, reluctantly, and in the face of international opinion, Norway supported the UN resolution which divided Palestine. Following the war of 1948, as Norwegian historian Hilde Waag puts it, Norway very quickly 'changed her mind' and supported Israel's application for UN membership. Following a plane crash in 1949, in which twenty-six Jewish children, who were being brought from Israel to Norway for education and medical purposes, were killed, public and governmental opinion swung more wholeheartedly behind support for the fledgling Jewish state. The Norwegian Labour movement funded a Kibbutz in the 1940s and 1950s. Also, the Labour movement believed in the socialist experiment that was Israel's international image and Norway preserved its links with Labour Israel via the Socialist International. Finally, there is also the fact that, under the Quisling Regime, Norway suffered under the Nazis during the war. World War Two helped to define policy. Egeland stated, '[t]he Norwegian people were deeply shocked when they learned the truth about the fate of the Jews during the Holocaust. Many felt that more could have been done for their Jewish neighbours during the Nazi Occupation of our country.'

As a result of the Holocaust, there was a great deal of sympathy in Norway for what Pederson terms, 'the Israeli cause.' Pederson points to the role of Norwegian Labour Party secretary, a man named Haakon Lie, who, in Pederson's words, developed a 'very strong personal relationship' with leading figures in the Israeli Labour Party. The Norwegian Labour movement supported the creation of the state of Israel in 1948. (Norway voted in favour of the UN General Assembly Resolution 181 which partitioned Palestine into Jewish and Arab states.) And Norwegian Labour support for the fledgling Israeli state only strengthened with time. For example, Norway supplied Israel with heavy water for Shimon Peres's nuclear programme in the 1950s and 60s (although the Norwegian government denied any knowledge of this apparent support for Israel). The nature of the support given by the Norwegian Labour movement to Labour Israel, in the late 1940s and throughout the 1950s and 1960s, has led one historian to describe Norway as Israel's 'best friend' during the difficult formative years of the Israeli state.[8] Pederson concurs with this analysis. He claims that from the mid-1940s onwards, and right up until the late 1970s, all the Labour leaders in Norway followed 'whatever was Israeli policy'; Pederson adds: 'there was no criticism whatsoever'.

Importantly, as Jan Egeland states, 'a premise for playing a role as a third party is that you have the trust and the confidence of both sides.' In the 1970s, and following the Israeli occupation of the West Bank and Gaza Strip in 1967, the Norwegian Labour Party, after a trade-union initiative, began to develop ties with the Palestinians. The aim was to institute, as Egeland puts it, 'not a one-leg, but a two-leg policy.' Past and contemporary Norwegian Labour Party policy came to be viewed as biased and the Norwegian Labour Party began developing contacts with the PLO and Yassir Arafat. For example, there soon developed, between the PLO and the Norwegian Labour Party, as Egeland puts it, 'a long-standing . . . foreign aid relationship.' By the late 1980s, as Egeland states, referring to Norway, 'we were among the relatively few countries who had excellent relations both with Israel and the PLO.' Norway was well placed to be a facilitator in the Israeli–Palestinian conflict by the late 1980s. Pederson adds that the Norwegians were trusted by both parties.

Norway's role as facilitator did not begin in earnest until January 1993 and the start of the talks in Oslo. Prior to this date, though, and following the end of the Gulf War, Norwegian politicians were becoming more involved in the politics of the Israel–Palestine conflict.

Traditionally, it was Sweden which represented and promoted the Nordic, facilitative model of mediation in the politics of the Middle East.[9] However, with the accession to power of a Conservative government in Sweden in 1991, a government which had a more pro-European and, put broadly, an anti-third world orientation, ex-Swedish Foreign Minister Sten Anderson magnanimously advised the PLO to approach Oslo for any future help it required from Scandinavian states. As Pederson put it, a 'vacancy opened up' and 'another party, another country could play a role if needed.' Consequently, several PLO delegations headed towards Oslo and not Stockholm in 1991 and early 1992, requesting, among other things, financial help and Norwegian facilitation of direct contacts with the Israeli government.[10] These delegations included figures such as Faisal Husseini and Hanan Ashrawi from the 'Territories', plus Nabil Shaath, Abu Sharif and Abu Alaa from PLO headquarters in Tunis.

Perhaps most significantly, Abu Alaa, the PLO's banker, came to see Norway's foreign affairs staff in late February 1992 and solicited financial support for the PLO. Alaa met Egeland and was introduced by Mona Juul, an official at the Foreign Ministry, to Terje Rod Larsen, Mona Juul's husband.[11] The Oslo process began, as Pederson puts it, as a 'personal relationship with Abu Alaa' – a man searching for money in an attempt to avert the PLO's post-Gulf War financial crisis.

Larsen, at the beginning of 1992, was working on an academic study of welfare and living conditions in the Gaza Strip and the West Bank under the auspices of FAFO, his social science research organisation based in Oslo. Fathi Arafat, brother of Yassir, had suggested to Larsen, when Larsen and Yuul were living and working together in Egypt in 1989, that he conduct a study of Palestinian living and welfare conditions.[12]

Larsen decided to act on this suggestion. In pursuing his investigations into the Palestinian economy, Larsen travelled extensively throughout the region. His work forced him to negotiate, and develop contacts, with both senior Israeli and

Palestinian figures, figures who had both military and political connections. As Pederson put it, 'to successfully complete such an undertaking [i.e. the social science research] you needed to create an understanding among the Palestinians and the Israelis.' (Here we see the roots of the Norwegian facilitation.) Larsen needed to gain, as Pederson states, 'permission' from both the politicians and the military.

Among others, Larsen contacted Yossi Beilin, a 'dovish' Israeli Labour MP who had strong connections with Shimon Peres. In May 1992, Larsen made a trip to Jerusalem and met Beilin. During this meeting, Beilin, then busy with the Israeli Labour Party's election campaign, suggested that Larsen could help secure Palestinian support for the Labour Party in the forthcoming Israeli elections. Beilin also intimated that the Labour Party was looking for ways to bypass the stalled Washington process in the event of a Labour election victory in June. Larsen was intrigued by Beilin's ideas. One of the first meetings between Israelis and Palestinians, facilitated by a Norwegian, occurred when Larsen subsequently arranged for Yossi Beilin and Faisal Husseini to meet at the American Colony Hotel in Jerusalem later that May.[13] About the same time, Larsen also travelled to Tunis, where he was asked by Yassir Arafat whether or not the Norwegians would like to play a role in the area. At that time, Larsen was unsure whether to speak to the PLO or to the personalities from the territories.[14]

Meanwhile, Jan Egeland had been instructed by Thorvald Stoltenberg, Norway's Foreign Minister at the time, to monitor the Madrid/Washington process and 'reactivate the role that [Norway] had played at times in the past.'[15] Stoltenberg, Egeland claims, knew 'that the potential was there' for an influential Norwegian facilitation. Stoltenberg had long been pursuing a Norwegian intervention in the Israel–Palestine conflict. In 1983, Stoltenberg tried to bring Israeli and Palestinian 'moderates' together. His plans were deliberately thwarted when PLO official, Issam Sartawi, was assassinated by dissenting Palestinian gunmen outside a Socialist International meeting that Stoltenberg was attending in Portugal. Despite such setbacks, Stoltenberg obviously remained undeterred. In October 1991, under Stoltenberg's instructions, Egeland and Mona Juul went to Madrid with the aim of 'reactivating' a Norwegian facilitative role.[16]

Larsen could not act without the backing of the Norwegian Foreign Ministry. And, as Pederson points out, this backing was given by Egeland, who could secure support for the project from Stoltenberg. Egeland believed that Norway could introduce 'confidence-building measures' and what he termed 'pilot projects' in an effort to produce a more meaningful dialogue between the Israeli and Palestinian representatives in Madrid. He aimed to enquire whether the parties would be interested in a Norwegian role. Egeland states; 'we knew we were trusted by both sides and could play a role as a facilitator.' (Egeland mentions, however, that, at that time, 'no-one would even dream of an Oslo channel.' The aim was not to replace the Madrid/Washington process, but merely to 'service' it.) In Madrid, Egeland met Netanyahu and various figures on the Palestinian side, and formed the impression that the Madrid/Washington process was a 'circus' of journalists and police. The publicity surrounding the Madrid negotiations curtailed the possibility of meaningful dialogue, in Egeland's view. Egeland described the hotels in which the delegates were staying as 'fortresses.' It was not, according to Egeland, a situation conducive to deep-rooted and wide-ranging communication – the Nordic/facilitative model of conflict resolution. The Norwegians thus aimed, as Egeland put it, to 'service' the Madrid/Washington process through developing more 'informal' political contacts.

The Norwegians' ambitions were given a boost following the Labour victory in Israel in June 1992. Following the election, as Egeland states, Norway now had a 'unique possibility.' With the Labour victory, the pieces of the Oslo backchannel began to fall into place. In September 1992, Egeland made an official visit to Israel and held a clandestine meeting on the 12th of that month, attended by Juul, Larsen, Beilin and his confidant, Yair Hirschfeld. Egeland, bringing with him official Norwegian Foreign ministry backing, offered Norway's services as a third-party facilitator between the Labour Party and the Palestinians (although at this stage it was still not clear whether the dialogue was intended to be with the leaders in the territories, Husseini, etc., or the PLO itself). Beilin responded to Egeland's suggestion by saying that moves towards a dialogue with the PLO were desirable but too dangerous at that time, given that contacts with the PLO were illegal in Israel. Nevertheless, Beilin agreed to meet Faisal Husseini either in Jerusalem or in Oslo sometime in the near future. This meeting never took place. As Makovsky puts it, 'Beilin had become nervous about the endeavour. It was one thing to hold private conversations, but quite another to conduct what would be tantamount to backchannel negotiations.'[17] Despite the possibilities, the Norwegian backchannel remained quiet for almost the rest of 1992.

In any case, by December 1992, the focus of Israeli attention had shifted away from the leaders in the territories, Husseini, Ashrawi and so on, and towards the PLO itself – the 'organization' of the Palestinian diaspora. As the Madrid process continued, it became clear, as Pederson put it, 'that it was not possible to do anything without the PLO.' By this time, therefore, Beilin was interested in establishing a direct link with Arafat's men in Tunis. On 2 December 1992, a bill to revoke the law which made contacts with the PLO illegal received its first reading in the Knesset. The bill was sponsored by elements within the Israeli Labour Party headed by Yossi Beilin.

On the 3rd and 4th of December 1992, the multilateral talks of the Washington process were taking place in London. Beilin sent Hirschfeld to London to meet with PLO official Abu Alaa, who was coordinating Palestinian participation in the talks from behind the scenes.[18] Hirschfeld expressed some reservations about the legality of the act; although personally, and as a representative of Yossi Beilin, he actually wanted the meeting to take place. To help smooth things over, therefore, Hirschfeld called on the services of the Norwegian facilitator Larsen. Larsen was also in London at the time, allegedly discussing, with Hirschfeld, the financing of some academic projects.[19] Larsen, in the words of Pederson, was 'not to participate in the meeting [between Hirschfeld and Alaa] but to see that everything went alright' (a classic facilitative role). A meeting took place in which the two men, Yair Hirschfeld and Abu Alaa, discussed the progress of the Washington talks. They met again that same evening and agreed, if possible, to pursue their contacts further, in Oslo, using the facilitation of the Norwegians.[20]

Abu Alaa then returned to Tunis and submitted a report to Abu Mazen, a PLO official close to Arafat who was responsible for overseeing contacts with the Israelis.[21] Two weeks later Larsen went to Tunis and met Abu Alaa, Abu Mazen and Arafat himself. With Abu Mazen's permission, Alaa agreed to go to Oslo if certain conditions were in place.

The resources of small states

The Norwegians were able to provide a number of resources which ensured their place as facilitators. Egeland argues that, as a general rule, small states in the international system have a number of advantages: 'less complicated foreign policy objectives', 'less organisational tension', 'no legacy of foreign excesses', 'a good domestic record', 'a high level of foreign aid' and 'a consistent and active support of the decolonisation process.'[22]

In a more specific sense, the Norwegians could guarantee, first and foremost, absolute secrecy. In telephone conversations conducted between Egeland and Juul in Oslo and the Israelis in Jerusalem, Beilin insisted on secrecy and the possibility of 'full deniability.' Both Egeland and Pederson stressed that the provision of 'absolute secrecy' and a 'trusted environment' were the Norwegians' greatest assets at this point in the negotiations. Egeland argues that Norway could 'provide absolute secrecy' and a 'trusted environment.' Pederson stated that 'they would never have been successful if they were not able to do this behind closed doors.' From an Israeli perspective, Makovsky notes that the Oslo channel had some initial advantages:

> [f]irst the participation of private Israelis in a seminar under FAFO auspices would not violate Israeli law. Second, the nature of such discussions would be more academic than political, thereby allowing the exploration of PLO views without Israeli commitments. Finally, the backchannel could operate on FAFO funds, rather than Israeli funding that would have required an official government decision to conduct the talks.[23]

The Norwegians had other resources which ensured that they were sucessful as third parties. As Pederson points out, Norway was able to play a role because it was understood by the parties that they 'did not have any self-interest in the area.' Israel understood that if a deal was to be accepted by public opinion it should not be a deal that could be perceived as having been 'forced upon them.' Thus, a neutral third party was needed. Pederson adds that Israel viewed the conflict resolution process 'rightly or wrongly, as a question of life or death.' 'They are all concerned with security', he adds. Thus, if Israel was to construct a deal with the Palestinians, this would have to take place 'without any foreign pressure.' The circumstances were thus well suited to the potential role of Norway – a small state facilitator unable to generate pressure for an agreement which may, for example, grant Palestine a state. Yet Norway did have a 'generous aid policy' and a 'very good relationship with the United States.' It could coordinate compensating economic assistance to the Palestinian autonomous areas. These structural factors, plus 'the right people' and 'right historical connections', made the Norwegian facilitation a sucessful one.

It was decided that FAFO, Larsen's social science institute in Oslo, would provide, as Jan Egeland put it, 'a very good façade.' It was the 'perfect camouflage' for discussions between Labour Israel and the PLO. A meeting in Oslo was arranged for the 20th of January 1993. On 10 January 1993, the Israeli Parliament rolled back its ban on contacts with the PLO. The 'Oslo backchannel' was under way.

The opportunity and pressure of defeat

We have seen in the last section the circumstances which brought the Norwegians to the negotiating table. In this section we shall examine the geo- and regional political circumstances which drove the Israeli Labour government and the PLO to the negotiating table. The analysis focuses on the Gulf War, the problem of the Gaza Strip and its political repercussions. In keeping with the sociological cast of critical theory noted in the last chapter, the character of the Accords can be partially explained by the circumstances in which they were conceived.

Consider the political situation following the end of the Cold War. Broadly, the collapse of Soviet power meant a weakening of the forces which opposed US hegemony in the Middle East.[24] The movement for reform in the Soviet Union in the late 1980s caused a rolling back of Soviet foreign policy commitments right across the third world and in the Middle East.[25] Furthermore, likely Soviet reliance on future US economic aid boosted America's hand in its attempt to refashion global politics according to its own objectives. With the decline of Soviet power, and with the concomitant 'free hand', US policy-makers began to direct their attention to threats posed to US interests by specifically third-world regional powers and problems.[26]

The first real consequence of this changed international outlook and structure was the Gulf War. As Ken Matthews puts it: 'the Gulf Crisis can be seen to have been a manifestation of the end of the Cold War and indeed the first post-Cold War crisis.'[27] The Gulf War demonstrated that the USA could act and pursue its interests in the region without significant opposition. The decline of the Soviet Union removed one important element from the US calculation. Also, it is likely that the Soviet Union would never have allowed its client – Iraq – to invade Kuwait in the old Cold War days for fear of becoming involved in a superpower conflagration. The end of the Cold War, and its immediate consequence the Gulf War, are intimately linked to the emergence of the Oslo process. The Gulf War demonstrated to the Bush administration that the problems of the Middle East needed addressing in a comprehensive manner. In a speech to the UN in October 1990, for example, George Bush stated that when Iraq withdrew from Kuwait there would be opportunities 'for all the states and the peoples of the region to settle the conflicts that divide the Arabs from Israel.' Journalist Pinhas Inbari describes the Gulf War as the 'big bang' that gave rise to the Palestinian–Israeli peace processes of the early 1990s.[28]

The Gulf War had a number of immediate ramifications for the present case. First, as Makovsky writes, it greatly strengthened Israel's regional position:

> the Gulf War drastically weakened Israel's most powerful foe, Iraq, and crippled its nascent nuclear capability; buried the myth of a united Arab political front and left the radical Arab camp in disarray; and demonstrated that the United States, Israel's patron and the world's only post-Cold War superpower, would intervene in the Middle East to protect its vital interests.[29]

Second, in contrast, and owing to the support it gave Iraq during the Gulf War, the PLO was dealt an enormous blow, in both political and financial terms. The PLO had been developing contacts with Iraq throughout the 1980s. According to Mohamed Heikel, Arafat and the PLO began to look towards Baghdad following the expulsion from Lebanon in 1982. Heikel writes: '[t]he PLO chairman could hope that some day Iraq might help the PLO regain strength it had enjoyed before the fall of Beirut.'[30] In addition, during the mid-1980s Arafat was becoming increasingly concerned for his personal safety. After the Israeli bombing of PLO Headquarters in Tunis in 1985, Arafat spent a great deal of time in the Iraqi capital, where he was offered protection. The Israeli assassination of Abu Jihad – head of the PLO's military arm – in 1988 only served to increase Arafat's fears and push him further towards the Iraqi military government.[31] There was even talk of moving PLO headquarters to Baghdad. Describing PLO attitudes to Iraq, Yezid Sayigh writes: 'The Palestinian leadership was deeply impressed by Iraqi military and industrial capability, and hailed the end of the war with Iran . . . because Israel would now face a major new challenge.'[32]

Furthermore, during the intifada, Iraq, perhaps the most regular contributor to PLO funds, gave around $40 million a year towards the PLO's costs. This financial factor, which helped induce Arafat's support for Saddam Hussein, was compounded by the fact that the Gulf monarchies, especially Saudi Arabia, bypassed Arafat and the PLO and funded the Palestinian struggle against Israel on the ground via the Islamic opposition – Hamas.[33] Thus, by 1990, and in the wake of popular Palestinian support for Saddam Hussein in Gaza, the West Bank and Jordan, Arafat was prepared to be one of Hussein's small band of allies during the Gulf War period.

Arafat's support for Saddam Hussein, 'the fatal linkage', cost the PLO dearly in both financial and political terms. Around 400,000 Palestinians who worked in the Gulf monarchies were expelled by what Heikel calls 'the Arabs of the desert.' In addition, Arafat estimated that as a result of the crisis, the PLO had lost around $120 million in annual contributions. If other assets lost are added to this figure, then overall PLO losses amounted to around $10 billion.[34] Payments to hospitals, newspapers, community centres, armed units and the families of 'martyred' Palestinians were curtailed, or they ceased altogether.

On top of the economic costs, Arafat became politically isolated as a result of the PLO's Gulf War stance. Arafat's Gulf War policy, what Chomsky terms his 'absurd posturing', did not even enjoy the support of many of his closest allies.[35] For example, the head of the 'political' wing of the PLO, Salif Khalaf (Abu Iyyad), was publicly critical of Iraq's invasion of Kuwaiti and of Arafat's proposal of 'linkage' in accordance with the popular wishes of the Palestinian people. On 14th January 1991, Abu Iyyad was assassinated by a member of Abu Nidal's Revolutionary Fateh movement and Saddam Hussein was strongly suspected of being behind the assassination. The loss of Iyyad was a personal and political blow for Arafat. Iyyad, a former commander in the Black September movement, had some influence and contact with the US government.

In 1990 Iyyad had published an article in the prestigious US journal, *Foreign Affairs*, entitled 'Lowering the Sword', in which he had expressed a willingness to compromise and negotiate with US/Israeli positions.[36] According to Pinhas Inbari, senior members of Iyyadist circles also shared their fallen comrade's opinions. Amongst this group are names like Faisal Husseini, Ahmad Qrei (Abu Alaa) and Abu Mazen – all names that would play prominent roles in the then forthcoming peace talks. Pinhas Inbari argues that the PLO's Gulf War line raised the tension between the political/Iyyadist wing of the PLO (which supported diplomacy, a two-state solution, and which was largely based in the Occupied Territories) and the military/Jihadist wing which, largely based in the diaspora, wished to confront and, if possible, militarily overthrow the US-Israeli hegemony in the region.

Arafat's pro-Iraqi stance during the Gulf War meant that when the Bush administration's Madrid/Washington process began, it was the Iyyadist wing and the personalities from the territories which made up the Palestinian delegation. Under Faisal Husseini, with his base in Orient House in East Jerusalem, the centre of political gravity within Palestinian life shifted towards the West Bank 'personalities' as the Americans took steps to marginalise the PLO organisation of the diaspora, which was an absolutely unacceptable negotiating partner to Shamir's Likud government.

This rise to prominence of the personalities from the territories following the Gulf War, coupled with the political isolation of Arafat, was certainly a factor in accounting for the birth of the Oslo channel, which, contra Madrid and Washington, directly involved Arafat. However, opinions differ as to whether or not it was only – or mainly – Arafat's fear of an alternative leadership that prompted him to pursue the deal on offer through the Oslo channel. Inbari, for example, is clear that this was the primary reason behind Arafat's acceptance of the terms laid before him at Oslo. As he puts it:

> The danger reflected to Arafat's leadership from within the occupied territories was, in the end, the direct cause of his decision to accept the agreements prepared between Abu Mazen in secret in the period in which Arafat was conducting his bitter struggles against the formula imposed on him after the Gulf War.[37]

Others writers are less keen to place the causal emphasis in this factor alone. Arafat was not that isolated from the Washington Madrid process. In their biography of Arafat, for example, Gowers and Walker place less stress on Arafat's personal isolation during the period immediately following the Gulf War. They point out the following: that the delegation to Washington was always under the strict scrutiny of Nabil Shaath (Arafat's trusted aid); that the Washington delegates had repeatedly to travel back and forth to consult with Arafat in Tunis; and that Arafat was keen to make public shows of friendship with Washington figures like Abd 'al-Shafi, Faisal Husseini and Hanan Ashrawi.

Instead of relying solely on the isolation of Arafat from the Washington/Madrid focus, and the fact that emphasis was being placed on the personalities from the 'territories', Gowers and Walker point to additional explanatory circumstances in accounting for the emergence of the Oslo channel. Or, rather, and this is a slightly weaker argument, the political isolation of Arafat and the PLO has to be situated in a slightly wider context if its influence is to be properly understood. If we expand on these hints, we can specify the following themes: the situation in Gaza, the threat from Hamas, the bankruptcy of the PLO, Israel's desire to be rid of Gaza, Arafat's move towards the Egyptians following his isolation after the Gulf War, and Egyptian support for the Gaza-first option. To these factors, I would also want to add the sheer pressure placed by the Israeli government on Palestinians on the ground. As we shall see, the new Rabin government, elected, in part, on a peace ticket, was fierce in its use of repressive methods against Palestinian political activism in Gaza and the West Bank. To my mind, accounts of the origins of the Oslo channel often fail fully to emphasise this fact.

The problem of Gaza

Gaza is probably the key which unlocks the whole explanation of the Oslo Accords. The problems in Gaza are linked to all relevant explanatory factors: Arafat's fear of isolation, Rabin and Peres's fear of terrorism, PLO bankruptcy following the end of the Gulf War and pressures emanating from the Palestinian population. The Oslo Accords put Gaza first; an explanation of the Accords should do this also.

Begin with the role of Hamas and the situation in the Gaza Strip. The rise of Hamas and the deteriorating situation in Gaza placed political pressures on both the PLO and the Israeli government. It concerned Arafat, given that support for Arafat's Fatah was being threatened by the growth in support for Hamas. (For example, Hamas avoided the type of sanctions imposed on the PLO through a more nuanced diplomatic response to the Gulf crisis.)[38] It concerned Rabin and Peres, given that the Gaza Strip was, under Hamas, and in Graham Usher's words, 'teetering on the brink of an anti-colonial war.'[39] Gaza is the fulcrum around which all the players in the Oslo Accords turn.

Sarah Roy points out that social conditions in the Gaza strip by around 1990/1 were appalling. The Gulf War had a devastating impact. Both aid and earnings from outside countries, such as Saudi Arabia and Kuwait, had ceased to flow into the Strip. Also, under pressure from measures imposed by the Israeli government in response to the intifada, the GNP of the Gaza Strip had fallen around 35 per cent from 1988 to 1990. In January 1991, for example, Israel imposed a 'comprehensive and prolonged' curfew on Gaza and the West Bank, which, in Roy's words, 'virtually shut down the economy.' Curfews and closures continued into 1992. The net effects were devastating. In the Autumn of 1992, for example, 11,655 people applied for eight advertised jobs of garbage collectors. As Sarah Roy points out, this figure amounts to around 10 per cent of Gaza's total labourforce.[40]

The Gaza Strip has always differed from the West Bank in its leaning towards religious Orthodoxy. The overcrowding, the political repression, the boredom, the high ratio of refugees, the refugees from refugee camps, the economic dependence – all these factors created a more turbulent social situation than the one that existed in the West Bank. What Janin Di Giovanno calls 'the sheer weight of despair' has created a groundswell of support for the Islamic-based national movements, which are seen, by Palestinians, as being more aggressively opposed to US/Israeli hegemony than the PLO.[41]

The Islamic Resistance Movement – Hamas – first appeared in Gaza in February 1988. It grew out of the Muslim Brotherhood in Palestine, a broad Muslim Arab organisation which has its roots in the Egyptian nationalism of the 1920s.[42] Funded at the outset, primarily, by Saudi Arabia, the Islamic resistance movement, under the tutelage of Sheikh Ahmad Yassin, has its power-base in the

Mosques and Islamic universities in Gaza. At first, the movement was encouraged, perhaps even supported, by the Israelis and the Americans as part of a strategy which aimed at undermining the secular-nationalist PLO.[43] However, as conditions in Gaza dramatically worsened, in the late 1980s and early 1990s, the problem of controlling Hamas's increasingly frequent and successful military activity moved to the top of the political agenda for both the PLO and the Rabin government.[44]

The volatile and desperate situation in Gaza had always presented something of a problem to successive Israeli governments. In 1948, following the war of independence, Israel balked at taking over the Gaza Strip on discovering the density of its (Arab refugee) population.[45] Despite these early doubts, Israel captured the Strip in the Six-Day War of June 1967. By 1990, though, and following three years of the Gaza-born intifada, Israel's military 'top brass' had realised that the Strip was spinning out of their control. (Famously, Rabin once told François Mitterand, for example, that he wished Gaza would sink into the sea.[46]) With the deadlock of the Washington negotiations bogged down, as they were, in questions of the West Bank, settlements, Jerusalem and so on, and with the increasing violence emanating from Gaza in the early 1990s, the Gaza-first option moved to the top of the Israeli government's 'peace' agenda.

In his memoirs *Battling for Peace*, Shimon Peres outlines some of the attractions of pursuing the Gaza-first option in the period immediately following the Gulf War.[47] First, he writes, '[t]he Gaza strip presented neither of the daunting problems that we faced on the West Bank' – Peres is referring to the problem of Jerusalem and the settlements, to the demands of the 'personalities' from the 'Territories.' Second, Peres refers to the poverty of Gaza. He refers, with no sense of irony, to 'this woe-begotten stretch of land' that gave us 'nothing at all save a growing, festering sense of shame at our inability to relieve any of its problems.'

To these points, we can add two other considerations. First, Israel paid for the Gaza born intifada in both financial and ideological terms. Financially, the cost of occupation during the intifada ran into millions of dollars a day.[48] On a more ideological level, Israel's international reputation was damaged by the publicity surrounding its brutal methods of dealing with the uprising. Second, note that Israel did not just want to be rid of Gaza. Makovsky argues that Rabin took a long-term view of Israeli security, whose principal concern was Islamic extremism emanating, but not exclusively, from Iran. According to Makovsky, in his mind, Rabin linked this particular threat to the growth of Hamas in Gaza. Makovsky writes that Rabin 'realized that Gaza's appalling poverty and festering discontent fuelled the trend and made it ripe territory for extremist agitation.'[49] Thus, in some fashion, Gaza had to be dealt with. Following the Hamas military strikes in February 1993, Rabin probably realised that the Washington delegation from the territories was not in a position to meet the rising 'security' challenge from Hamas. Thus Rabin switched from Washington to Arafat's PLO through Oslo.

Through ceding Gaza a degree of autonomy, and by placing Arafat in charge of its security, Rabin hoped to quell the support for the Islamic movements. As Peres writes, 'nobody wanted Gaza.' On this basis, Peres argues that 'the logical thing to do... was to place the responsibility for the future of Gaza in the hands of the people who lived there.'[50] In clearer terms, we learn what this means when Peres notes a few sentences later that, in January 1993, just as Oslo was getting under way, 'I suggested [to Rabin] that we propose to Arafat and his staff that they move to Gaza.'[51] Thus, we can perceive Israel's thinking at the beginning of 1993: Gaza is a huge problem, nobody wants it, and with the help of the Norwegians, it can be given to Arafat.

If we take Israel's desire to be rid of the Strip – with, of course, guarantees about (Israeli) security – and couple it with Arafat's fears about his shrinking power base within both the West Bank and the Gaza Strip, then the attractiveness of the Gaza-first option to both Rabin, Peres and Arafat becomes more clear. As Gowers and Walker put it:

> Hamas had adopted the classic guerrilla tactics with which Arafat had made his mark 30 years before, and was challenging the established Palestinian leadership as Fatah's young hotheads had done in the 1960s. The danger was that, if this continued, his control over events in the territories would slip away completely... The alternatives were stark. To align himself with the fundamentalists and other radicals would be to risk losing everything for which he had fought. Yet to rein them in, he simply did not possess the means. Not, that is, unless he contemplated the unthinkable: forging an unholy connection with the enemy, Israel itself.[52]

Arafat was moved towards the Gaza-first option as he wrestled with the post-Gulf War situation. As well as the distinction between the Jihadist and Iyyadist wings of the PLO, there was also a fault line within the Iyyadist wing between those who preferred a Gaza-first option and those who preferred that the emphasis be placed on the West Bank. The Gaza wing was headed by Abu Mazen, the West Bank wing by Faisal Husseini. Heikel notes that the PLO's insistence on a comprehensive settlement, i.e. one that included all the West Bank demands of Palestinian nationalism, was not without its internal critics. Abu Mazen, for one, had once argued that an 'interim settlement' would be acceptable, as it would create facts on the ground just as the Zionists had done following the Balfour Declaration.[53]

Arafat's search for funds, immediately following his Gulf War débâcle, brought him into contact with Abu Mazen and PLO banker Abu Alaa. Following the Gulf War, Arafat moved towards the Egyptian Gaza-first option. During this time Mazen was sent, by Arafat, to Saudi Arabia in January 1993 to elicit financial support and mend some fences with the 'Arabs of the desert.' This occurred shortly after Abu Alaa's trip to Norway, the trip where Alaa met Larsen, who was then working on the living conditions survey in Gaza and the West

Bank. Arafat launched his political career from Egypt. In the political wilderness following the Gulf War, and in the search for funds, Arafat seems to have been drawn towards what is the Egyptian-orientated Gaza-wing centred around Abu Mazen. Indeed, Heikel reports that, in February 1993, Arafat was often meeting with President Mubarak of Egypt, urging him to, in Heikel's words, 'persuade Saudi Arabia to come to the aid of Gaza.' (I will return to the sheer desperation of the Palestinian situation as an explanatory factor below.) Furthermore, Heikel notes that Arafat and Mazen were keen to brief Mubarak on the progress of the Oslo talks and, after meetings in April '93, Mubarak travelled to Washington for talks with Clinton and Warren Christopher.[54]

The role of the Egyptians in the peace process at this precise point in time is an interesting one, though hard to detect. In an article entitled 'The Half-Empty Glass of Middle East Peace', published in 1990, Walid Khalidi notes that the Egyptians had been a conduit for American diplomacy during the opening shots of the Bush administration's post-Gulf War initiative.[55] Lines of communication also went from Israel out and through Egypt. Peres, for example, notes that he transmitted his idea of a Gaza-first option to the Egyptians sometime in 1992, with the aim of getting the Egyptians to persuade the PLO of its efficacy. 'The Egyptians', he adds, 'saw the logic of my argument and began to act.'[56]

The Egyptians had 'Gaza-type' ambitions of their own. For example, they needed Arafat and the PLO to grant a retrospective legitimacy in the Arab world to the Camp David Accords by pursuing a political solution which embodied at least the spirit of the agreement which had so isolated Egypt from the Arab world back in the 1980s – i.e. functional autonomy in parts of Palestine and not a Palestinian state. In addition, and owing to the geographical and historical proximity of Egypt and Gaza, Egypt felt the need to curtail the radical Islamic influence which Gaza might have on groups inside Egypt itself (Egypt has, of course, been the subject, in recent years, of an Islamic movement 'terror' campaign). Of course, as Peres writes, 'nobody wanted Gaza. [Even] the Egyptians were probably relieved to have lost it.' However, with Arafat's PLO in charge, the Egyptians could hope to curtail the Islamic influence without appearing to the wider Arab world as supporters of military occupation. As Inbari writes, '[i]t is, then, no coincidence that Egypt backed the Oslo agreements.'[57] One can speculate about lines of global communication here: from Washington to Egypt, from Egypt to Tunis, from Tunis to Norway, from Norway to Tel-Aviv and from Tel-Aviv back to Washington (such is the possible nature of the Norwegian 'facilitation'). Although this is speculation, what we can establish is the importance of a Gaza-first option to Peres, Rabin, Arafat and the Egyptians. As we shall see, in the next chapter, right from the outset, it was Gaza first, and only ever Gaza first, that was on the table at Oslo.

The Gaza-first option also had a distinct economic dimension to it. It skirted around the more complex, normative questions posed by the West Bankers. Abu

Alaa had written a well-received paper on regional economic development, which chimed with Peres's liberal institutionalist vision of the Middle East as an economic community modelled on the EEC.[58] Peres claimed that '[m]odern technology can make the Gaza port one of the most useful on the Mediterranean.'[59] Terje Rod Larsen was also working, with his FAFO institute, on improving the economic conditions of Gaza residents. Arafat was pushed towards these economic considerations, given his desperate search for funds which were needed to maintain his popular support. Thus the four main Oslo protagonists shared an 'economic' view of the way forward, and this shared economic world-view was part of the 'success' of Oslo. Of course, the problem is that agreement on the big political and moral questions was either ignored or postponed. This is precisely what happened in the Accords, as we shall see. The key normative issues, Jerusalem, refugees, settlements and nationhood, were postponed. And two out of four annexes to the Oslo Accords concerned regional development programmes.

Pressures on the Palestinian population

Alongside, and intertwining with, the key role played by Gaza lies an aspect of the mechanics of Oslo which is often ignored in explanations of its inception: the sheer pressure being placed on Palestinians 'on the ground' during the early 1990s. The Oslo Accords grew out of this situation. This pressure has, roughly, three dimensions: economic collapse, immigration and settlement, and human rights considerations.

Return to the economic analysis. In March 1993, the Israeli government sealed off the West Bank and Gaza Strip. According to Sarah Roy, '[t]he economic damage incurred by the Palestinian economy after March 1993 had no precedent under Israeli Occupation.'[60] The effects in Gaza were devastating. Unemployment rose to 55 per cent. Food purchases declined by over 50 per cent. The UN Relief and Works Agency (UNRWA) predicted child malnutrition. GNP per-capita fell to levels equivalent to the poorest of third world nations. Demand for credit grew. Exports declined and the amount of expensive imports rose. As Roy puts it: '[t]hese conditions, coupled with Gaza's near-total dependence on Israel for income generation, actually deepened Palestinian dependence on Israel at a time when Israel was preparing to transfer political control over the territory to a new Palestinian authority.'[61]

A second pressure bearing down on Palestinian leadership was increasing numbers of Israeli settlements and expanding Soviet-Jewish immigration. The Soviet collapse prompted massive Soviet-Jewish immigration into Israel. Graham Usher estimates that figure to be around 390,000 between 1990 and 1992.[62] Such large-scale immigration, coupled with expectations about future immigration, led to the Israeli government approving the construction of 45,000 housing units per year between 1990 and 1993.⁶³ Estimates of the extent of Soviet settlement on the Palestinian side of the 1948 green line are hard to come by. However, Hilterman argues that 50% of settlers who moved to the Jerusalem area settled in the city's eastern annexed part.⁶⁴ In any case, Soviet-Jewish immigration increased the general pressures on housing, driving up rents and making housing in the settlements of the West Bank economically more attractive. In 1991, the number of settlement starts was a worrying 60% greater than the average number between 1967 and 1990.⁶⁵ The effects on the Palestinian mind of Soviet-Jewish immigration and continuing settlement in the West Bank is of a certain qualitative nature. As Edward Said puts it, 'it made the time factor singularly punishing.'⁶⁶

By 1993, Palestine was indeed 'a tortured land' with a 'captive people.'⁶⁷ Rabin's disregard of human rights considerations, coupled with his sealing off of the Occupied Territories, 'was intended', according to Graham Usher, 'to compel the Palestinians to come round to Israel's way of thinking at the negotiations.'⁶⁸ Rabin's election to power in June 1992 was only possible given his promotion as a man who would be tough on 'terrorism.' The security-minded centrist gained the support he needed by promising that there would be no 'terror' inside the green line. Rabin's efforts to crack down on 'terrorism' led to increases in the number of Palestinian deaths. In the last six months of the Shamir government, for example, 57 Palestinians were killed by the Israeli army. The equivalent figure for the first six months of the Rabin government is 78.⁶⁹ Between February and May 1993, 67 people were killed in the Gaza Strip alone, bringing the total of Palestinian deaths at the hands of Israeli soldiers since the beginning the of intifada to around 1,200.

In addition, thousands were injured by live ammunition, rubber bullets and tear-gas during this period. Particularly worrying was the dramatic increase in the number of children killed. From the start of the intifada around 232 children aged 16 or under were killed by the Israeli Defence Forces (IDF). Of these, 38 were killed between December 1992 and June 1993 – the precise scope of the Oslo period.⁷⁰ During this time, evidence also came to light of the existence of IDF undercover death squads who were given licence to kill 'wanted' Palestinians.⁷¹ By the time of the Oslo backchannel, tens of thousands of Palestinians were in Israeli jails. The use of administrative detention and torture continued.⁷² Buildings and houses continued to be demolished. Between the summer of 1992 and April 1993, 21 operations were carried out, of which 17 took place in the Gaza Strip, where a total of 121 buildings were destroyed or damaged. To this we must add the February closure of the West Bank and Gaza, the expulsion of 415 people to the hills of Lebanon in December and the execution of Operation Accountability directed towards Lebanon on July 1993, which killed 130 and destroyed 10,000 homes.

The significance of Rabin's security policies can be disputed. Usher, above, makes it plain that he believes that they were intended to place direct pressure on the Palestinians while they were negotiating. David McDowell is more circumspect. He argues that 'the pressure... *may* have been to force the PLO to an agreement.'[73] Israeli journalist David Makovsky, from a different angle, claims that such policies were intended only for Israeli domestic consumption in order to bolster Rabin's image in Israeli public eyes as a trustworthy actor who could be trusted with security issues. If Rabin wanted to make peace, he had to appear to be tough on terror. Makovsky writes:

> the three important decisions Rabin made prior to Oslo – the Hamas expulsions, closure of the territories, and air strikes in Lebanon . . . were not made with an eye toward a breakthrough with Arafat, but rather to calm a restive public following a wave of Arab violence and in doing so to ensure the political survival of a government committed to peace.'[74]

Where the truth exactly lies, it is hard to tell. Suffice it to say that, objectively, i.e. irrespective of intentions, there were immense pressures being placed on the Palestinian population at a time when it was negotiating its way through the politics of the post-Gulf War period.

In this chapter I have detailed the Norwegian road to the Oslo Accords and have also suggested some of the reasons which drove Arafat, Peres and Rabin to accept and pursue the offer of Norwegian facilitation. I cannot hope to be exhaustive. However, at the root of any analysis would be the explosive position of the Gaza, which, following the 'fatal linkage' of the Gulf War, was on the verge on an anti-colonial war. Arafat, fearing for his vanishing authority, decided to accept the offer of Gaza first which Rabin and Peres placed on the negotiating table in order to deal with the security threat to Israel. Arafat, Peres and Rabin needed allies to combat the threat from Hamas, and, in the uncertainty following the Gulf War, they broke with precedent and turned to each other.

From this rather feverish environment, a mediation known as the Oslo backchannel was born. The Norwegian mediation attempted to establish political contacts which would bring together the two sides in an effort to break the cycle of conflict and violence. The Norwegian facilitators wre the right people to deliver the secure environment for negotiations, an environment that would place no international pressure on Israel.

The next chapter pursues the line of analysis from another angle. Specifying the reasons and motivations for a particular act does not, of course, exhaust an account of that act's normative significance. Something could be done for X and Y reasons but actually have implications and consequences which, from the moral point of view, transcend the reasons and motivations which brought it into being. Normative analysis comprehends reasons, causes, motivations and consequences, plus the moral character of the whole. This is what makes normative analysis different from an empirical or narrative history. I mentioned in the introduction how the Accords embody, distil and crystallise an idea. The Oslo Accords make a claim, as their very name suggests, to normative validity. The next chapter will pursue normative analysis, using the tools of critical theory, to ascertain whether or not that claim to normative validity can be satisfactorily redeemed.

NOTES

1 M. A. Heller and S. Nusseibeh, *No Trumpets, No Drums: A Two-State Settlement of the Israeli–Palestinian Conflict* (London: IB Tauris and Co. Ltd, 1991).
2 F. Halliday, 'The future of International Relations', in S. Smith, K. Booth and M. Zalewski (eds), *International Theory: Positivism and Beyond* (Cambridge: Cambridge University Press, 1996), pp. 324 and 325.
3 For the perspective of the Israeli government see D. Makovsky, *Making Peace With the PLO* (Westview Press, 1996) and S. Peres, *Battling for Peace* (London: Orion, 1995). Palestinian perspectives can be found in M. Abbas, *Through Secret Channels* (Reading: Garnet, 1995) and P. Inbari, *The Palestinians: Between Terrorism and Statehood* (Brighton: Sussex University Press, 1996). Inbari is an Israeli journalist. Nevertheless, his book tracks the internal politics of the PLO following, roughly, the end of the Gulf War in 1991. The Norwegian perspective can be found in J. Corbin, *Gaza First: The Secret Norway Channel to Peace Between Israel and the PLO* (London: Bloomsbury, 1994). (Corbin's book is a little anecdotal and journalistic. It comments on the key actors' dress sense. However, Corbin does offer insights into the Norwegian perception of facilitation.) Needless to say, none of the above perspectives is to be viewed as definitive.
4 See, for example, E. Said, *Peace and its Discontents* (London: Vintage, 1995); G. Usher, *Palestine in Crisis: The Struggle for Peace and Political Independence After Oslo* (London: Pluto Press, 1995); N. Chomsky, *Powers and Prospects: Reflections on Human Nature and the Social Order* (London: Pluto Press, 1996) chapter 6; N. G. Finkelstein, 'Whither the Peace Process', *New Left Review*, 218 (1996), pp. 138–49.
5 In August 1996 I interviewed Jan Egeland and Geir Pederson. Jan Egeland was Deputy Foreign Minister of Norway at the time of the Oslo talks. Pederson's personal involvement in the backchannel was limited. Nevertheless, as an official at the Foreign Ministry and a close confident of Terje Rod Larsen, the key facilitator, Pederson was very close to events. Pederson notes that Terje Rod Larsen could not have played his role 'without the strong political backing of the foreign ministry.' That backing was given by Egeland who, in the words of Pederson, 'secured support for the whole project from the then Foreign Minister Mr Stoltenberg.' Pederson, as we shall see, gives a detailed account of the ideas and general philosophy lying behind Norwegian foreign policy. Unless otherwise indicated, all quotes in this and the following chapter stem from these interviews.
6 *Palestine Report*, 1 November 1996. JMCC Larsen took up the UN post in the summer of 1994.
7 *Norway Now*, 10 June 1996.
8 Waag, Hilde-Henriksen Waag, *Norge-Israels Beste Venn?: Norsk Midt-østen Politkk 1949–56'*, Universidetsforlaget, Oslo 1996; J. Egeland, *The Norwegian Channel: The Secret Peace Talks between Israel and the PLO*. Paper given to the JFK School at Harvard, 23 March 1995.
9 R. Mohamed, 'The US–PLO Dialogue: The Swedish Connection', *Journal of Palestine Studies*, XXI:4 (1992), pp. 54–66. The Swedish Social Democratic Party and Swedish Foreign Minister Sten Anderson were instrumental, during the 1980s, in building contacts between the PLO, Jewish Americans and the US State Department. Interview with Geir Pederson, 8 August 1996.

10 Egeland, *The Norwegian Channel*.
11 Interview with Geir Pederson, August 1996.
12 Corbin, *Gaza First*, pp. 12–13. Yuul was working in the Norwegian Embassy in Egypt.
13 *Ibid.*, p. 19. Note that Beilin and Hirschfeld (a confidant) had in fact maintained their own backchannel to Husseini since 1989 but did not tell this to the Norwegians at the time (Makovsky, *Making Peace*, p. 14). Pederson thus wrongly states that the American colony meeting was 'one of the very first contacts.'
14 Interview with Geir Pederson, August 1996.
15 Interview with Jan Egeland, August 1996.
16 *Ibid.*
17 Makovsky, *Making Peace*, pp. 16–17.
18 *Ibid.*, p. 27. Abu Alaa was well known in Israeli government circles as an economist who had proposed economic cooperation with Israel, a policy close to the Peres vision of a Middle East modelled on the European community. Corbin, *Gaza First*, p. 28.
19 Interview with Geir Pederson, August 96.
20 Incidentally, at this time, the Americans, in the form of official Dan Kurtzer, were told, by Hirschfeld, probably with the knowledge of or at the request of Beilin, of the contacts with the PLO. According to Hirschfeld, Kurtzer said that the talks would be useful as long as they remained unofficial (Makovsky, *Making Peace*, p. 19). When Egeland went to Washington in December 1992, he had reported to the Americans that Norway could possibly pursue more informal contacts. The response was very much a policy of 'wait and see.' As Mohamed Heikel demonstrates, international politics is riddled with such backchannels and a Norwegian one, at this stage, had no special reason to stand out – *Secret Channels* (London: Harper Collins, 1996).
21 Incidentally, Mohamed Heikel claims that Mazen elected not to tell Arafat about the London meeting (*Secret Channels*, Reading: Garnet, 1995, p. 437). Mazen himself writes, 'Abu Alaa returned to Tunis and submitted a brief report to Arafat who referred it on to me for evaluation and a decision' (*Through Secret Channels*, p. 113). Corbin notes that Arafat was recovering from a stroke. According to Corbin, Larsen, who visited Arafat during this time, was 'concerned that the PLO might be drifting and he feared therefore that Abu Alaa and Abu Mazen might be taking the decision to open clandestine talks with the Israelis on their own initiative'(Corbin, *Gaza First*, p. 34.) The potential weakness of Arafat is a theme to which we shall return.
22 J. Egeland, *Impotent Supowerpowers, Potent Small States* (Norwegian University Press, 1988), p. 5.
23 Makovsky, *Making Peace*, p. 19. With regard to the second point, note the critique of the facilitative model of mediation articulated by Edward Said in his piece 'The Limits to Cooperation', published in *Peace and its Discontents*, Said's critique of the Oslo process. Said notes that, in the facilitation workshop, Americans and Israelis always benefited more than the Palestinians, as 'they could get to know and to a certain extent penetrate Palestinian ranks by slowly changing our agenda from struggle and resistance to accommodation and pacification' (*Peace and its Discontents*, p. 35).
24 For a discussion of the position of the region in the Cold War, see T. Y. Ismael, *The Middle East in World Politics: A Study in Contemporary International Relations* (Syracuse University Press, 1974).
25 As Ken Matthews puts it, '[t]he fostering of client states in the Middle East has been an important foreign-policy priority for the Soviet Union since the mid-1950s . . . More specifically the Middle Eastern states were regarded as particularly important for the Soviet Union because it had legitimate security and economic interests in the area. The region occupied a crucial geopolitical position on the southern flank of the Soviet Union and

Soviet leaders saw the need to foster clients in the region in order to counter the western attempt to forge anti-Soviet alliances all around the Asian land mass' (*The Gulf Conflict and International Relations* (London: Routledge, 1993) pp. 52–3.)

26. A. Safty, *From Camp David to the Gulf* (Montreal: Black Rose Books, 1992), pp. 186, 187 and 188. This policy was outlined and considerably enhanced by Martin Indyk, former executive director of the American Israeli Political Action Committee (AIPAC). Indyk's comments are illuminating as they admirably sum up Washington's attitudes to the Middle East in the wake of the end of the Cold War. As head of the Washington Institute for Near Eastern Affairs, Indyk outlined the situation which the first Clinton administration had inherited: '[A]s a result of the Iran–Iraq War and the Gulf War', he writes, 'we are fortunate to inherit a balance of power in the region and a much reduced level of military capability to threaten our interests. The million-man Iraqi army of seventy divisions is no more.' Furthermore, 'in the wake of the collapse of the Soviet Union . . . came the collapse of the radical, rejectionist front in the Middle East' (e.g. Syria). (Special Assistant to the President Martin Indyk, Remarks on the Clinton Administration's Approach to the Middle East, Washington, DC 18 May 1993. Text presented in *Journal of Palestine Studies*, XXII (1993).
27. Matthews, *The Gulf Conflict*, p. 53.
28. Inbari, *Statehood and Terrorism*, p. 118.
29. Makovsky, *Making Peace*, p. 107.
30. Heikel, *Secret Channels*, p. 365.
31. A. Gowers and T. Walker, *Arafat: The Biography* (London: Virgin, 1990), p. 418.
32. Y. Sayigh, *Armed Struggle and the Search for a State: The Palestinian National Movement 1949–1993* (Oxford: Clarendon Press, 1997), p 640.
33. Inbari, *Terrorism and Statehood*. Furthermore, in the 1980s, Iraq was seen as a bulwark by the Gulf monarchies and the Americans against revolutionary Iran. Throughout the 1980s, therefore, Arafat's move towards Baghdad did not contradict moves towards an understanding with the Americans, a goal he also wanted to pursue. Under pressure from the intifada, contacts with the Americans had increased in frequency during the late 1980s. This growing, although limited, rapprochement, enhanced by King Hussein of Jordan's renunciation of claims to the West Bank, culminated in Arafat's Geneva statement and in the PLO declaration of 1988 which declared a Palestinian state in the West Bank and Gaza thus accepting Israel and the principle of partition. This more inclusive dynamic ground to a halt when on 30 May 1990 the Palestine Liberation Front attacked a beach resort south of Tel-Aviv. Bush demanded that Arafat should condemn the raid on 20 June 1990, and the dialogue with the USA was broken off. (Gowers and Walker, *Arafat*, chapter 17).
34. Gowers and Walker, *Arafat*, p. 472.
35. Chomsky, *Powers and Prospects*. Arafat's understanding of the Gulf War situation seems rather flawed. He proposed that the Gulf Crisis could be resolved by simultaneous negotiations of all Middle East conflicts, the lifting of international sanction against Iraq, withdrawal of American forces from the Gulf and an 'Arab solution' in which the PLO would act as neutral mediator. See Sayigh, *Armed Struggle*, p. 642.
36. The article extolled, among other things, the advantages to the Palestinian national movement of pursuing a diplomatic solution to the conflict under American auspices. Iyyad advocated a two-state solution, a modified approach to the 'right of return' and a demilitarisation of the Occupied Territories. (see Inbari, *Terrorism and Statehood*, chapter 1).
37. Inbari writes that 'in the wake of the Madrid conference Arafat's policy toward the Palestinian delegation was consistent, with one goal: foil the delegation' (*Terrorism and Statehood*, p. 139.) There is some evidence that Arafat tried to undermine the Washington talks. For example: following the expulsion of 415 Palestinians from Gaza in December

1992 the PLO announced on 16 February that it was suspending the Washington negotiations until UN Security Council Resolution 799, calling for full repatriation had been implemented by Rabin's government. Abd 'al-Shafi, a Washington Palestinian negotiator, was adamant that negotiations would not resume until the deportation crisis had been sorted out and Arafat supported this line. On 3 March 1993, Abu Mazen outlined a PLO four-point plan setting out conditions for the resumption of negotiations. During February and March the Oslo negotiations were in full swing with, of course, the full knowledge of Arafat and Abu Mazen.

38 Sayigh writes that Hamas 'sought safety' by calling for withdrawal of foreign forces from the Gulf, evacuation of the Iraqi army from Kuwait, and freedom for the Kuwaits to choose their own future. As Sayigh adds, 'Hamas was rewarded with continued financial assistance' – *Armed Struggle*, p. 651.
39 Usher, *Palestine in Crisis*, p. 7.
40 S. Roy, *The Gaza Strip: The Political Economy of De-Development* (Washington, D.C., 1995), pp. 309–12.
41 J. Di Giovanno, *Against the Stranger: Lives in Occupied Territory* (London: Penguin 1993).
42 G. Usher, 'What Kind of Nation? The Rise of Hamas in the Occupied Territories', *Race and Class*, 37:2 (1995).
43 Inbari, *Terrorism and Statehood*, chapter 4. The early month of 1993, for example, witnessed interesting developments in this regard. On 24 February 1993, Secretary of State Warren Christopher told territory delegates that the USA. had no plans to resume a dialogue with the PLO. On 25 February, a Hamas representative in Amman reported that US officials had held regular meetings with Hamas spokesmen in recent months. Predictably, the PLO expressed surprise at these developments, coming as they did after the recent bout of Hamas military activity. (Bush ordered the severing of links with the PLO after the abortive beach raid in May 1990.) The developments seem to indicate, as Inbari argues, that there have been links with the USA, the conservative monarchies of Saudi Arabia and Hamas in the Gaza Strip.
44 In late 1992 Hamas prosecuted some of the most successful operations against the Israeli military in years. In December 1992, the Izzadin el-Qassim brigade – the military wing of Hamas – launched a series of guerrilla actions in the West Bank and Gaza which claimed the lives of six Israeli soldiers in as many days. The political repression that followed, exemplified by Rabin's expulsion of 415 individuals to the mountains of Lebanon, derailed the Washington negotiations, as the Palestinian delegation refused to participate until the crisis was resolved.
45 D. McDowell, *The Palestinians: The Road to Nationhood* (London: Minority Rights Publications, 1994), p. 32.
46 Heikel, *Secret Channels*, p. 390.
47 Peres, *Battling for Peace*, pp. 376–9.
48 J. Gabriel, 'The Economic side of the Intifada', *Journal of Palestine Studies*, XVIII:69 (1988).
49 Makovsky, *Making Peace*, p. 112.
50 Peres, *Battling for Peace*, pp. 376 and 378
51 Ibid., p. 378.
52 Gowers and Walker, *Arafat*, p. 500. In July 1992 street battles between Hamas and Fatah supporters had erupted in Gaza leaving 100 injured and 3 dead.
53 Heikel, *Secret Channels*, p. 438. Heikel dryly observes that '[t]his argument overlooked important differences. Zionist settlers were able to grow from small beginnings in Palestine because of British support and because of the wealth and power of world Jewry. The Palestinians, on the other hand, had nothing but a defeated camp, an empty bank balance, and a worn out population.'

54 Heikel, *Secret Channels*, pp. 440 and 441.
55 W. Khaladi, 'The Half-Empty Glass of Middle East Peace', *Journal of Palestine Studies*, XIX:75 (1990) pp. 14–38.
56 Peres, *Battling for Peace*, p. 378.
57 Inbari, *Terrorism and Statehood*, p. 173. The Egyptians seem to have been instrumental in the public rift that broke out between Arafat and the delegation from the territories in early August 1993. The crisis broke out after the Palestinian delegation had refused to give US Secretary of State Warren Christopher a document prepared by the PLO office in Cairo; the document was supposed to be a response to a recent American attempt to bridge respective Palestinian and Israeli positions. The delegation from the territories found the document unacceptable as it pursued the Gaza-first option. The Egyptian government denied interfering in PLO decision-making, but a report published at the time allegedly revealed that the delegations were convinced that Egypt was 'tutoring' the PLO leadership in Cairo. Also, it is not coincidence that Egypt lent top lawyer Taher Shash to Arafat, on his request, in August 1992 to look over the final draft of the Oslo Accords. According to Heikel, Shash responded by saying that the problem with the document was not with the legal language but with the content. 'This is Camp David only even worse', he told Arafat on the phone (Heikel, *Secret Channels*, p. 452.)
58 S. Peres, *The New Middle East* (New York: Henry Holt 1991).
59 *Ibid.*, p. 139.
60 Roy, *The Gaza Strip*, p. 312.
61 *Ibid.*, p. 316.
62 Usher, *Palestine in Crisis*, p. 2.
63 J. R. Hilterman, 'Settling for War: Soviet Immigration and Israel's Settlement Policy in East Jerusalem', *Journal of Palestine Studies* XX:2 (1991) pp. 71–85.
64 *Ibid.*, p. 7.
65 Usher, *Palestine in Crisis*, p. 4.
66 E. Said, 'Reflections on Twenty Years of Palestinian History', *Journal of Palestine Studies*, XX:4 (1991), pp. 5–22.
67 These phrases were used in Haider Abd 'al-Shafi's opening statements to the Madrid conference, 31 October 1991.
68 Usher, *Palestine in Crisis*, p. 6.
69 Palestine Human Rights Information Centre (PHRIC), Comparison of Israeli Human Rights Violations during the Shamir and Rabin Administrations, 1992–3, Jerusalem, April 1993.
70 B'Tselem, 'The Killings of Palestinian Children and the Open-Fire Regulations', Jerusalem, 13 July 1993.
71 *Middle East Watch*, 'A License to Kill: Israeli Undercover Operations Against "Wanted" and Masked Palestinians', New York, 7 July 1993. The US State Department human rights report of 1992 itself noted that two-thirds of those shot by such units were unarmed at the time.
72 Amnesty International Report 1993, 'Israel and the Occupied Territories.'
73 McDowell, *The Road to Nationhood*, p. 117. My emphasis.
74 Makovsky, *Making Peace*, p. 87

7

From Oslo to where?
The radical intimacy of the hearth

NORWAY IS A country with a good international record. It established the world's first peace institute – PRIO – in 1959 with the backing of the government. As a proportion of GNP, its contributions to foreign aid are the best in the world. The UN has set an ODA/GNP ratio target at 0.7 per cent. (overseas aid as a proportion of Gross National Product). Norway has consistently spent over 1 per cent of its GNP on overseas development aid, and year after year it comes at the top of the international league tables in this regard. The average amount given by the world's leading nations has never excceeded 0.35 per cent. Norway is no international aggressor. It is a committed member of the UN. The first secretary of the UN, Trygve Lie, was a Norwegian.

The Norwegian intervention in the Israeli–Palestinian conflict in 1993 was based on the facilitative model of third-party intervention, which we examined in an earlier chapter. Makovsky writes: '[t]he Norwegians served as facilitators but did not mediate disputes.'[1] Corbin notes that Larsen believed that 'the gap between them [Israelis and Palestinians] was not as great as they or the outside world felt it to be. It was their hostile image of each other, forged by war and terror, which prevented any real understanding.'[2] Egeland and Pederson both described their role as being a facilitative one.

Facilitation is a form of politics that wills the good. It is about communication, empathy, mutual recognition and removing psychological obstacles to dialogue. Thus, how could Norway and facilitation be added together to produce a form of international politics directed against the struggle for justice in the Israeli–Palestinian conflict?[3]

In an article in third-party roles and the Oslo process Aggestam and Jonsson describe the Oslo process as one of 'bargaining' with the aid of facilitation.[4] In this model, the peace process is a 'long road' beset by dangers and difficulties, where disputing parties, propped up by third parties which help smooth the way, jostle for position in a post-conflict era. Such is the conventional wisdom. The central motif to arise from the following analysis, however, is a different one. Here the peace process is one where a stronger party slowly and deliberately crushes the aspirations of the weaker party. Analysis can identify the methods, the victims, the culprits and the regional and international actors involved. The correct model here, as Norman Finkelstein has demonstrated, is the structure of an expanding imperial power gradually removing a native or previously resident population.[5]

The case for the Accords: the dynamic of mutual recognition

In this and the following sections we examine the *normative* dimension of Linklater's threefold designation of the critical theory of international relations. We then move on to the *sociological* and *praxeological* elements.

The Oslo Accords consist of the following two sections: a 'Declaration of Principles on Interim Self-Government Arrangements' (DoP), signed in Washington, DC on 13 September 1993, and Letters Exchanged between PLO Chairman Arafat, Israeli Prime Minster Rabin, and Norwegian Foreign Minister Holst, between Tunis and Jerusalem on 9 September 1993.

The Accords make a claim to normative validity. The opening paragraph of the DoP announces that the 'State of Israel' and 'the PLO team ... representing the Palestinian people' must 'recognise their mutual legitimate and political rights, and strive to live in peaceful coexistence and mutual dignity and security and achieve a just, lasting and comprehensive peace settlement and historic reconciliation through the agreed political process.'[6]

The DoP consists of seventeen articles, four annexes and a set of minutes. The articles specify the following: the aims of the peace process, the jurisdiction of the 'Palestinian Interim Self-Government Authority', the concept of a transitional period and permanent status, the powers and responsibilities of the Palestinian Authority, arrangements for public order and security, the redeployment of Israeli forces, arrangements for Israeli–Palestinian cooperation and arrangements for liaison with Jordan and Egypt. The annexes concern the details of Israeli withdrawal from the Gaza and Jericho area and protocols of cooperation in economic matters.

The Letters of Mutual Recognition mark the negotiation of mutual recognition. In his letter to Yitzhak Rabin, Chairman Arafat, on behalf of the PLO, agrees to 'recognise the right of the State of Israel to exist in peace and security', to accept UN Resolutions 242 and 338 and to renounce those articles of the Palestinian covenant which 'deny Israel's right to exist.' In his letter to Norwegian Foreign Minister, Johan Jorgen Holst, Arafat also states that, 'the PLO encourages and calls upon the Palestinian people of the West Bank and Gaza Strip to take part in steps leading to the normalisation of life, rejecting violence and terrorism, contributing to peace and stability and participating actively in shaping reconstruction, economic development and cooperation.' Rabin, in his letter to Arafat, states that, 'the Government of the State of Israel has decided to recognise the PLO as the representative of the Palestinian people.'

We will deal with this issue of mutual recognition first. Those who have supported the Oslo Accords fasten onto this issue when constructing arguments in favour of the Accords. The existence of mutual recognition between Israel and the PLO is seen, by many commentators, as being the most important consideration in the defence of Oslo. The Oslo facilitation process broke decades of non-recognition and changed the conflict's existential nature. The pro-Oslo argument is this: for the first time in the history of the Israel–Palestine conflict, the PLO, considered as the representative of the Palestinian people, was granted a public and recognised place at the international negotiating table alongside Israel. There may be many issues that have to be addressed in the conflict resolution of the future. However, so the argument goes, Oslo has changed the basic rules of the conflict. The political boundaries encompass all the actors and issues that they ought to. It is this consideration that gives the Oslo Accords their fundamental legitimacy.

Not surprisingly, Shimon Peres is the lead figure in this approach. At the Oslo signing ceremony he claimed that Israel and Palestine 'have agreed to move decisively on the path of dialogue, understanding and cooperation.' The concept of mutual recognition is the cement of the entire Oslo edifice, and Peres's analysis is repeated by others. In his article 'National Vision and the Negotiation of Narratives: The Oslo Agreement', Jeffrey Michels argues that the Oslo Accords constitute the first genuine recognition of the Palestinian people within the history of Zionism. For the first time, Zionist narrative has publicly admitted the existence of a Palestinian people. And it did so within the context of an internationally recognised agreement.

Article III of the DoP refers to the 'legitimate rights of the Palestinian people.' In reference to this, Michels writes: 'if Zionism was founded by denying the very existence of a legitimate, indigenous Palestinian people [and we are not claiming a particular point of view here] then by admitting the existence of the "just requirements" of Palestinians, the foundations of Zionism are shaken.'[7] By including reference to a Palestinian people in the Accords, and by admitting the Palestinian narrative, Zionism has substituted an inclusive, and therefore legitimate, narrative for an exclusive, and therefore illegitimate narrative. Michels also points out that the text of the Accord refers to the West Bank and not just to Judea and Samaria – the biblical or Hebrew names for the same geographical area. Again, according to Michels, the Oslo Accords contain an additional recognition of Palestinian rights, aspirations and identity. Zionism, through the Oslo Accords, includes a recognition of Palestinian aspirations and paves the way for a legitimate and long-lasting peace.

Michels also argues that these elements of mutual recognition change what he calls 'the narrative telos' of the Israeli–Palestinian conflict. Mutual recognition alters the future trajectory of the relationship between Israel and Palestine. As one actor recognises the other, so future narratives will include rather than exclude the other. If the logic of the Accords has its way, previous narratives of rejection or blindness will be marginalised. Narratives of mutual recognition will be encouraged. The relationship between Israel and Palestine will be based on an evolving intersubjectivity – one present in embryonic form in the Oslo process and Accords. Given this shift in perspective, future agreements, as Michels puts it, 'will be less of a shock to national vision.'[8] And as agreements become less of a shock, and narratives become more intertwined, so legitimate political agreement in the future becomes more likely.

Nabil Shaath, a long-standing adviser to Arafat and a key political figure in the PLO's negotiations with the Israeli government over the years, also claims, in a 1993 article, that the Oslo process enabled Israel and the PLO to create their 'own dynamic' – a dynamic that was independent of the superpower policies of Washington, policies which have served only to exclude proper Palestinian participation over the years.[9] Oslo was important in that, for the first time since 1948, Palestinians were directly negotiating matters relating to 'their own land, future and fate.'[10] The fact that the Israeli government dealt directly with the PLO, in sight of international public opinion, is seen, by Shaath, to be of vital importance. Shaath claims, echoing Michels, that reaching an agreement with the PLO – the representative of the Palestinian people – 'strikes against Zionist ideology.' This is an ideology which, according to Shaath, has always doubted the existence of a specifically Palestinian people.[11] Of equal importance, for Shaath, was the inclusion of such issues as Jerusalem, the Jewish settlements and the refugee problem within the text of the DoP. Although, according to the DoP, these issues are to be dealt with only in the final status negotiations, their inclusion in the text of the Accords 'calls into question the legality and finality of the annexation [of the West Bank and Gaza post 1967].' By including reference to these issues within the Oslo Accords, Shaath claims that Israel is admitting that the Israeli annexation of the West Bank and Gaza is not final and that it still needs to be negotiated – i.e. rendered legitimate.[12] Thus the Oslo Accords include rather than exclude the concerns of Palestinian nationalism. And the concerns of Palestinian nationalism, by being included, are treated as legitimate political issues. This is deemed to be an important breakthrough. As Uri Savir, an Israeli negotiator at Oslo put it, '[m]utual recognition is more important than the DoP, because it is the center of the conflict. It turns the Israeli–Palestinian conflict from an existential to a political conflict.'[13] (As we have seen, in the chapters on facilitative theory, it is argued that removing existential barriers between adversaries is a vital step in the process of conflict resolution.) Removing the existential barriers to dialogue was seen, by many, to be the basic achievement of the whole Oslo process.

Avi Shlaim writes, as Michels and Shaath, of the symbolic implications of the Oslo Accords. He argues that the Accords reconcile Jew and Arab to the fact that both peoples have to share 'the cramped living space between the Jordan River and the Mediterranean Sea.'[14] In his support of Oslo, Shlaim reiterates his general historical position. His *Collusion Across the Border* is an account of the relations between Jordan's King Abdullah and the leaders of the Israel national movement from the 1920s up to Abdullah's assassination in July 1951. Shlaim's narrative documents the twists and turns of Israeli and Jordanian policy. Shlaim is critical of bungling, incompetence, short-sightedness, ambition and greed of all parties during these crucial years. However, he also wishes to rescue the idea that negotiations between Arabs and Israelis, and the principle of partition, have been present in the politics of the region right from the beginning. There is a historic relationship, which, though flawed, may provide the foundations for a new beginning.[15] Shlaim's article supporting the Oslo Accords extends the analysis in his book and focuses on the fact that the 'historic reconciliation' was based on 'a historic compromise: acceptance of the principle of partition.'[16]

We could go on documenting how issues of mutual recognition are supposed to support the Accords, but the general point has been made.[17] Efraim Karsh, for example, echoes the arguments about symbolism and mutual recognition. He writes:

> The Declaration of Principles . . . signed on the White House Lawn on 13 September 1993, was a watershed in the one-hundred-year war between Arabs and Jews. After a century of denial and rejection, of blood-letting and bereavement, Arabs and Jews have finally agreed to bury the hatchet and settle for peace, based on mutual recognition and acceptance.[18]

According to those who support the Accords, their importance lies, for the most part, in the facilitation of mutual recognition. Palestinian agreement to reject those parts of the PLO covenant, which 'deny Israel's right to exist', are set alongside the State of Israel's recognition of the PLO as the 'representative of the Palestinian people.' Although the details of the new relationship still need to be ironed out, and many difficulties will lie ahead, supporters of Oslo argue that the 'dynamic', 'narrative telos' and 'rules' of the relationship between Israel and Palestine have been fundamentally rearranged for the better. Although it is only a small step, this basic recognition of the other is the foundation of the future.

Mutual recognition and the power to exclude the validity claims of statehood

In this and the following section we contrast the claims made about mutual recognition with the way in which the PLO was prevented from raising validity claims pertaining to Palestinian statehood during the entire Oslo process. And notwithstanding the references, embedded in Oslo, to UN Security Council

Resolution 242 and the concept of an interim period, the capacity of the Oslo-inspired process to redeem the claim to Palestinian statehood must be placed in question given the exclusion of substantial references to Palestinian self-determination in the text of the Oslo Accords.

As David Makovsky notes, the Oslo process was dominated by the twin issues of statehood and security.[19] The Palestinian delegation hoped, eventually, to create a Palestinian state. The Israeli delegation, on the other hand, looked to ensure the security of an Israel expanded, to a greater or lesser degree, into the West Bank. On the Palestinian side, discussing statehood meant raising validity claims about the following core components of Palestinian nationalism: Jerusalem, refugees, land, borders, self-determination and the economy. For Israel, the issue of security breaks down into combating terrorism, acquiring land, strategic depth, demographic depth, settlements and secure borders.

Based only on secondary sources, it is difficult to specify the exact claims that the PLO delegation intended to raise at Oslo. In the light of the pressures placed on the authority of Arafat detailed in the last chapter, the PLO may well have begun Oslo with a minimal set of goals. Abu Mazen offers some clues, but his account cannot be considered too definitive.[20] Despite these problems, it is possible to chart the path of exclusion down the various phases of Oslo with reference to the various drafts of the DoP. These can be compared to each other and to the generally recognised, historical goals of Palestinian nationalism.

In *Battling for Peace*, Shimon Peres makes clear that Israel had a fairly exclusionary agenda from the outset. None of the core demands of Palestinian nationalism was to be discussed. He writes, for example, that '[t]hroughout the Oslo process we were determined not to make any concessions on Jerusalem.' He continues:

> [t]he Palestinians did not give up without a fight. As their opening position, they demanded that the seat of the autonomous self-government be in Jerusalem. And they clung doggedly to their demand that East Jerusalemites be eligible both to stand and to vote in the election for the self-governing Council.[21]

Thus Jerusalem as an element of Palestinian national rights was excluded from the agenda right from the outset. This is the case, despite the fact that Palestinians can lay claim to the city as the historical capital of the region, which has intricate cultural and economic ties to other Palestinian cities.

Similarly with the idea of an international trusteeship and the idea of a Palestinian state. Peres writes:

> international trusteeships in recent history were almost always established prior to full independence. Israel's declared position was that it opposed the creation of an independent Palestinian state . . . we were not prepared to commit ourselves at the outset of the interim period to accepting the Palestinian's demand for eventual independence.[22]

Peres also makes it clear that he intended to exclude all claims to Palestinian sovereignty. For example, as he puts it, the Israeli team 'laid great stress on the need to ensure that the IDF's redeployment . . . be clearly defined in the Declaration of Principles as a matter *for Israel's sole discretion*.'[23] Again, this proposal would surely negate any realistic claim to Palestinian territorial sovereignty.

The Oslo process can be divided into two stages: five rounds of exploratory negotiations and five rounds of more official negotiations. The DoP went through various phases before it was signed in August (Oslo) and September (Washington): the Sarpsborg DoP, the Gressheim DoP, the PLO objections at Halvorsbole and the final DoP which took shape in the first weeks of August 1993. When the details are examined, it is clear that each phase of the negotiations progressively excluded more of the core demands of Palestinian nationalism while placing the core Israeli demands for security in an expanded state at the centre of the political process. The result was an Accord which addressed the core demands for Israeli security but which postponed the core demands of Palestinian nationalism. At least, these demands were postponed until the creation of a final status solution, couched in terms of the famous UN resolutions (242 and 338) and conditional upon the fulfilment of the security demands which made up the core character of the Oslo document.

The Sarpsborg document – DoP number one – contained fifteen articles and was accompanied by annexes on the status of Jerusalem in Palestinian elections, Palestinian economic development and regional economic development. Among other things, Sarpsborg stated the following: that the aim of the peace process was to implement UN Resolutions 242 and 338; that a Palestinian Interim Council would cover the territory of the West Bank and the Gaza Strip; that Israel would withdraw from the Gaza Strip within two years and that the region would be administered by an international trusteeship; that an Arbitration Committee would be established consisting of the two sides and the co-sponsors of the Madrid conference; and that the Palestinians of Jerusalem could participate in elections for the Palestinian Interim Council and cast their votes *in* Jerusalem.[24] Remaining articles reflected the strong technocratic impetus behind all the versions of Oslo and detailed plans for economic and scientific cooperation.

On 13 March 1993, the Oslo talks were upgraded, as Rabin sent the diplomat Uri Savir and the lawyer Joel Singer to Oslo to negotiate on behalf of the Israeli government. As talks moved beyond the initial academic and exploratory stage, Singer and Savir began to renegotiate Sarpsborg. The result was the Gressheim DoP, signed at the beginning of July 1993. The Gressheim document differed from Sarpsborg in a number of respects: Israel agreed to withdraw from Gaza and Jericho within two months and not two years of signing; there was to be no international trusteeship and no international arbitration (a fact which, as Peres notes, is highly significant); the Palestinians maintained their insistence on full jurisdiction throughout the Occupied Territories, but the accompanying minutes excluded settlements, settlers and Israeli military locations from Palestinian control; Palestinians in East Jerusalem were no longer able to vote in elections to the Palestinian Interim Authority in Jerusalem – as this was seen to imply that they had political rights as residents of Jerusalem; furthermore, the Gressheim DoP did not commit Israel to negotiate either settlements, water, the status of the 1948 refugees or Palestinian national sovereignty until *after* an interim period.

Although, considered against the historically articulated Palestinian national goals, Sarpsborg was an exclusionary document in itself, between Sarpsborg and Gressheim more of the core demands of Palestinian nationalism were excluded from the Oslo process and postponed to the final status negotiations. By the time of Gressheim, the issues of Jerusalem, refugees, land, borders and settlements had been moved off the immediate political agenda altogether.

The final version of the DoP, finalised in August 1993, reflected the central dynamic of Oslo – a dynamic which placed the core Israeli demands for security in a partially expanded state at the centre while marginalising the Palestinian national demands. Consider, for example, Article IX and Article VII(5) of the agreed minutes to the DoP. Article IX states that 'both sides will review jointly laws and military orders presently in force in remaining spheres' – the 'remaining spheres' being defined as those spheres that are not the responsibility of the Palestinian Council. Thus, in the West Bank and Gaza *as a whole*, first, Israeli military orders would remain in place after Oslo and, second, they are subject only to the *review* of the joint Israeli–Palestinian Liaison Committee (there are no commitments to repeal them). This may seem like an interim or compromise position, one that reflects the realities of facts on the ground. Indeed, Article VII promises that, eventually, 'after the inauguration of the Council, the Civil Administration will be dissolved and the Israeli military government withdrawn.' However, lest there be any misunderstanding, any undertaking to withdraw militarily is negated by article VII(5) of the agreed minutes. This states: '[t]he withdrawal of the military government will not prevent Israel from exercising the power and responsibilities not transferred to the Council.' Powers transferred to the Council include only education and culture, health and social welfare, direct taxation and tourism. Thus, military and security policy in the West Bank and Gaza – as a whole – remains subject to Israeli sovereignty. The Palestinian police, set up in Article VI, will enforce Israeli-defined conceptions of security. As Article VIII states, 'Israel will continue to carry the responsibility for overall security of Israelis for the purpose of safeguarding their international security and public order.' Responsibility for overall Israeli security means retaining effective control over the Occupied Territories.

Paragraph 3b of Annex II – 'Protocol on Withdrawal of Israeli Forces from the Gaza Strip and Jericho Area' – states that the Palestinian authority has no authority over external security, settlements, Israelis and foreign relations. Peres underlines what this means. He writes:

> the Palestinians demanded that the Declaration of Principles provide (Article VII) that, 'after the inauguration of the Council, the Israeli Civil Administration and military government will be dissolved.' We countered that the whole Civil Administration would be 'dissolved' once the autonomy was in place, the military government could only be 'withdrawn', not 'dissolved' – *because legally the military government would remain the source of authority in the territories.* The Palestinians agreed, in the end to that distinction.'[25]

Thus it is no accident that, as the Oslo process has proceeded, Israel has retained effective military control over the West Bank and Gaza. A map of the West Bank five years after the signing ceremony in Washington reveals pitifully small amounts of territory under complete Palestinian control. So small are these amounts that it is meaningless to speak of Palestinian sovereignty or national self-determination. Instead, the picture is one where the Palestinian National Authority, with its many security agencies, police small pockets of the Palestinian population within the context of overall Israeli military dominance. Five years after the Washington ceremony, Zone A, 3 per cent of the West Bank, was under complete Palestinian control – i.e. both security and civilian policy is directed by the Palestinian National Authority. Zone B, 24 percent of the West Bank, was under Israeli security and Palestinian civilian control and Zone C, 73 percent of the West Bank was under complete Israeli control, as if the Oslo Accords had never happened.

Yezid Sayigh, in his history of the Palestinian national movement, claims that, despite the flaws associated with the Oslo agreements, the PLO has managed to achieve an historic attachment to Palestinian territory which has been missing ever since 1948. For Sayigh, the Oslo Accords mark the beginning of an new historical phase, where 'the centre of national politics, primary social constituency, and statist institutions were based in one and the same location, the occupied territories.'[26] However, first, the pockets of territory left to the Palestinian authority are so small that they circumscribe the possibility of meaningful autonomy and, second, given the strength of the right wing in Israel's politics, there are no guarantees that the so-called state-building impetus will not wither or go into a complete decline. Political institutions are like biological entities in the sense that they need a certain critical mass in order to exist. Deprived of this 'critical mass' they are unsustainable. The possibility that the nascent state institutions created by the Oslo Accords will reverse into decline is not circumscribed by the Oslo process. On the contrary, the prospect of irreversible decline is built into a process which postponed too many of the core components of Palestinian nationalism to the final status, while providing no guarantees about the nature of either the interim or final status during the interim period.

Cosmopolitan mediation?

How the text negates mutual recognition

All in all, three aspects of the Oslo Accords serve to marginalise the brief references made to Palestinian national demands included in the Oslo Accords: first, the overriding emphasis on Israeli security; second, the ambiguity surrounding UN Security Council Resolution 242; third, the ambiguity surrounding the concept of an interim period.

The central position of Israeli security in the Oslo Accords, noted in the DoP, is amplified in the Letters of Mutual Recognition. In Arafat's Letter to Rabin, as we have noted, he states that the 'PLO recognises the right of the State of Israel to exist in peace and security.' Also, the same letter states that 'the PLO renounces the use of terrorism and other acts of violence and will assume responsibility over all PLO elements and personnel in order to assure their compliance, prevent violation and discipline violators.' Arafat then promises that 'those articles of the Palestinian Covenant which deny Israel's right to exist and the provisions of the Covenant which are inconsistent with the commitments of this letter are now inoperative and no longer valid.' In the letter to Holst, Arafat continues: 'the PLO calls upon the Palestinian people in the West Bank and Gaza Strip to take part in the steps leading to the normalisation of life, rejecting violence and terrorism, contributing to peace and stability.' For his part, Rabin merely promises to 'recognise the PLO as the representative of the Palestinian people and commence negotiations with the PLO within the Middle East peace process.'

The inequality embodied in these commitments is, in a sense, startling. When these words are coupled with the provisions in the DoP (above), it is hard to see the Oslo Accords as anything but abject Palestinian surrender to the core demand of Israeli nationalism – security in an expanded Israeli state. The Oslo Accords institutionalise a state of affairs in which Arafat and the PLO security apparatus promise to become the enforcer of Israeli law and sovereignty in parts of the Occupied Territories where there is a dense Palestinian population – most obviously in the Gaza Strip. (Here, the security concerns about Hamas, detailed in the last chapter, shed a great deal of light on the rationale behind Oslo.) Furthermore, Palestinian claims to eventual national independence following the interim stage are made contingent on the enforcement of Israeli security, in the West Bank, the Gaza Strip – *in Israeli Occupied Territory* – and in Israel. The PLO is to look after the security of the occupiers and if it does not, then there will be no *discussion* of self-determination – let alone self-determination itself. Thus, it is no accident that, since 1993, the security provisions of the DoP have continually been used by the Israeli right wing to obstruct chances for progress.[27] The Oslo process can be passed like a baton from the so-called 'left' of the Labour party to the Israeli right wing, which can easily exploit the central provisions and rationale to pursue its exclusionary goals. The media often claim that Oslo enshrines the principle of land for peace. However, this argument misses a crucial aspect of the Accords. The problem is that Arafat cannot point to a single aspect or clause of the Accords which states that the PLO is entitled to resist a failure to relinquish land using violence. On the other hand, there are many clauses in the Accords which state that their implementation is contingent on the end to the Palestinian armed struggle. Given this, it is easy for a more intransigent government not to relinquish land and claim that the resulting violence nullifies the agreement.

The problems are further compounded. The meaning of UN Security Council Resolution 242, which specifies the aims and goals of the peace process, is disputed. Netanyahu, for example, subscribes to a very minimal interpretation. Referring to the clause specifying the right of every state in the area 'to live in peace within secure and recognised boundaries', Netanyahu argues that 'the bulk of the resolution is a demand that the Arab states make peace: by ending the state of war against Israel, recognising Israel's right to exist and assuring that Israel's borders will be secure ones.'[28] Referring to the call for Israeli withdrawal from Occupied Territory, he continues, 'has Israel withdrawn from "territories occupied in the conflict"? It certainly has.'[29] Netanyahu refers to the 1979 Israeli withdrawal from the Sinai desert and the Camp David Accords and implies that Israel has already complied with the obligations imposed by UN Resolution 242. Further references to 242 must, according to the leader of Likud, refer to the obligations of Arab states and the PLO, as Israel has discharged its moral and political responsibilities.

Other commentators point to the ambiguities in Resolution 242. Heller and Nusseibeh argue that '[r]esolution 242 does not oblige Israel to withdraw to the 1949 armistice lines.'[30] Edward Said agrees with Netanyahu, Heller and Nusseibeh about the meaning of The Resolution. According to Said, as it does not even refer to Palestinians, 'insistence on 242 is tantamount to asking Palestinians to renounce their national aspirations.'[31]

David McDowell also notes that 'Israel has argued that the wording of the second requirement [that Israel withdraw from territories] did not necessarily mean all the territories it had occupied.'[32] Nevertheless, McDowell argues that 'the first principle [concerning the inadmissibility of the acquisition of territory by war] precludes such casuistry.'[33] He may be correct in his interpretation of the withdrawal clause – in principle. However, the political uncertainty surrounding the interpretation of Resolution 242 was well known at the time of Oslo. It is problematic, therefore, that Oslo did not attempt to clear up these ambiguities. As Netanyahu's comments reveal, these ambiguities could be exploited to the disadvantage of the Palestinian case.[34]

The DoP states that the core demands of Palestinian nationalism will be discussed in the final status negotiations following an interim period of five years.[35] There is nothing necessarily wrong with the concept of an interim period. As Walid Khalidi puts it, '[o]ne cannot leap from the present situation to a final settlement in one go.'[36] However, the character and nature of the final status and interim period need to be very clearly defined. They require what Edward Said has called 'a discipline of detail', as opposed to what may only be 'a wish for autonomy and Israeli withdrawal.'[37] The Oslo Accords marginalised the demands of Palestinian nationalism until the arrival of a final status solution couched in the famous UN resolutions. However, these resolutions can be misinterpreted and exploited and this fact was known at the time of Oslo. The resolutions are the only principles underlying the interim period. The faults of the former thus serve to undermine the rationale of the latter.

When we look at the Letters of Mutual Recognition and the parts of the DoP pertaining to ideas of mutual recognition, this relationship of sovereignty to non-sovereignty is precisely what we find. Arafat's letter of recognition refers to the 'State of Israel.' Rabin's letter refers merely to the PLO as the 'representative of the Palestinian people.' The DoP refers to the 'State of Israel', but only to the 'PLO team.' The 'PLO team', under the Oslo implementation process, is to become a 'Self-Governing Authority' – an 'elected Council.' The jurisdiction of this 'Council' 'will cover West Bank and Gaza Strip territory' (the omission of 'the' here is obviously significant). Control of this territory is to be handed over to 'authorised Palestinians.' This group is to control education and culture, health and social welfare, direct taxation and tourism, while Israel retains overall responsibility for 'defending against external threats, as well as the . . . responsibility for overall security of Israelis for the purpose of safeguarding their internal security and public order' (thus, only Israel has international capabilities – the necessary agreements of sovereignty and statehood according to international law).

Performative contradiction: coherence vs. shattered identity

In this and the following section we examine the *sociological* dimension of Linklater's threefold characterisation of the tasks of a critical theory of international relations. We concentrate on the idea of performative contradiction, inadequate modes of political agency and the role and nature of a facilitation process.

In the Oslo process, the intersubjective DoP was negotiated *before* the identity defining Letters of Mutual Recognition. At first sight, this appears contradictory. How is it possible to negotiate an intersubjective agreement when mutual recognition has not even been achieved, let alone defined? The Oslo Accords therefore raise important and general questions of subjectivity or agency and its relation to intersubjectivity within procedures of political negotiation. Habermas writes: 'I call interactions communicative when the participants coordinate their plans of action consensually, with the agreement reached at any point being evaluated in terms of the *intersubjective* recognition of validity claims.'[38]

There are two ways to evaluate intersubjectivity, i.e. that which takes place between subjects. First, we can question the nature of the relationship *between* parties. We may ask questions such as the following: to what extent did the various parties in a process agree to a particular outcome? Was the outcome a matter of consensus, compromise or force? These are the intersubjective considerations that make up the bulk of Habermas's 'Discourse Ethics' and the cosmopolitan approach to international relations detailed in the preceding chapters. Second, though, there are questions of subjectivity or agency. These arise, as there can be no intersubjective agreement without clearly defined and autonomous subjects. An intersubjective ethics, as presented by Habermas, highlights the importance of subjectivity or agency and its character and situation. Agency must be sufficiently mature to bear the weight of a cosmopolitan communicative action.

In Habermasean terms, there is a 'performative contradiction' involved in negotiating the intersubjective DoP *before* the Letters of Mutual Recognition. This performative contradiction has the following aspects.

Heller and Nusseibeh argue the need for technical expertise in the negotiation of an Israeli–Palestinian peace agreement.[39] Similarly, Said calls for a 'discipline of detail.'[40] Groups may be prevented from engaging in negotiations and communicative action – from raising relevant validity claims – through having fractured identities or inadequate modes of political agency. Edward Said, for example, has been sharply critical of the lack of preparation and incompetence on the part of the PLO delegation at Oslo: of Arafat's posturing, lack of international understanding, ignorance of detail, international law and the processes of government. Said writes of 'the technical incompetence of the PLO, which negotiated in English, a language that neither Arafat nor his emissary in Oslo knows, with no legal adviser.' He continues, describing how 'Arafat and his three or four subordinates alone faced an entire corps of Israeli Foreign Ministry experts.' Said argues that Palestinian agency is hampered by 'Arafat's dictatorial ways, his single-handed control over money, the circle of sycophants... the absence of accountability.' Said concludes: '[t]he march towards self-determination can only be achieved by a people with democratic aspirations and goals, or it is not worth the effort.'[41]

In his *Secret Channels*, Mazen unwittingly supports Said's view. He writes, for example:

> I must admit that throughout the Oslo negotiations we did not review the texts with a legal consultant for fear of leaks. We had therefore to depend on our own experience and knowledge of handling texts. I tried to make use of the remnants of the legal knowledge I had acquired while studying law at Damascus University, but I could not draw much comfort from them.[42]

Corbin makes a similar point, noting that Hasson Asfour joked that the agreement would have to be simple because he could only understand, in English, the main points.[43]

This problem was compounded, given that, while the Israeli party was negotiating the state of intersubjectivity during the DoP discussions, i.e. their intersubjective relationship with the PLO, the PLO was negotiating this same intersubjectivity *and* the nature of their own subjectivity, which was, at this time, radically insecure. The PLO delegation carried an extra burden. Israel's identity as a state was never in question during the Oslo process. The boundaries of the state may have been in question, but not the existence of the state itself. Israel, quite clearly, to use Netanyahu's own phrase, had 'a place among the nations.' Although Israel has had to fight for its survival on many occasions, and although it has experienced fierce international criticism over the years, by the time of Oslo, Israel was undergoing, to use Aharon Klieman's words, a 'diplomatic renaissance.'[44] Israel's identity as a sovereign state was – relatively – secure at the time of Oslo.

However, while Israeli identity going into the Oslo negotiations was relatively secure, the same cannot be said of Palestinian identity.[45] We have already touched upon the issue of Palestinian political and legal incompetence. This hampered the ability to negotiate. Also, consider the leadership crisis and the prospect of financial meltdown following the Gulf War as an immediate background to the Oslo channel. In addition to this, however, Palestinian identity in general is notoriously insecure.[46] The root of the Palestinian predicament is precisely the lack of statehood – a problem of self-definition and organisation. Palestinians in Occupied Territories, in Lebanon and in Kuwait are not citizens of Israel – but nor are they citizens of an independent Palestinian state. They exist, as it were, in a political and legal no man's land.[47]

Because Palestinian identity was not sorted out before the intersubjective negotiations, Israel was able to exploit the more vulnerable position of the Palestinians to its own advantage. This is recognised by Makovsky. He writes that in July 1993 'Savir had cabled his superiors from Oslo saying that the Palestinians wanted a "package deal" – the DoP in exchange for mutual recognition.'[48] Makovsky continues, 'although Arafat's approval was a *sine qua non* for any deal, the symbolism of his return [to Gaza] was a chip that Israel could use to extract substantive concessions.'[49] Corbin describes the promise of mutual recognition as Israel's 'trump card.' It was a card presented to the Palestinian delegation at a difficult moment in the peace process, when the Palestinian delegation, at Halvorsbole, presented objections to Joel Singer's tough approach which led to the Gressheim DoP. Singer, according to Corbin, 'dangled the prospect of mutual recognition before the PLO' as a means of obtaining a number of Palestinian concessions: that the Israeli army should continue to protect the settlers; that it should control the borders between the Jericho areas and Jordan, and between Gaza and Egypt; that Palestinian institutions in Jerusalem should not be linked to the Interim Council; that the Palestinian authority should not have judicial, legislative as well as executive powers. These Palestinian demands were traded in for mutual recognition. As Corbin writes of mutual recognition: 'it was something that Arafat, shut out of the Washington process, longed for.'[50] The exploitation of vulnerable subjectivity runs counter to the cosmopolitan spirit of negotiations specified in the concept of a 'dialogic community.' And the inadequate treatment of political agency within the process partially explains why the Accords have the normative character that they do.

The radical intimacy of the hearth

The problems discussed in the previous sections are linked *intrinsically* to the facilitative role of the Norwegians. The Norwegian facilitation helped constitute a state of affairs where Palestinian claims to national self-determination were marginalised. In this section we investigate a further aspect of the sociological aspect of Linklater's threefold designation of the tasks of a critical theory.

The Norwegian facilitative model, based on the radical intimacy of the hearth, was the appropriate channel in which to institutionalise a relationship between Israel and the PLO, whereby the latter is maintained in the space that exists between the international and the domestic. Historically, Palestinians are neither citizens of Israel nor citizens of an independent Palestine. To institutionalise this state of affairs, Israel needed to sign an agreement with the PLO but the agreement, and the process of agreement, had also to exist in a space between the international and the domestic. Israel could not sign an international agreement, as this would grant an implied recognition to Palestinian claims to statehood. At the same time, Israel could not deal with the Palestinians as if they were citizens of Israel. This strategy confronts what is called, in Israeli political discourse, the demographic problem. The small-state, facilitative mediation offered by the Norwegians is the perfect solution to this dilemma. The Oslo process and the Accords are not part of Israeli domestic politics. But, existing in the radical intimacy of the hearth, neither are they part of a full-blooded international politics. The Oslo Accords and process offered the appearance of international politics, without creating any international obligations. It is the perfect form of politics by which to institutionalise a neo-colonial arrangement. The previous chapter outlined the political structures which emerged following the end of the Cold and Gulf Wars: PLO political and economic bankruptcy and US/Israeli hegemony. The Oslo process and the Oslo Accords helped bring the new contours of the Middle East into being. The new structures of power which emerged following the end of the Cold War needed to be legitimated and the Oslo process was the right type of mediation for the job.

Much is made of the Norwegian mode of conflict resolution – the Oslo spirit. Jane Corbin's account of the process and Accords, described by Egeland as 'the Norwegian perspective', emphasises the friendships which were created between the main players, the small group setting, the secrecy and intimacy of the facilitative approach. In this approach, as we have seen in previous chapters, the emphasis is on breaking down stereotypes, smoothing over existential obstacles, clearing up misunderstandings and overcoming a lack of willingness to talk. This view of conflict resolution uses the radical intimacy of the hearth to melt the vast, frozen structures of international politics. As the warmth and intimacy of the Norwegian household contrasts with the vast ungovernable landscape of Norway, so, in the Oslo process, the radical intimacy of the hearth was used to warm the frozen and ungovernable structures of the Cold War in order that a new international order could be eased – facilitated – into being.

Norwegian facilitation is poised somewhere between the domestic and the international. It emphasises the relations of the hearth – warmth, intimacy, empathy, friendship and so on. Yet it promotes these relations as appropriate in the international world. Norway wants to play an international role. However, it is too small and powerless a state to project its sovereignty safely in the international world in which it moves. Owing to its weakness, the facilitator can act 'internationally' only by radically domesticating international politics. Owing to the weakness of the small-state facilitator, international politics must be radically tamed. International politics is safe, for the facilitator, only if everyone is a 'friend.' The line between the international and the domestic is thus blurred by the small-state facilitation. And in the case of the Israeli–Palestinian conflict, this blurring is highly inappropriate.

The Oslo process – being part of Norwegian foreign policy – helps sustain the existential status of Palestinians. The Palestinians are maintained in the space between the domestic and the international by a peace process and treaty which also exist in this space. The Oslo process was not a fully fledged example of international politics. There were two states and one quasi-state entity involved in the Oslo process. But Norway intervened as a facilitator not as a state, thus diminishing rather than enhancing the international status of the PLO. The PLO is allowed to participate in a facilitative exercise but not an international conference. Yet neither was the Oslo process a form of Israeli domestic politics – for either the Palestinians or the Israelis. (Presumably it is safe to assume that Israel and the PLO do not normally conduct their 'domestic' political interaction in hotels in Oslo.)

Similarly with the Oslo Accords. Legally, they are not a normal part of Israeli domestic politics; they point, as it were, outside the borders of the nation. However, given that the Accords, in international terms, are a unilateral declaration of sovereignty, they do not bind Israel into commitments with other states.[51] In terms of international law, the DoP is more like an unilateral declaration. As international lawyer, Ian Brownlie, writes: '[a] state may evidence a clear intention to accept obligations vis-à-vis certain other states by a public declaration which is not an offer or otherwise dependent on reciprocal understandings' – at least at the international level.[52]

The normative understanding of the Norwegian facilitator reveals this blurring of the international and the domestic. Towards the international public, the facilitator can present views which are committed, principled and substantial. The facilitator can appear as a sovereign power would like to appear, as a confident voice in the conversation of nations. To the conflicting parties in their charge, however, the facilitator is moved by the radical intimacy of the hearth – the need to gain and promote the warmth and friendship of both sides.

When asked about the issue of legitimacy, it is noteworthy that Geir Pederson used the resources of domestic political legitimacy to underpin what he believes to be an act of international politics. Pederson argued that 'we were dealing with an elected government and an organisation, the PLO, which is recognised internationally and also by the Palestinians as their organisation.' Similarly, '[we] needed to trust that the political leaders of the parties you are dealing with will actually give the whole thing to the democratic process afterwards.' Here, according to Pederson, as the two parties legitimately represent their own people, any agreement they enter into between themselves must also be legitimate. There is some sense to this argument. If the leaders were illegitimate, then any agreement between them would not bind those they purport to lead. However, Pederson's analysis tries to use resources that would guarantee domestic legitimacy to legitimise something which exists at the international level. This analysis ignores whether or not agreement between communities is legitimate. This particular argument, if pushed to a logical conclusion, banishes questions of legitimacy from the international realm.

Egeland draws a sharp distinction between the facilitator's public and private roles. Publicly, the Norwegians are allowed to develop a stance of the sovereign power – one which is committed, principled and substantial. As a facilitator, however, the role is formal and strictly limited. Egeland says of the Oslo process that:

> The whole trick was to keep it secret. As long as the parties knew that the world knew nothing about the Oslo channel, it was not that important what we would say in public as long as they felt that we did not try to manoeuvre them into any kind of any kind of position or help any one or other of the two . . . They were never really concerned with what I would say on the television, for example, as long as I didn't try to push either side to meet the other.

Egeland continues:

> we were very good in Oslo at mathematically giving them the same kind of treatment: always the same sized rooms, the same kind of cars, we met them at the airport whether they would be this or that side. But we were not in the negotiations room. We made a point of not being there. We felt it was important not to be involved.

The facilitator trod a fine line between promoting a substantial Norwegian line in public and promoting a formal and limited Norwegian facilitation in private. Thus, as Egeland argues:

> we would certainly not be neutral to the main subjects. We would be against the use of violence, against terrorism, against the Israeli settlements, against the Israeli occupation. We were in favour of Israeli withdrawal. We did not compromise our Norwegian stance and it was well known by the parties. But it was more clear that we would take an impartial side on some of the issues that were up for negotiations: what would be the final status of Jerusalem? Should there be anything of Jerusalem or not in the text? Would we have a view on the final status of the Palestinian areas? Would we feel that Gaza plus Jericho would be enough to start with? What should the status of the settlements be in the future? Many have asked does our role as an intermediary and a facilitator mean that we could criticise either one of the parties. We could criticise them for human rights abuse, for lack of democracy, for settlements etc. But we would be impartial as regards sympathy to one or other of the parties. We felt a *friend to both sides*.

Egeland is keen to stress that the facilitators had political goals of their own. However, these were stated in public, where there was no real influence, and never in the facilitation process itself, where substantive interventions would have been inappropriate and ineffective.

Pederson also argues that the Norwegians did have policy commitments of their own. These policy commitments, however, had to be kept out of the negotiations. Pederson argued:

> We thought that by playing an active part in facilitating contact between what we saw as the representatives of the Palestinian people and the Israeli government, this could create a climate conducive to a peaceful development in the area. And hopefully to contribute to a solution that would give the Palestinians what the international society said they should have. [Nevertheless, argues Pederson, it was important that the third party had to stay out of the discussions when they concerned issues of substance]. It would be truly wrong for a third party to interfere in the process ... it was absolutely the correct strategy not to interfere in the discussions or in the negotiations. We would interfere only to the extent that we would try to keep it on track.

Where the Norwegians had little or no influence, they acted as sovereign powers – proclaiming their ambitions for the nature of the international world. Where they were able to exercise some influence, however, they did so, but only as facilitators, where issues of substance are brushed aside. This position reflects the weakness of the small-state facilitator who, in a world of playground bullies, has to act as the 'friend of both sides' to survive. This may well be the rational approach of a small state in the international world which wants to develop a foreign policy. But the facilitative small state cannot concentrate only on its own needs. Domestic-type facilitation in the international world has to be applied with great care. *Its application can be flawed when struggles for national self-determination are involved.* A facilitation process preserves what Sayigh calls the 'enduring contrast between the PLO's statist character and its lack of stateness internally, and . . . its pseudo-sovereign juridical standing and non-state empirical reality, externally.'[53]

Significantly, the Oslo Accords and the Norwegian style of international politics represented a rational strategy for Israel. Israel, as a whole, is not that keen on having a Palestinian state on its borders. Rabin, for example, stated to the *Jerusalem Post* shortly after Oslo: 'I stick to my position: no Palestinian state, Jerusalem must remain united under Israeli sovereignty, and be our capital forever.'[54] Peres adopts a similar attitude. Referring to Israel's historic position, he states: '[o]ur basic position was that we opposed the creation of a separate Palestinian state. Such a state, as we saw it, would split Western Palestine down the middle, leaving Israel with an untenable and indefensible narrow waist.' Referring to the time of Oslo, he writes, 'Israel's declared position was that it opposed the creation of an independent Palestinian state following the interim period of self-government.' Peres adds: 'the Palestinian negotiators pressed repeatedly for the wording, "mutual legitimate, national and political rights" in the preamble to the Declaration of Principles. We eventually agreed, reluctantly, to "political", but refused to accept "national".'[55] Netanyahu's position is the same. He writes that a Palestinian state 'would leave the Jews with a state ten miles wide, its cities crowded along the Mediterranean, with the likes of Yasser Arafat and George Habash peering down at them from the Samarian and Judean mountains that dominate the country.'[56]

While Israel is not keen on the idea of a Palestinian state, it is also not keen to develop a large domestic Palestinian population. This scenario is called the 'demographic problem.'[57] In these contradictory circumstances, where Israel is caught in a pincer which is basically of its own making, the country has to develop a rather unique strategy. This is a strategy of dilemma-management. Palestinians are not to have a state of their own. But nor are they to be made citizens of Israel. A unique strategy has to be formulated to deal with this situation. What is this strategy if it can be given a name? The most accurate description is this: the Oslo Accords represent a form of concealed occupation.

An international conference?

Recognising that the struggle for self-determination lay through international recognition, the PLO had always sought a conflict resolution process based on an international conference. This position supporting an international conference has been proposed many times. The Palestinians have argued that the third party needs international standing to boost the power of communicative action. The Palestinian National Council's Declaration of Palestinian Independence in 1988 stated that 'the State of Palestine herewith declares that it believes in the settlement of regional and international disputes by peaceful means, in accordance with the UN charter and resolutions.' The Fifth General Congress of Fatah called, in 1989, for the following:

> an effective international conference with full powers for peace in the Middle East which must be convened on the basis of international legitimacy under UN supervision and patronage, with the participation of the Security Council and the concerned parties including the PLO on an equal footing and with equal rights as other states.

The position was repeated in the PLO's response to the suspension of US–PLO dialogue on 21 June 1990 and in PLO statements during the entire Madrid process.

Faisal Husseini described the reasons for this position in 1991.

> We Palestinians, we the PLO, are strong when the game is governed by rules ... it is this same approach that leads us to demand an effective role for the UN and Europe, that makes us demand that the negotiations unfold under the twin banners of international legality and the implementation of UN decisions.[58]

Interestingly, the international conference was also a position supported by the Nordic foreign ministers right up until the onset of the Oslo process. For example, a communiqué on the Middle East issues by the Nordic foreign ministers on 16 August 1989 stated that:

> the ministers continued to regard an international peace conference under the auspices of the UN with the participation of the five permanent members of the Security Council and all the parties concerned, including the PLO, as the best chance of bringing the parties together in binding negotiations.

This communiqué affirmed Palestinian rights to 'self-determination.' This position was repeated in March 1990.

Egeland was asked why there was a change in Norwegian state policy, with a change from a Conservative to Labour government in Norway. He replied that there was 'not a very active Norwegian foreign policy around that [the previous] idea.' He stressed Norway's commitment to the UN, pointed to Israel's alienation from the UN, and argued that the call for UN resolutions was only 'the best show in town in the 1980s.' For Egeland, the Conservative government's policy involved paying lip service to UN resolutions, nothing else. The Gulf War and the Madrid process altered the political landscape for Egeland, and a new policy initiative seemed more appropriate and possible. The Norwegians, the small-state facilitator, decided to shoulder what were previously seen to be international responsibilities.

In the post-Oslo period, the call for a greater international presence has been repeated. Hanan Ashrawi states: 'It has always been a common strategy of the United States and Israel to exclude others. This is why it is important for us to include others.'[59] Abd' Al Shafi reiterates this point. He states: 'Leaving the solution to the Israelis and Palestinians cannot lead anywhere because of the crushing asymmetry of power. A neutral mediator is needed.'[60]

A more neutral third party is needed to strengthen the forces of democracy and compromise. This is a third party, inspired by the cosmopolitan ideal of international mutual recognition, which can insist that a political settlement moves towards national rights for both Israel and Palestine – whether it be a dual state or bi-national paradigm. A conflict resolution process in this part of the world will continue to demand the attention of outside powers: to help shape a balance of power, to oversee implementation, to offer guarantees, financial and technical help. This outside role cannot be left to the power-political role of the United States nor can it be left to the powerless small-state facilitator which is unable to shape the real dynamics of the conflict. A cosmopolitan mediation needs the power of the nation-state without the dangerous and potentially arbitrary unilateralism of the superpower. A cosmopolitan mediator needs the ideological aims of facilitation without the concomitant weakness. A cosmopolitan mediator is most likely to be a coalition of states or an international organisation representing a coalition of states. In this regard, the future of the EU in the Middle East peace process is an interesting question which should receive attention in the future. Thus, European leaders are increasingly frustrated at the lack of progress and are seeking a greater role in the region.[61]

A critic might charge that the application of a strong cosmopolitan morality to this particular conflict would result in immediate disqualification for the mediator, with the result that conflict just continues. However, conflict resolution in this context means national rights for both parties. And this is all cosmopolitanism would require. Interim stages are possible. But they must be grounded in an overall consensus about final status. Given the fact that both sides require national rights for the conflict to cease, the view from the 'ideal speech situation' is a necessary goal not some wild abstraction. Cosmopolitan solutions are the only solutions capable of delivering long-term stability. The alternative involves extinguishing the national claims of one party or, for that matter, both.

Concluding remarks

Back in Madrid in 1991, during the peace process following the Gulf War, the Palestinian delegation in Washington understood the forces of Israeli rejectionism. Accordingly, they refused to be drawn into an agreement about interim status which offered no guarantees about settlement construction, human rights, the economy and the ultimate promise of national self-determination. Arafat, locked out of this process, took advantage of the fact that Madrid/Washington floundered on the rocks of sensible Palestinian demands and Israeli intransigence. He believed that, through offering a plethora of concessions and by pleasing the United States, he could steer the interim period towards a Palestinian state in the absence of any real guarantees about the nature of final status. This was an incredibly risky strategy from the outset, a strategy easily derailed by inherently predictable events such as a suicide bomb in Jerusalem or the election of a Prime Minister from Israel's other and now seemingly majority political tradition. The nature of the Oslo document, with security in an expanded Israel as its central motif, is easily exploited by the right wing in Israel. In the years following Oslo, security responsibilities came to mean everything, anything and, as a result, absolutely nothing.

For example, the US proposals drafted in March 1998 for a 13.5 per cent withdrawal from Zone C, which were *rejected* by Netanyahu's government on the grounds that they gave too much away, carried with them exacting clauses concerning, yet again, the maintenance of Israeli security. For example, in exchange for an initial redeployment of 2 per cent (of the 13.5 percent of Zone C), the Palestinian Authority would be required to issue orders banning 'incitement.' Incitement, of course, could mean any opposition to the status quo. Should 'incitement' occur, redeployment would cease.[62] It is an impossible situation, and it should be no surprise to future historians that Oslo never really managed to find its way from interim to final status. The facilitative distinction between these two stages postponed all the tough cosmopolitan decisions until later, with the result that the interim stage just ran out of steam.

With no outside power willing to exert pressure, the forces of compromise and democracy are crushed. Thus, as the Oslo interim period drew to a close it is just like old times in this part of the Middle East, with Israel refusing to grant Palestinians national rights unless the latter clamp down on 'terrorism.' This is a logic which can only fail to bring peace. Or, at least, it is a logic that can bring peace only if Palestinian national resistance is completely extinguished. An occupying power will always face acts of violence from those whose land it occupies.

It is recognised across the world that Palestinian statelessness is in the roots of the Israeli–Palestinian conflict. Of course, Israeli fears about national security in the unstable Middle East are also at the roots of the conflict. But 'peace with security' can only be achieved in the context of an agreement with Palestinian political forces which grants a strong measure of national rights. The Norwegian facilitation sidestepped the issue of Palestinian national self-determination. By its very nature it could do little else. We are unlikely to welcome either the short- or long-term consequences.

The problems with the Oslo Accords stem from a misuse of language and the concomitant political ideals surrounding the logic of a cosmopolitan communicative action. The Oslo Accords make a claim to mutual recognition. The very fact that negotiations took place creates an illusion of communicative action. And the fact that these negotiations took place under the auspices of Norwegian facilitation serves further to create the image that the logic of communicative action was respected. However, when we look at the details, when we peer beyond 'language in the service of propaganda', the chimera of communicative action disappears. The Oslo process and Accords free-ride on commitments to truth and rationality; they claim the benefits of certain political ideals without accepting the serious responsibilities that go with them. The process and Accords make use of the cosmopolitan ideals of a 'dialogic community' without accepting the political and moral implications. This is problematic. Language and communicative action are vital to the reproduction of society. It is the task of a critical theory of international relations to ensure that language, communicative action and the cosmopolitan ideals of democratic public law remain resources which future generations are able to use. To fulfil this purpose, criticism of political projects which fall short of this ideal is vital and necessary. In normative, sociological and practical terms, a critical, cosmopolitan approach to international mediation seeks to guarantee that those who subscribe to its principles accept that they make a claim on scare resources. The justification for applying a robust cosmopolitan critique is that it becomes a voice of contradiction and dissonance. But this is a contradiction intimately related to political practice. In the case which we have been examining, a cosmopolitan ethic is not a wild idealism. Rather, with its defining motif of mutual recognition, it is the central strategy involved in creating a stable future.

NOTES

1 D. Makovsky, *Making Peace with the PLO* (Boulder, Col.: Westview Press, 1996), p. 22.
2 J. Corbin, *Gaza First* (London: Bloomsbury, 1994), p. 13.
3 I will not write with the benefit of hindsight. Rather, I will engage in a textual analysis. At the time of writing, spring 1998, it looks as though the Oslo process is about to die. We cannot necessarily infer from this situation that the Accords must have been flawed right from the beginning. However, it is totally legitimate to wonder whether there is a relationship between the Accords, considered as a text, and the political realities and dynamics that followed them. Ideas and discourse do have an influence on reality. As Goldstein and Keohane write, borrowing from Weber, ideas are like 'switchmen.' They turn 'action onto certain tracks rather than others' and they 'obscure other tracks from the agent's view' (*Ideas and Foreign Policy* – New York: Cornell University Press, 1993), p 12. We can wonder which courses of action were obscured by the Oslo procedure and which courses of action were initiated.
4 K. Aggestam and C. Jonsson, '(Un)Ending Conflict: Challenges in Post-War Bargaining', *Millennium: Journal of International Studies*, 26:3 (1997) pp. 771–93.
5 N. G. Finkelstein, *The Rise and Fall of Palestine* (London: University of Minnesota Press, 1996).
6 This document and a whole host of documents relating to various peace negotiations, treaties and so on can be found in *The Palestinian–Israeli Peace Agreement: A Documentary Record* (Institute for Palestine Studies: Washington DC, 1993). Future references to either the DoP or the 'Letters of Mutual Recognition' are to this source.
7 J. Michels, 'National Vision and the Negotiation of Narratives: The Oslo Agreement', *Journal of Palestine Studies*, XXIV:1 (1994). The point raised by Michels's argument is an interesting one and we shall return to it. For now, note the following: the Oslo Accords grant the 'legitimate rights of the Palestinian people' – it is true. But what are the legitimate

rights of the *Palestinian* people? Michels's arguments are explicitly directed at Edward Said's *Peace and its Discontents*, perhaps the most articulate criticism of the Oslo Accords (London: Vintage, 1995). We shall examine Said's arguments with regard to mutual recognition in due course.
8   'National Vision', p. 37.
9   N. Shaath, 'The Oslo Agreement: An Interview with Nabil Shaath', *Journal of Palestine Studies*, XXIII:1 (1993), pp. 5–13.
10 *Ibid.*, p. 8.
11 Of course, the various attitudes of Zionism to the Palestinian population is a vast topic and is one that cannot be detailed here. Suffice to say that Shaath refers to a strain of Zionism that speaks and writes as though Palestinian Arabs, given they are first and foremost Arabs, are not particularly attached to Palestine; that they would be happy living in, for example, Jordan or Syria. The early Zionist leader, Israel Zangwill, for example, who adopted the phrase 'a land without a people for a people without a land', knew, as David McDowell writes, that Palestine was populated. (McDowell, *The Palestinians: the Road to Nationhood* (London: Minority Rights Publications, 1994), p 10. Zangwill merely thought, as McDowell quotes him as saying, that, '[t]here is no particular reason for the Arabs to cling to these few kilometers' (*ibid.*). Such attitudes persist. Benjamin Netanyahu who became Prime Minister of Israel in May 1996, addresses the Palestinian Arabs and says, 'you already have a Palestinian state – called Jordan' – *A Place Among the Nations* (New York: Bantam Books, 1993), p. 150.
12 N. Shaath, 'The Oslo Agreement', p. 8.
13 Cited in Makovsky, *Making Peace With the PLO*, p. 69/70.
14 A. Shlaim, 'Prelude to the Accord', *Journal of Palestine Studies*, XXIII:2 (1994).
15 A. Shlaim, *Collusion Across the Border: King Abdullah, the Zionist Movement, and the Partition of Palestine* (Oxford: Oxford University Press, 1988).
16 *Ibid.*, p. 26.
17 The diplomatic correspondent for the Jerusalem Post, David Makovsky, also highlights the issues of mutual recognition. He writes: 'mutual recognition was the *sine qua non* for creating a climate among the Israeli and Palestinian populations within which a peace process was possible.' Makovsky continues: 'the importance of symbolism should not be dismissed. For Palestinians, the idea that Israel no longer regarded the PLO as a terrorist organization amounted to a genuine breakthrough marking a new level of respect from a once contemptuous foe. For Israelis, Arafat's pledge to renounce terrorism and annul the section of the 1964 Palestinian National Charter calling for Israel's destruction was seen as a highly significant indicator of a serious commitment to peace.' Makovsky points to the very apex of symbolic politics here when he writes that '[t]he handshake between Rabin and Arafat on September 13, 1993 is evidence of the importance of symbolism.' Of course, Makovsky is right, this was a media image of profound importance. But what is its real significance? (*Making Peace*, p. 134).
18 E. Karsh, *Peace in the Middle East: The Challenge for Israel* (Ilford, Essex: Frank Cass, 1994), p. 1. In the same volume another contributor writes of 'the momentous historical and psychological significance of the secret agreement' (P. J. Vatikiotis, 'Peace by the End of the Century?', pp. 5–13). Vatikiotis employs some interesting arguments against Edward Said who he acknowledges as being a 'virulent and vociferous opponent of the Oslo Accords.' Vatikiotis argues that Said's 'property-owning bourgeois background in Palestine' has raised his expectations of economic reward in a future Palestinian state. He continues: '[g]iven the likely size and nature of such a state [his] expectations are unrealistic' – the implication being that Said resists the Oslo Accords because they are not economically fruitful enough for Edward Said (no evidence is offered to support this view). Vatikiotis also

criticises Said for attacking Arafat's despotism. He writes: 'the difficulty is that virtually all rule and ruling institutions in the Arab Middle East have been autocratic in the main, and it is most unlikely that were any of Arafat's opponents to replace him in power . . . they would hasten to abandon that kind of rule.' (What are the implications? That Said is an autocrat in the making? That criticism of power of pointless if you are an Arab?) Vatikiotis concludes, referring to Said, that 'one cannot take such critics too seriously, and especially when their credibility is otherwise in question.' Vatikiotis's remarks hardly establish that Said's credibility is in question. More likely that these kinds of remark are a substitute for real argument against the critics of Oslo.

19 Makovsky, *Making Peace*, p. 47.
20 In *Through Secret Channels* Mazen states that he met Abu Alaa and Hasson Asfour 48 hours before they travelled to Oslo. They agreed on the following points: peace was to be based on Resolutions 242 and 338; the territory over which the Palestinian Interim Authority will exercise power includes the territories occupied in 1967; the Palestinian Interim Authority will be chosen by all Palestinian residents registered in the West Bank on 4 June 1967; an Arbitration Committee will be established to review all disputes, the committee will contain representatives from the UN; the permanent status would commence after two years – *Through Secret Channels* (Reading: Garnet, 1995), p. 116–17.
21 S. Peres, *Battling for Peace* (London: Orion, 1995), p. 389.
22 Ibid., p. 390.
23 Ibid., p. 391. My emphasis.
24 Note, however, that voting was to take place in or near to religious or historic monuments. As Peres puts it in *Battling for Peace*, '[o]n the issue of voting in Jerusalem, for instance, the suggestion put forward was that East Jerusalemites cast their ballots in the Holy Places – the Moslems at the Mosque of al-Aksa and the Christians at the Church of the Holy Sepulchre. Hirschfeld and Pundak (the two academic negotiators) felt that this could be acceptable to Israel, as it could claim that its concession on this point was linked somehow to the Palestinian's religious rights at the Holy Places – and did not signify a direct political nexus between Jerusalem and the autonomy' – p. 383.
25 Peres, *Battling for Peace*, p. 392. My emphasis.
26 Y. Sayigh, *Armed Struggle and the Search for a State* (Oxford: Clarendon Press, 1997), p. 663.
27 Thus Likud use these provisions in the Oslo Accords to criticise the Palestinian Authority. Likud publishes a document called 'Major PLO Violations of the Oslo Accords.' Among them, the following are included:
(i) 'The Accords require that the Palestinian police act to prevent violence and cooperate with Israeli security forces (see, for example, Annex I, Article II). The conceptual foundation of the Oslo Accords is a rejection of violence and force in the conduct of bilateral relations. By initiating violence against Israelis, the PA has violated a cornerstone of the agreement' (the document refers to the violence that followed the opening of a tunnel near the Temple Mount in September 1996). Of course, one violation does not necessarily justify another. Also, Arafat has been heavily criticised since 1993 for allowing the military wing of the PLO – the Tunisians as they are known – to become a force which cracks down on opposition to Oslo. The Oslo requirement that the PLO clamp down on 'terror' has meant that judicial process has been abused and undermined by the Palestinian National Authority. This has involved, for example, the use of torture and extrajudicial execution. (See, for example, *Birzeit Human Rights Record* No. 17 April–September 1996; *Friends of Birzeit Newsletter* Summer 1996). David Hirst has written about PNA abuses of power in *The Guardian* newspaper. He estimates that there is one policeman for every citizen – as compared with one for every 2,000 in Los Angeles. (6 July 1996). Also see 'Shameless in Gaza', *Guardian*, 21 April 1997).

28 Netanyahu, *A Place Among the Nations*, p. 290.
29 Ibid.
30 M. Heller and S. Nusseibeh, *No Trumpets, No Drums: A Two-State Settlement of the Israeli–Palestinian Conflict* (London: IB Tauris and Co. Ltd., 1991), p. 79. Heller and Nusseibeh argue that the Green Line that delineated the post-1949 boundaries should form the basis of peace negotiations.
31 Said, *Peace and its Discontents*, p. 141.
32 McDowell, *Making Peace*, p. 154.
33 Ibid.
34 Consider, also, that US policy under the Clinton administration in 1993 did not view the West Bank and Gaza as occupied territory. For example, in a letter to the then Secretary of State James Baker, future vice-President Al Gore stated that the West Bank and Gaza were not occupied. He asks Baker: '[h]ow can the US support UN resolutions that refer to the territories administered by Israel since 1967 as "occupied Palestinian territories" when US policy is that the status of those territories is to be determined through direct negotiations between the parties?' Furthermore, Warren Christopher described these views as the 'correct position' during his confirmation hearing as Secretary of State before the Senate Foreign Relations Committee in January 1914. (*Journal of Palestine Studies*, XXII (1993) pp. 153–4. See also Donald Neff, 'The Clinton Administration and UN Resolution 242', *Journal of Palestine Studies*, XXIII (1994) pp. 20–30). In two papers drafted by the Clinton administration in May and June 1993 – the precise scope of the Oslo process – references to Occupied Territory were dropped. The June paper, for example, stated that '[t]he two sides concur that the agreement reached between them on permanent status will constitute implementation of resolutions 242 and 338 in all their aspects.' These remarks reflect the positions adopted by Gore and Christopher that the territories are disputed, not occupied.
35 These arrangements are stated in Article One – the aim of the negotiations.
36 W. Khalidi, 'The Half Empty Glass of Middle East Peace', *Journal of Palestine Studies*, 3:75 (1990). Heller and Nusseibeh concur with this analysis. They write, '[p]hased implementation of an Israeli–Palestinian settlement is necessary for both political and practical reasons. Politically, it provides a mechanism and period of time for risk management and confidence building . . . On the practical level phased implementation will be required to permit the orderly redeployment of Israeli personnel and facilitate the relocation of Jewish settlers . . . and to create or consolidate the constitutional order and the political and administrative institutions of the Palestinian state' – *No Trumpets, No Drums*, p. 136).
37 Said, *Peace and Its Discontents*, p. 25.
38 J. Habermas, 'Discourse Ethics', in *Moral Consciousness and Communicative Action* (Cambridge: Polity Press, 1991), p. 58.
39 Heller and Nusseibeh, *No Trumpets, No Drums*, pp. 149–50.
40 Said, *Peace and Its Discontents*, p. 25.
41 Ibid., pp. 13–14.
42 Mazen, *Through Secret Channels*, p. 162.
43 Corbin, *Gaza First*, p. 143.
44 See, A. Klieman, 'New Directions in Israel's Foreign Policy' in Karsh (ed.), *The Challenge for Israel*, pp. 96–117. Israel had good reasons to be confident about its international status by the time of Oslo: GA Resolution 3379 was revoked in 1991; the 1988 PLO Declaration of Independence referred to UN Resolution 181 which partitioned Palestine into two states, the strength of the intifada was ebbing; Arafat had declared on French television that the parts of the PLO covenant denying the right of Israel to exist were 'obsolete'; the Madrid process included Israel as a state and never questioned the existence of the state; and by 1993 Israel had formal diplomatic relations with more than 115 countries.

45 The PLO has received recognition from the UN. UNGAR 181 (1947) partitioned Palestine into two states – one Jewish and one Arab. In 1974, the General Assembly expressed the view that the PLO should be entitled 'to participate as an observer' in all UN bodies. On 1975, the Security Council invited the PLO to participate in a debate, the invitation conferring on the PLO 'the same rights are conferred when a member state is invited.' Furthermore, following the 1988 Declaration of Statehood, the PLO received recognition from states worldwide, the bulk of the recognition coming from the Arab and third world (in Western Europe, for example, only Austria, Portugal, Turkey, Malta, Yugoslavia and Cyprus granted recognition. (*Journal of Palestine Studies* XVIII:3 (1989)). However, despite the gestures towards international recognition, the legacy of occupation since, at least, 1967 has left both the idea and reality of Palestinian statehood hanging in the balance. The annexation of Jerusalem, Jewish settlement, land confiscation, economic dependence, the military occupation and the dispersal of the Palestinian population have all made precarious both the idea and reality of a Palestinian state.

46 The fractured nature of Palestinian society can be seen when we look at, for example, the dispersal of the Palestinian population. Note the following table. Estimated and projected Palestinian population:

Country	1995
Inside Palestine	
W.Bank/E.Jerusalem	1,250,000
Gaza Strip	880,000
Israel	810,000
Outside Palestine	
Jordan	2,170,000
Lebanon	395,000
Syria	360,000
Other Arab States	517,000
Rest of the World	500,00047

(Source: Mcdowall, *The Road to Nationhood*, p. 126.)

47 This position of statelessness affects Palestinians inside Israel, the Occupied Territories and the Palestinian diaspora. In Israel itself – defined by the Knesset in 1985 as Jewish state – Palestinians have been subject to legal, social and economic discriminations. See, for example, A. Haider, *The Arab Population in the Israeli Economy*. (Tel Aviv: International Center for Peace in the Middle East, 1991); A. Haider, *Social Welfare Services for Israel's Arab Population* (Boulder, CO: Westview Press, 1991); D. McDowell, *Making Peace*, pp. 81–93. For the situation in Occupied Territories, see R. Shehadeh, *Occupier's Law: Israel and the West Bank* (Washington: Institute for Palestine Studies, 1985). The problems of statelessness obviously affect the 1.5 million or so Palestinian Refugees who live in neighboring Arab states. As McDowell writes, 'Jordan went for headlong integration ... conferring full citizenship. Syria extended equal rights to the refugees, allowed them to maintain their Palestinian identity [..] Lebanon was a good deal less hospitable, placing the refugees in an indeterminate category, *neither foreigners nor nationals*' (pp. 65–6). See, for example, L. Brand, *Palestinians in the Arab World* (New York and Oxford, 1988) and R. Sayigh, *Too Many Enemies: The Palestinian Experience in Lebanon* (London, 1994).

48 Makovsky, *Making Peace*, p. 62.
49 Ibid.
50 Corbin, *Gaza First*, p. 136.

51 Despite having all the appearance of international politics, of crucial importance is this simple fact: the facilitating state and all the other states involved only witnessed the agreement. They did not sign it. They were not parties to the Accord, they only assert that they saw others become party to it. And among those who signed the Accord there was only one state. The agreement is not part of international politics – it is not between nations – and it is not internationally binding.
52 I. Brownlie, *Principles of Public International Law*, 4th edn (Oxford: Clarendon Press, 1990), p. 638.
53 Sayigh, *Armed Struggle*, p. 667.
54 *Jerusalem Post*, International edition, 16 October 1993.
55 Peres, *Battling for Peace*, pp. 352 and 392.
56 Netanyahu, *A Place Among the Nations*, p. 6.
57 In *Handshake in Washington: The Beginning of Middle East Peace*, John King writes the following: 'It should also be seen that the problem of peacemaking is firmly rooted in the demography of Israel and the Occupied Territories. The population of Israeli proper is almost five million, of whom some 900,000 are Arabs. A million Palestinians live in the West Bank and ¾ million in the Gaza Strip. The total numbers of Arabs in Israel and the Occupied Territories is therefore 2.65 million, almost half the overall population of 6.65 million . . . If the Occupied Territories were ever to have been annexed, the Arabs would have soon of outvoted the Jews, or [to maintain Israel as a Jewish state] two classes of citizen would have to be instituted, one without the vote.' (J. King, *Handshake in Washington* (Reading: Ithaca Press, 1994), p. 5.
58 *Journal of Palestine Studies*, XX:4 (1991), p. 107.
59 Interview in *Journal of Palestine Studies*, XXVI:3 (1997).
60 'Moving Beyond Oslo', *Journal of Palestine Studies*, XXV:1 (1995), pp. 76–85.
61 A European Commission Report in 1998 criticised Israel and the Netanyahu government for causing increasing poverty in the Occupied Territories and European Commission President Jacques Santer has demanded that Europe be given a more prominent role (see *Middle East International*, nos. 567 and 568).
62 *Middle East International*, 10 April (1998), p. 5.

Conclusion

CHAPTER ONE DESCRIBED how the concept of mediation is contested in the existing literature. We noted the many different meanings which can be located in the existing mediation literature and how commentators disagree over the many aspects of a mediation process. Despite this theoretical and practical complexity, two basic approaches to the theory and practice of international mediation were discerned: the power-political approach and the approach based on facilitation or the problem-solving workshop.

The power-political approach works with the concept of strategic or technical rationality. It emphasises the idea of the mediator as manipulator or problem-solver working with the levers of executive and administrative power in a condition of structural anarchy, where normative questions are pushed onto the backburner. Facilitation theory works with the concept of contextual rationality. It emphasises hermeneutic understanding, problems of poor communication, feelings of existential danger, 'the demonisation of the other' and the importance of breaking cycles of mistrust through small-scale negotiations conducted in secret, where a trusted, disinterested and neutral third party acts to create and maintain a momentum for an emancipatory dialogue.

Chapter two set the scene for the critical turn. Mediation operates in the following context: protracted social conflict, fragmentation plus globalisation, the existing state of weapons technology and the crisis surrounding the tradition of western political thought. In this context, the study of mediation is governed by institutional and discursive questions. As an institution, mediation serves the task of the historical reproduction of societies in crisis. It carries the past, through the present and into the future. It preserves the historical moment from the threat of destruction. As a form of agency, mediation must respect the condition of plurality. This truth leads, eventually, to the development of a cosmopolitan analysis.

Chapter three began to reflect upon and criticise the theoretical and practical assumptions of existing mediation theory by subjecting the power-political or geostrategic paradigm to normative analysis. In theoretical terms, the power-political approach was found to operate with a problematic empiricist assumption which separated questions of fact and value. Theoretical enquiry was found to be unreflective and to lack an awareness of the broader cultural consciousness which can operate to shape political thought. Theoretical enquiry is more politically contentious than the 'objective' power-political approach would imply. We noted that the power-political approach runs the risk of reifying existing social reality, and shades of ideology began to be seen, if only very briefly, in certain so-called objective analyses of US mediations in the Middle East. Furthermore, the power-political relegation of normative questions to the backburner of analytical priorities was found to be unsupported by the arguments from structural anarchy. These arguments do not rule out the possibility of political agency, and the conditions of normative theorising – ought implies can – remain satisfied.

Finally, the practice of power-political mediation was found to ignore the 'phenomenology of the moral.' Here, mediation becomes a depoliticised form of technical control, which can obscure the wider context of conflict. Instead, it was demonstrated that mediation ought to be connected to the social roots of a conflict through the exercise and promotion of communicative reason. In a time of historical crisis, it is the reproduction of society, not states, which is at stake.

Kissinger's disengagement policies and the way in which Israel was developed as a strategic asset to superpower interests throughout the 1970s is a testimony to the dangers of the geostrategic paradigm. Kissinger primed a regional conflict with all the tensions of a global Cold War, as the conflict between Israel and the PLO became subsumed into the more ferocious ideological currents of the century.

Chapter four subjected the approach of facilitation theory to normative analysis. The facilitative arguments concerning the limitations of instrumentalism were described as being full of insight. However, problems began to emerge for facilitation theory when the philosophical tension between understanding and critique was described. Facilitation theory does attempt to move beyond a pure hermeneutics. However, facilitation theory's attempt to embrace normativity was found to be wanting, in both theory and practice. The model of needs as drives construes language and conflict resolution in instrumental terms, and it obscures questions of normative legitimacy. The simple equation of the act of reflection with liberation and emancipation was also described as being too simplistic. The view of conflict as arriving out of 'legitimate concerns' and not 'lawlessness' is a contingent assumption and criticism is needed to link the practice of facilitation to the normative goals which define its aspirations. In concentrating too heavily on symbolic and psychological issues, the practice of facilitation was described as a flight from the realities of genuine political action, and the attempt, made by facilitation theory, to embrace normativity was deemed to raise more questions than it answered.

Conclusion

The more recent attempts to ally facilitation theory with a theory of communicative action are a welcome development. However, there are two implications. First, facilitation theory must recognise an authority outside itself. Second, the theory of communicative action cannot be equated with the problem-solving workshop. The appeal to communicative reason can be vindicated by alternative forms of practice. Shades of the cosmopolitan idea that mediation aims to strengthen the forces of democracy in the region began to emerge. The more facilitation attempts to deliver substantial goals, the more it merges into an approach associated with a robust cosmopolitan international political theory.

In chapter five we noted how normative questions impinged on the consciousness of theory following the collapse of the Cold War. In both historical and theoretical terms, mediation theory can no longer resist the claims of normative analysis. The normative approach described in this thesis stems from critical theory, and the roots of critical theory in the work of Jürgen Habermas were described. Critical theory was contrasted with Kantianism, Marxism, postmodernism and instrumentalism. Habermas's ideas about the importance of communication were described, as was the concept of 'performative contradiction' and the concept of 'discourse ethics.' The theoretical foundation of critical theory was then compared with a traditional question in the theory of international relations concerning the relations between men and citizens, and the chapter discussed the work of Andrew Linklater and David Held. The cosmopolitan ideal emerged with the concepts of 'democratic public law' and the 'dialogic community.' These forms of practice are designed to redeem the unfinished project of modernity in a post-Westphalian form of international politics.

In a more sceptical moment, we noted the importance of historical and contextual enquiry. If critical approaches to international relations are to avoid the postmodern charge of presuming to speak with a sovereign voice beyond politics and contestation, they need to adopt historical and contextual analysis.

We also discussed the tension between process and outcome. Despite the criticism that a robust cosmopolitanism would exacerbate a conflict rather than alleviate it, we concluded that incremental facilitation cannot proceed without the notion of final status, and that the latter can only be uncovered with the aid of a more robust cosmopolitan ethic.

Finally, I suggested that cosmopolitanism may overemphasise the existence of a moral world order in its favour. With Nietzsche, it is possible to argue that the moral resources of the West are exhausted or even in decline.

Despite the difficulties, critical themes apply to the work of mediators who are now charged with enlarging the domain of moral responsibility, and with ensuring that the logic of communicative action, built into the structure of linguistic reality, can unfold.

In chapter six, the descent into the case study began, with a description of the origins of the Oslo Accords. The Norwegian facilitation arose from strong ties between the respective Labour movements in Norway and Israel, the political and financial bankruptcy of the PLO, the Israeli desire to be rid of Gaza, Arafat's political isolation, the pressures being placed on the Palestinians on the ground and the political deadlock in Washington. Into this situation stepped a group of Norwegian politicians and academics who could provide a 'perfect camouflage' and 'trusted environment', where the post-Cold War order in this part of the Middle East could be eased into being.

Chapter seven took the text of the Oslo Accords and the Oslo process itself and subjected them both to a normative analysis stemming from the perspective outlined, primarily, in chapter five. The Oslo process and Accords were found to reproduce structures of inequality and domination. Too many of the key demands of Palestinian nationalism were illegitimately excluded by the Accords. In addition, the particular concept of an interim period, the ambiguities in UN Security Council Resolutions 242 and 338 and the overriding emphasis on Israeli security ensure that the Oslo process was unlikely to redeem the claims of Palestinian national self-determination. The Oslo process was also flawed given that is was premised on, and institutionalised, a 'performative contradiction.' The advent of negotiations raised the spectre of the ideal speech situation, where validity claims are redeemed in an unrestrained act of communication. However, owing to their weakness, the Palestinians could not carry through the project which they began. The Palestinians are politically weak, and given that the DoP was negotiated before the Letters of Mutual Recognition, the DoP has the status of an Israeli sovereign voice.

Unfortunately, the Norwegian facilitation process was found to be intrinsically linked to the inequalities embodied in the Accords. Norwegian facilitation exists in a space between the international and the domestic, as do the Palestinian people and the Oslo Accords themselves. Norwegian facilitation was a peace process which sustained the existential status of the Palestinians, a status which many believe to be at the root of the conflict between Israel and Palestine. The Oslo Accords create a state of concealed occupation and they contradicted the historical demand of the PLO for an international conference, where a state or coalition of states acts as a guarantor of the international status of the peace process and resulting peace agreement. The Palestinians needed a peace process which enhanced their international standing and their ability to act and negotiate on an international stage. They did not need a peace process which preserves their suspended animation in an international political no man's land. The Norwegian facilitation failed to boost the power of communicative action in this crucial part of international relations.

The analysis of the Oslo Accords is designed to vindicate the claims of a distinct critical position. The Oslo process and Accords were based on a 'performative contradiction.' The properties of communicative action associated with mutual recognition and the rational redemption of validity claims were used to cover up and legitimise what would otherwise appear to be naked strategic action. A resource – language – which has developed and evolved for communicative purposes was used to promote sectional and factional interests, thus threatening a universal interest in the 'well-being' of a resource vital in the reproduction of society. The themes of mutual recognition, discourse ethics, 'performative contradiction' and issues of inclusion and exclusion are employed in the analysis. The focus is on the ideas of learning and rationalisation in the moral or practical spheres, and the underlying social philosophy emphasises how social and political realities are constructed in an arena of political contestation structured by boundaries whose status can be assessed for normative legitimacy. Moral, practical learning or rationalisation take place according to the extent to which conflict resolution is structured by the key themes articulated by critical or cosmopolitan theory.

Given that 'anarchy is what states make of it', to quote Wendt, realists cannot even *explain* the particular characteristics of the Oslo Accords, let alone assess its normative character.[1] Explanation requires investigation into the social construction of international political reality. As Linklater writes: '[c]ritical theory invites observers to reflect upon the social construction and effects of knowledge and to consider how claims about neutrality can conceal the role knowledge plays in unsatisfactory social relationships.'[2] On this basis, we reflected on how the Accords were 'socially constructed.' We focused on the particular role that Norwegian facilitation played in maintaining the ambiguous status of Palestine. Like the Oslo facilitation process itself, and the Oslo Accords, Palestinians are not internationally recognised, but nor are they a recognised part of a domestic state politics. From the critical point of view, the Oslo facilitation process is a socially constructed process well suited to keeping Palestinians in Israeli-occupied territory. There is an intimate relationship between all these elements: the place of the Palestinians, the nature of the facilitation and the Accords themselves. All the elements serve to reinforce an unequal and unjust socially constituted reality. And this claim is not undermined by the concept of an interim status, and UN Resolutions 242 and 338 are politically ambiguous. The overriding emphasis on Israeli security plus the complete lack of *any* mention of Palestinian claims to national self-determination in the text of the Accords means that the Accords were always unlikely to redeem the claim to Palestinian statehood. The Accords are part of a socially constructed reality designed to exclude the claims of Palestinian statehood. The history of the Oslo process since 1993 is a testament to this conclusion.

The implications of this analysis for the nature of post-positivist international theory are slightly more difficult to ascertain. Chapter three contained the details of the criticism of geostrategic thinking in the theory of international relations. Apart from the theoretical arguments, the case study proposes that post-positivist thinking in the theory of international relations ought to think carefully about the details of particular circumstances before announcing the validity of its ideals. Post-positivist theory, whether in its critical or postmodernist guise, is generally critical of state-centrist approaches to international politics. The analysis of the Oslo Accords, however, was based on the failure to construct an international agreement. The use of critical theory in this thesis seems, therefore, to embody a contradiction. Critical theory seeks to transcend the state, yet the case study highlighted the importance of state structures. This contradiction can, however, be easily ironed out. In the case of critical theory, at least, the importance of post-sovereign considerations lies in the extension of moral community beyond the boundaries of the nation state. As Linklater writes:

> discourse ethics cannot be completed by a number of separate experiments in democratic participation within independent sovereign states. Discourse ethics clashes with the idea of sovereignty which restricts the capacity of outsiders to participate in discourse to consider issues which concern them.

Linklater adds that 'discourse needs to be embodied transnationally' and rightly points out that critical theory may, potentially, clash with the concept of a nation-state and seek to overcome it altogether.[3] The central point, however, is that there is nothing in this analysis – the idea of, for example, the trans*national* – which necessitates the abolition of the idea of state-sovereignty altogether – i.e. irrespective of history and circumstances. Rather, it is a case of critical theory working, in particular circumstances, with the idea of interstate relations in order to improve the moral obligations which the members of those states have to outsiders. Communicative action needs to be bolstered in international politics. Post-positivism calls the validity of the state into question, but does not necessarily abolish, in its entirety, the idea or reality of the state without reference to particulars. As we have seen in the case study, extending the bounds of moral responsibility beyond the state *can* mean creating and respecting the claims of national self-determination in others.

This point was made in chapter 7. Palestinians are seeking entry into an international society consisting of sovereign states. While one may be interested in ultimately abolishing the concept and reality of a state, at the end of history, as it were, it is undeniable that the state *can* offer a degree of legal, physical and existential protection to its members, at the present time. This does not imply that realist structures of state relationships are immutable nor does it mean that normative questions are entirely abandoned in the international realm. If we take the need for contextual knowledge seriously, it follow that extending moral responsibly and moral equality into international politics can mean, in certain circumstances, respecting deeply felt claims to national self-determination in others. As I noted in the discussion of 'performative contradiction', it was Palestinian political weakness and the existing norms of an international society which stifled the possibility of communicative action. Palestinians, at Oslo, could not have claimed to have negotiated an international treaty, and therefore buttressed their claims to

Conclusion

national self-determination. But what needs to be altered in these circumstances is the political and legal power of Palestinian negotiation, relative to other actors, not the norms of 'international society.' Palestinians require the reality of statehood, not a different idea of statehood. It is important to shape the themes of critical theory to circumstances as they exist. The post-national and post-sovereign is important. What is also important, however, is to recognise that post-national identity rests, to some extent, on a transcended national identity. The security and coherence of the state is a good basis to move into post-national politics. *It is hard to lecture the sub-national about the importance of the post-national from the comfort of nationhood itself.* And there is no reason why critical theory or post-positivism should do this. It can emphasise the importance of respecting the structure of communicative action without rejecting, universally, the concept of the state.

In essence, the critical theory of international mediation asks a very simple question. This is a question which respects rationality and canons of truth without falling into dogmatism. It is a question which recognises the fundamental communicative quality of language. In approaching an instance of mediation, we want to know whether it respects 'no force except that of the better argument' where 'all motives except that of the cooperative search for truth are excluded.' If these conditions are not fulfilled, then we are not dealing with or viewing an instance of moral and practical learning in international relations. Rather, we are viewing a situation where one party is attempting to impose its vision of the world on another party. Of course, in trivial matters such acts may pass unnoticed. But in dealing with fundamental historical matters, such as national recognition, the destiny of humanity is at stake.

The history of modernity is a history of vanishing cultures and world-views. Mediation is the preservation of an aspect of global plurality which faces the prospect of abolition. My fear is that the Oslo process has failed to accomplish this task. It is more like the careful management of a disappearance. The idea of a bi-national state in the part of the world under investigation is vanishing hour by hour, day by day, and year by year. These processes are historical in nature and are almost imperceptible to the everyday consciousness of time. Yet, unfortunately, and despite their incremental nature, they exist. Without a more effective process of international mediation, historical reproduction will break down as one part of the plurality of global life fades from view.

NOTES

1. A. Wendt, 'Anarchy is What States Make of It: The Social Construction of Power Politics', *International Organization*, 46:2 (1992), pp. 390–425.
2. A. Linklater, 'The Achievements of Critical Theory', in S. Smith, K. Booth and M. Zalewski (eds), *International Theory: Positivism and Beyond* (Cambridge: Cambridge University Press, 1996), p. 279
3. *Ibid.*, p. 294.

SELECT BIBLIOGRAPHY

Abbas, M., *Through Secret Channels* (Reading: Garnet, 1995).
Arendt, H., *The Human Condition* (Chicago: The University of Chicago Press, 1958).
Arendt, H., *The Origins of Totalitarianism* (London: Allen and Unwin, 1967).
Arendt, H., 'Truth and Politics', in *Between Past and Future* (London: Faber and Faber, 1961).
Ashley, R. K. and Walker, R. J. B., 'Reading Dissidence/Writing the Discipline: Crisis and the Question of Sovereignty in International Studies', *International Studies Quarterly*, 34:3 (1990) pp. 367–416.
Bailey, S. D., *Four Arab–Israeli Wars and the Peace Process* (London: Macmillan, 1990).
Bercovitch, J. and Rubin, J. Z. (eds), *Mediation in International Relations* (London: The Macmillan Press, 1992).
Burton, J. (eds), *Conflict: Human Needs Theory* (London: The Macmillan Press, 1990).
Burton, J., *Conflict and Communication* (New York: Free Press, 1969).
Burton, J., *Violence Explained* (Mancester: Manchester University Press, 1997).
Bull, H., *The Anarchical Society* (Basingstoke: The Macmillan Press, 1977).
Calhoun, C. (eds), *Habermas and the Public Sphere* (Cambridge, Mass.: MIT Press, 1992).
Carr, E. H., *The Twenty Years Crisis* (London: Macmillan, 1962).
Chalmers, A. F., *What is this Thing Called Science?* (Buckingham: Open University Press, 1980).
Chomsky, N., *Chronicles of Dissent: Interviews with David Barsiman* (Stirling, Scotland: AK Press, 1992).
Chomsky, N., *The Fateful Triangle* (Boston: South End Press, 1983).
Chomsky, N., *Powers and Prospects* (London: Pluto Press, 1996).
Cook, T. E., *Criteria of Social Scientific Knowledge: Interpretation, Prediction, Praxis* (London: Rowman and Littlefield, 1994).
Corbin, J., *Gaza First* (London: Bloomsbury, 1994).
Cox, R., 'Social Forces, States and World Order: Beyond International Relations Theory', *Millennium*, 10:2 (1981).
Dajani, B., 'The September 1993 Israeli/PLO Documents: A Textual Analysis', *Journal of Palestine Studies*, XXIII (1994).
Egeland, J., *Impotent Superpowers, Potent Small States* (Norwegian University Press, 1988).
Egeland, J., *The Norwegian Channel: The Secret Peace Talks Between Israel and the PLO*. Paper presented to the JFK School in Harvard, 23 March 1995.
Ferrara, A., *Modernity and Authenticity: A Study of Social and Ethical Thought of Jean-Jacques Rousseau* (Albany, New York: New York State University Press, 1993).
Finkelstein, N., 'Whither the Peace Process?', *New Left Review*, 218 (1996), pp. 138–49.
Folger, J. P. and Jones, T. S. (eds), *New Directions in Mediation* (London: Sage Publications, 1994).
Frost, M., *Ethics in International Relations*, 2nd edn (Cambridge: Cambridge University Press, 1996).

Select bibliography

George, J., *Discourses of Global Politics: A Critical (Re)Introduction to International Relations* (Boulder: Lynne Rienner, 1994).

Geuss, R., *The Idea of a Critical Theory* (Cambridge: Cambridge University Press, 1981).

Goldstein, J. and Keohane, R. O., *Ideas and Foreign Policy: Beliefs, Institutions and Political Change* (Ithaca and London: Cornell University Press, 1993).

Gowers, A. and Walker, T., *Arafat: The Biography* (London: Virgin, 1990).

Habermas, J., *Communication and the Evolution of Society* (London: Heinemann, 1979).

Habermas, J., 'Hannah Arendt's Communications Concept of Power', in S. Lukes (ed.), *Power* (New York: New York University Press, 1986).

Habermas, J., *Justification and Application: Remarks on Discourse Ethics* (Cambridge: Polity Press,1993).

Habermas, J., *Knowledge and Human Interests*, trans. J. Shapiro (Boston: Beacon Press, 1971).

Habermas, J., *Legitimation Crisis* (Cambridge: Polity Press, 1988).

Habermas, J., *Moral Consciousness and Communicative Action* (Cambridge: Polity Press, 1990).

Habermas, J., *On the Logic of the Social Sciences* (Cambridge: Polity Press, 1988). First published in Germany in 1967.

Habermas, J., *The Philosophical Discourse of Modernity: Twelve Lectures* (Cambridge, Mass.: MIT Press, 1987).

Habermas, J., 'Systematically Distorted Communication', *Inquiry*, 13 (1970).

Habermas, J., *The Theory of Communicative Action*, Vol I (Cambridge: Polity Press, 1991). The book was first published in Germany in 1981.

Halliday, F., *Rethinking International Relations* (London: The Macmillan Press, 1994).

Held, D., *Democracy and the Global Order* (Cambridge: Polity Press, 1995).

Held, D., *Introduction to Critical Theory* (Cambridge: Polity Press, 1980).

Heller, M. and Nusseibeh, S., *No Trumpets, No Drums: A Two-State Settlement of the Israeli–Palestinian Conflict* (London: IB Tauris and Co. Ltd., 1991).

Herz, J. H., 'The Rise and Demise of the Territorial State', *World Politics*, 9:4 (1958) pp. 473–93.

Hobbes, T., *Leviathan* (London: Penguin Classics, 1985).

Hobsbawn, E., *The Age of Extremes* (London: Abacus, 1994).

Hoffman, M., 'Defining And Evaluating Success: Facilitative Problem-Solving Workshops in an Interconnected Context', *Paradigms: The Kent Journal of International Relations*, (Winter 1995).

Hoffman, M., 'Third Party Mediation and Conflict Resolution', in Baylis, J., and Rengger, N. J. (eds), *Dilemmas of World Politics* (Oxford: Clarendon Press, 1992).

Inbari, P., *The Palestinians: Between Statehood and Terrorism* (Brighton: Sussex University Press, 1996).

Jabri, V., 'Agency, Structure and the Question of Power in Conflict Resolution', *Paradigms: The Kent Journal of International Relations*, 9:2 (1995).

Jabri, V., *Discourses on Violence* (Manchester: Manchester University Press, 1995).

Keohane, R., *Neorealism and its Critics* (New York: Columbia University Press, 1986).

Koestler, A., *The Sleepwalkers* (London: Penguin, 1988).

Kolb, D., 'Expressive Tactics in Mediation', *Journal of Social Issues*, 41:2 (1985), pp. 16–24.

Select bibliography

Kressel, K. and Pruiit, D. G., 'Themes in the Mediation of Social Conflict', in Vasquez et al. (eds), *Beyond Confrontation* (1995).

Kuhn, T., *The Structure of Scientific Revolutions* (Chicago: The University of Chicago Press, 1962).

Kuttab, J., 'The Pitfalls of Dialogue', *Journal of Palestine Studies*, XVII:2 (1988), pp. 84–108.

Levine, E. P., 'Mediation in International Politics', *Peace Research Society: International Papers*, 8:18 (1972), pp. 23–42.

Linklater, A., *Beyond Realism and Marxism: Critical Theory and International Relations* (Basingstoke: Macmiilan, 1990).

Linklater, A., *Men and Citizens in the Theory of International Theory*, 2nd edn (London: Macmillan, 1990).

Linklater, A., *The Transformation of Political Community* (Cambridge: Polity Press, 1997).

Linklater, A., 'The Question of the Next Stage in International Relations Theory: A Critical-Theoretical Point of View', *Millennium*, 21:1 (1992), pp. 78–98.

Linklater, A. and Macmillan, J. (eds), *Boundaries in Question: New Directions in International Relations* (London: Pinter Publishers, 1995).

Little, R. and Smith, S., *Belief Systems and International Relations* (Oxford: Basil Blackwell, 1988).

Makovsky, D., *Making Peace With the PLO* (Bolder, Col.: Westview Press, 1996).

Mattingly, G., *Renaissance Diplomacy* (Boston: Houghton Mifflin, 1955).

McCarthy, T., *The Critical Theory of Jürgen Habermas* (Cambridge: Cambridge University Press, 1978).

McDowell, D., *The Palestinians: The Road to Nationhood* (London: Minority Rights Publications, 1994).

Michels, J., 'National Vision and the Negotiation of Narratives: The Oslo Agreement', *Journal of Palestine Studies*, XXIV:1 (1994).

Mitchell, C. R. and Webb, K. (eds), *New Approaches to International Mediation* (Westport, Connecticut: Greenwood, 1988).

Moore, C., *The Mediation Process: Practical Strategies for Resolving Conflict* (San Francisco, London: Jossey-Bass, 1986).

Neufeld, M., *The Restructuring of International Relations Theory* (Cambridge: Cambridge University Press, 1995).

Orwell, G., 'Politics and the English Language' in *The Penguin Essays of George Orwell* (London: Penguin, 1984).

Peres, S., *Battling for Peace* (London: Orion, 1995).

Princen, T., *Intermediaries in International Conflict* (Princeton: Princeton University Press, 1992).

Pruitt, D. G. and Carnevale, P. J., *Negotiation in Social Conflict* (Buckingham: Open University Press, 1993).

Roberts, A. and Kinsbury, B. (eds), *United Nations, Divided World* (Oxford: Oxford University Press, 1988).

Roderick, R., *Habermas and the Foundations of Critical Theory* (London: Macmillan, 1986).

Rothman, J., *From Confrontation to Cooperation* (London: Sage Publications, 1992).

Select bibliography

Roy, S., *The Gaza Strip: The Political Economy of De-Development* (Washington: Institute for Palestine Studies, 1995).
Safty, A., *From Camp David to the Gulf* (Montreal: Black Rose Books, 1992).
Said, E., *Culture and Imperialism* (London: Vintage, 1993).
Said, E., *Peace and Its Discontents* (London: Vintage, 1995).
Said, E., *The Question of Palestine* (London: Vintage, 1979).
Shaath, N., 'The Oslo Agreement: An Interview with Nabil Shaath,' *Journal of Palestine Studies*, XXIII:1 (1993), pp. 5–13.
Shaw, M., *Global Society and International Relations* (Cambridge: Polity Press, 1994).
Shlaim, A., 'Prelude to the Accord', *Journal of Palestine Studies*, XXIII:2 (1994).
Smith, S. and Booth, K., *International Relations Theory Today* (Cambridge: Polity Press, 1995).
Smith, S., Booth, K. and Zalewski, M. (eds), *International Theory: Positivism and Beyond* (Cambridge: Cambridge University Press, 1996).
Touval, S., *The Peace Brokers: Mediators in the Arab–Israeli Conflict, 1948–1979* (Princeton: Princeton University Press, 1982).
Touval, S., and Zartman, W. I., 'International Mediation: Conflict Resolution and Power Politics', *Journal of Social Issues*, 41:2 (1985), pp. 27–45.
Touval, S. and Zartman W. I. (eds), *International Mediation in Theory and Practice* (Boulder, Colorado: Westview Press, 1985).
Usher, G., *Palestine in Crisis: The Struggle for Peace and Independence After Oslo* (London: Pluto Press, 1995).
Vasqeuz, J. A., Johnson, J. J., Jaffes S. and Stameto, L. (eds), *Beyond Confrontation: Learning Conflict Resolution in the Post-Cold War Era* (Michigan: University of Michigan Press, 1995).
Waltz, K., *The Theory of International Politics* (Reading, Mass.: Addison Wesley, 1979).
Waltz, K., *Man, the State and War: A Theoretical Analysis* (New York: Columbia University Press, 1959).
Welch, D., *Justice and the Genesis of War* (Cambridge: Cambridge University Press, 1993).
Wendt, A., 'Anarchy is what States Make of it: the Social Construction of Power Politics', *International Organization*, 46:2 (1992), pp. 390–425.
White, S., *Political Theory and Postmodernism* (Cambridge: Cambridge University Press, 1991).
White, S., *The Recent Work of Jürgen Habermas* (Cambridge: Cambridge University Press, 1988).
Whittaker, D. J., *United Nations in Action* (London: UCL Press, 1995).
Wight, M., *Power Politics* (London: Leicester University Press, 1995).
Williams, R., *KeyWords: A Vocabulary of Modern Culture* (London: Fontana Press, 1988).
Zubek, J. M., Pruitt, D. G. and Peirce, R. S., 'Disputant Behaviours Affecting Short Term Sucess in Mediation', *Journal of Conflict Resolution*, 36 (1992).

Jan Egeland and Geir Pederson were interviewed August 1996.

INDEX

Abdullah, King of Jordan, 133
abstract universalism, 67
'Accord', meaning of, 105
action, need for, 73–4; *see also* communicative action
aesthetic consciousness, 84
Afghanistan, 52
Aggestam, K. and Jonsson, C., 129
aid programme, Norwegian, 129
Alaa, Abu, 109, 111–12, 119–21
anarchy in international relations, 36–40, 158, 161
Anderson, Sten, 109
anomie, 40
anthropomorphic thought, 93
Arafat, Fathi, 109
Arafat, Yasser, 18, 95, 106–23 *passim*, 130, 132, 134, 138–43 *passim*, 147, 149
  isolation of, 115–17, 160
  support for Saddam Hussein, 115
Arendt, Hannah, 26, 28–30, 46, 95
ARI (adversarial, reflexive and integrative) conflict framework, 66
Aristarchus of Samos, 44
armed forces, 27
arms trade, 27
Asfour, Hasson, 141
Ashley, Richard, 38, 41–2
Ashrawi, Hanan, 109, 111, 116, 148
'assisted' and 'unassisted' dispute resolution, 12–13
astronomy, Ptolemaic, 84

Babbit, E. F., 12–13; *see also* Kolb, D. M.
back-channel relations, 18, 106, 111–13, 116, 123
Bailey, S. D., 49–50
Banks, M. and Mitchell, C., 58, 62–3, 67, 74–5

bargaining processes, 129
Baynes, Kenneth, 86
Begin, Menachim, 51
Beilin, Yossi, 110–12
Benhabib, Seyla, 67
Bercovitch, J., 14
  and Rubin, J. Z., 15
biological weapons, 27
Bismarck, Prince, 12
Black September, 49
Britain, 83
Brownlie, Ian, 144
Bull, Hedley, 90
Burton, John, 24, 42, 63–4
Bush, George, President, 81, 114–15, 120
Buzan, B., 36

Camp David Accords, 43, 51–2, 120, 139
Camus, A., 24
Carnevale, P. J. *see* Pruitt, D. G.
Carter, Jimmy, President, 51
Centre for the Analysis of Conflict, 58
chemical weapons, 26–8
Chomsky, Noam, 9, 48, 52, 115
Christopher, Warren, 120
civil society, 14
Clark, Ian, 25
Clinton, Bill, President, 120
coalitions of states, 96, 149
Cobb, Sarah, 11, 18
coercive intervention, 60, 73
'committed engagement', 81
communication problems, 13, 17, 159
communicative action, 67, 85–6, 88, 92, 98, 150–1, 159–63
communicative discourse, 66
communicative ethics, 67, 69, 91
communicative politics, 58–9
communicative power, 18
communicative reason, 92, 99, 158–9

Index

The Communist Manifesto, 83
community-based standards, 44
compromise, 105
'concealed occupation', 147, 160
confidence-building measures, 110
conflict and its resolution, 40, 42, 66
conscription, military, 27
contextual rationality, 16
conventional weapons, 26–7
Cook, Terence E., 61
Copernicus, Nicolas, 44
Corbin, Jane, 129, 141–3
cosmopolis, definition of, 88–9
cosmopolitan (or critical) theory, 2–7, 31, 58, 62, 65–72 *passim*, 80–100, 105, 140–1, 149, 151, 157, 159, 161–3
  problems with, 4–5, 92–100
cosmopolitanism, contemporary, 87–90
'crisis', concept of, 3, 23–4
critical theory of international relations *see* cosmopolitan (or critical) theory
Crone, Hugh, 27–8
Cronin, Ciaran P., 87

Darwin, Charles, 36–7
Dayan, Moshe, 50
decision-making power, mediators' lack of, 11
Declaration of Palestinian Independence (1988), 147
Declaration of Principles (DoP) on Palestinian self-government, 130–44 *passim*, 147, 160
  successive drafts of, 134–6
'deep conceptual structures', 66
democratic institutions and procedures, 88–9, 94–5, 159
democratic public law, 81–2, 88–9, 91, 94–5, 151, 159
'demographic problem', the, 143, 147
demonisation, 18, 60, 157
Devetak, Richard, 90
Di Giovanno, Janin, 117
dialogic community, 59, 90–1, 151, 159
dialogic ethics, 67

'discipline of detail', 140–1
discourse ethics, 67–8, 86, 88, 90–1, 98, 141, 159, 161–2
dispassionate theory, 63
Doyal, L. and Gough, I., 65
drives, needs seen as, 65–6

Eban, Abba, 50
educational role of mediation process, 17
Egeland, Jan, 18–19, 71, 107–13, 129, 143, 145–6, 148
Egypt, 35, 48–52, 120
emancipatory processes, 59, 68, 94
'emergent' mediation, 11
empathy, 60–1, 66
empiricism, 43–4, 62
empowerment, 95
Enlightenment, the, 31, 83
ethics, 67–8; *see also* communicative ethics; dialogic ethics; discourse ethics
ethnic conflict, 64
European Union, 95–6, 107, 149
evolutionary approach to society, 99
excluded groups, 90, 93

facilitation of human need, 63–6
facilitation theory, 4–7, 13–18, 53, 58–76, 81, 94, 96, 129, 157–9
  problems and limitations of, 59, 70
facilitators
  advantages of small states as, 112–13
  function of, 18, 65
  goals of, 63, 146
  political commitment of, 63
  power and weakness of, 18–19
  public and private roles of, 145
fact/value distinction, 43–7, 62, 158
FAFO research organization, 109, 112–13, 121
Fatah, Fifth General Conference of, 148
Ferrara, Alessandro, 15
Finkelstein, Norman, 105, 130
First World War, 25, 27
Fisher, R., 13

Index

Folger, J. P. and Jones, T. S., 12
Foreign Affairs (journal), 115
Foucault, M., 81, 92
fragmentation
   of international environment, 12, 25–6
   of nation-states, 88
France, 29
free-rider problems, 35–6
Freudian theory, 65
friendship towards both sides, 146
Frost, Mervyn, 35, 62

Gadamer, Hans-George, 61
Galileo, 44
game theory, 41
'Gaza-first' option, 118–23
Gaza Strip, 5, 24, 51, 71, 106, 109, 113, 116–23, 132, 135–8, 140
   Israeli desire to leave, 118–19, 160
generalisable interests, 86–7, 91, 105
Geneva Protocol on chemical warfare, 28
geostrategic mediation, 3–4, 7, 13–16, 34–53, 60, 76, 157–8
   conclusions about, 47
   limitations of, 40–3, 161
   nature of, 34–5
Geras, Norman, 83
German philosophy and sociology, 58, 61
globalisation, 25–6, 88
Godal, Bjorne Tore, 107
Goldstein, Judith, 92
Gough, I., *see* Doyal, L.
governance-based approach to international relations, 95–6
Gowers, A. and Walker, T., 116, 119
Gressheim document, 135–6, 142
guaranteeing of agreements, 13
Gulf War, 27, 80, 113–15, 117, 148; *see also* Iran-Iraq War
Gulf War syndrome, 28

Habash, George, 147
Habermas, Jürgen, 2, 4, 16, 23–4, 35, 40–1, 47, 58–9, 62, 65–9, 81–100 *passim*, 140–1, 159
   concept of rationality, 82
   limitations of political theory, 67–9
   on cosmopolitan theory, 87
Hague Convention, 27
Halliday, Fred, 37, 44–5, 63, 106
Halvorsbole, 142
Hamas resistance movement, 115–19, 123, 138
Hampson, F. O., 95–6
Hebron, 107
Hegel, G. W. F., 84
Heikel, Mohamed, 49–50, 114–15, 119–20
Held, Colbert C., 47
Held, David, 2, 4, 81, 88, 90–1, 96–8, 100, 159
heliocentrism, 44, 46
Heller, M. and Nusseibeh, S., 139, 141
Herz, John, 42
Hilterman, J. R., 122
Hirschfeld, Yair, 111–12
historical analysis, 36–7
   neglect within cosmopolitan theory, 81, 92–3
Hobbes, Thomas, 7, 14, 36, 41, 98
Hobsbawm, Eric, 10, 27, 29
Hoffman, Mark, 17, 19, 59–62, 64, 66, 76, 80
Holst, Johan Jorgen, 107, 130, 138
Holst fund, 107
human dimension of international conflict, 42
human needs and purposes, 44, 63–6
Hussein, King, 49
Hussein, Saddam, 115
Husseini, Faisal, 109–11, 115–16, 119, 148

Ibrahim Mosque massacre, 107
'ideal speech situation', 71, 149, 160
identity
   ethnic, racial and linguistic, consciousness of, 60–1
   Israeli and Palestinian, 142
ideology, 34, 46, 131–2

Index

imperialism, 83–4
Inbari, Pinhas, 114–16, 120
incitement, banning of, 150
incremental facilitation, 71, 159
India, 29
instrumentalism, 158–9
interim status, 71, 94, 139–40, 149–50, 160–1
intermediaries, rewards for, 15
international and domestic politics, space between, 6, 143–5, 160
international conference (proposed), 147–8, 160
international governance and order, 10, 39–40
international law, 144
international organizations, 149; *see also* European Union; United Nations
internationalism, 92
interpretation of facts, 45–6
interpretive approach to social science, 62
intersubjectivity
 evaluation of, 141–2
 rebuilding of, 60–1
intransigent forces, 96
Iran, 27, 29, 52
Iran-Iraq War, 27, 114
Iraq, 27–8, 114
Islamic Jihad, 107
Israel
 as a strategic asset to the US, 4, 48–52
 denial of right to exist, 130, 133, 138–9
 exploitation of Palestinian weakness, 71, 73
 financial support from US for, 51–2
 military operations, 50
 nuclear programme, 29
 regional position of, 114
Israel-Palestine conflict, nature of, 6, 23, 64, 74–5
Israel-Palestine negotiations, circumstances promoting, 113–21, 123
Israeli Defence Forces (IDF), 122, 135

Italy, 28
Iyyad, Abu, 115
Iyyadist wing of PLO, 119

Jabri, Vivienne, 10, 60, 66, 72, 74–6
Jagland, Thorbjorn, 107
Japan, 28
Jericho, 135
Jerusalem, 71, 83, 134, 136, 147
Jihad, Abu, 114
Jones, T. S. *see* Folger, J. P.
Jonsson, C. *see* Aggestam, K.
Jordan, 49, 133
justice, distributive theory of, 2
Juul, Mona, 110–11

Kant, Immanuel (and Kantianism), 67–9, 74, 83–4, 86, 89–90, 94, 97, 159
Karsh, Efraim, 49, 51–2, 133
Kelman, Herbert C., 13, 64–5
Keohane, Robert, 92
Khalaf, Salif, 115
Khalidi, Walid, 120, 139
Kissinger, Henry, 4, 35, 48–53, 158
Klieman, Aharon, 142
knowledge, construction of, 38, 161
Kolb, D. M. and Babbit, E. F., 11–12
Korper, S. *see* Rouhana, N. N.
Kressel, K. and Pruitt, D. G., 14
Kuttab, Jonathan, 72–4
Kuwait, 114

Labour Party, Israeli, 5, 24, 107–8, 110, 113, 160
Labour Party, Norwegian, 107–9, 111, 160
land for peace, principle of, 49, 138–9
Larsen, Terje Rod, 106–7, 109–13, 121, 129
Lebanon, 46, 51, 122–3
legitimacy, 42, 145
Letters of Mutual Recognition, 130, 138, 140–1, 160
leverage, 11, 15
Lewis, Bernard, 48

172

Index

Lie, Haakon, 108
Lie, Trygve, 129
lifeworld, the, 85, 98–9
Likud Party, 51
Linklater, Andrew, 2, 4, 26, 44, 81–2, 88–93, 97–8, 100, 140, 143, 159, 161–2
   and Macmillan, J., 25

McDowell, David, 123, 139
Macmillan, J. *see* Linklater, Andrew
Madrid-Washington process, 80, 111–12, 115–16, 118, 148–9
Makovsky, David, 111–12, 114, 118, 123, 129, 134, 142
manipulation, mediation seen as, 3, 11, 157
Marx, Karl (and Marxism), 2, 31, 70, 82–3, 90, 97, 159
Matthews, Ken, 114
Mazen, Abu, 112, 115–16, 119–20, 134, 141
meaningful implication, method of, 39
mediation
   as an institution and as a form of agency, 3, 29–31
   family resemblances between forms of, 13
   goals of, 2, 4, 14
   history of, 9
   meanings of, 1, 7, 9–11, 82, 157
   nature of, 13–14, 30, 91
   role in international affairs, 9–10
   types of actors involved in, 11–12
Meir, Golda, 50–1
Metternich, Prince, 48
Michels, Jeffrey, 131–2
Middle East, geopolitical significance of, 47–8
military control of West Bank and Gaza, 136–7
military technology, 3, 26–30
Mitchell, C. *see* Banks, M.
Mitchell, C. R., 15
Mitterand, François, President, 118

modernity, 85, 90, 98, 159
monitoring of agreements, 13
monologicality, 68–9, 84
Moore, Christopher, 10–11, 13
moral community, 90, 162
moral development, 71
moral discourse, 87, 94
moral law, 89
moral resources, 98, 100
moral world order, 96, 100, 159
morality, cosmopolitan, 87
motivations, examination of, 65
Mubarak, Hosni, President, 120
Muslim Brotherhood, 117
mutual acceptability, 11
mutual recognition, 17, 131–2, 142–3, 150–1, 161; *see also* Letters of Mutual Recognition
myths, 18

Napoleon, 47–8
natality, 29
nation-states
   coalitions of, 96, 149
   nature of, 41–2
   power of, 88–9
nationalism
   Arab, 49–50
   Palestinian, 132–7, 140
need-fulfilment, 59
needs theory, 63–4
negotiation
   as a social practice, 60
   borders of, 91
   'scripts' for, 72
   strengthening of forces committed to, 95
neo-colonialism, 143
neo-realist approaches to international relations, 34, 38, 41
nerve gas, 28
Netanyahu, Binyamin 106–7, 111, 139, 142, 147, 150
Neufeld, Mark, 38, 44–5, 60
neutrality of mediators, 11, 19

Index

Nietzsche, F. W., 5, 26, 31, 82, 93, 97, 99, 100, 159
Nixon, Richard, 49, 51
Nixon Doctrine, 49
Nobel Peace Prize, 107
normative analysis, 80–1, 123–4, 130, 157–8, 160–1
norms, 39
  of public discourse, 86–7
  validity of, 68–9
Norway
  foreign policy of, 148
  international record of, 129
  political stance on main subjects of negotiation, 146
  resources for facilitation, 112–13
  role in Israel-Palestine negotiations, 106–10, 116, 123, 129
Nuclear Non-Proliferation Treaty, 29
nuclear weapons, 26–9, 108
Nusseibeh, S. *see* Heller, M.

Operation Accountability, 122
oppression, forms of, 82
Organisation for African Unity, 9
Organisation for Security and Cooperation in Europe, 9
Orwell, George, 9–10
Oslo Accords, 3–6, 18, 24, 51, 59, 69, 71, 74–5, 80, 92–3, 100, 105–6
  inequality embodied in, 137–8, 160–1
  problems with, 150
  sections of, 130
  social construction of, 161
Oslo process
  stages in, 135
  symbolic meaning of, 132–3
Oslo spirit, 143
'otherness', perceptions of, 18, 60, 64, 66, 75, 84, 157
Outhwaite, William, 87

Pakistan, 29
Palestine
  first Norwegian links with, 108
  killings by Israeli soldiers, 122
  National Authority, 95
  partition of, 108
  pressures on, 121–3, 160
  statehood of, 6, 52, 71, 106, 109–21, 133–8, 147, 150, 160–1
Palestine Liberation Organisation (PLO), 5, 24, 49, 51–2, 148
  financial problems of, 114–17, 121, 142, 160
  illegality of contacts with, 111–13
  incompetence in negotiations, 141–2
  initial goals at Oslo, 134
  recognition of, 131–3, 138, 161
participant observation, 63
peace, concept of, 10
peace processes, 5–6, 10, 46, 160
Peace Research Institute Oslo (PRIU), 107
'peace with security', 150
Pederson, Geir, 71, 107–8, 110–13, 129, 145–6
Peres, Shimon, 48, 106–10, 117–23, 131, 134–5, 137, 147
performative contradiction, 6, 85, 140–1, 159–62
peripheral issues, 71
permissive cause, 39
'phenomenology of the moral', 41, 158
'philosophy of consciousness', 84
plurality, human, 29–31, 163
police, Palestinian, 136
political commitment and goals of facilitators, 63
political ideals, 151
positivism, 62–3
postmodernism, 2, 81, 90, 159
  problems and contradictions of, 84–5
post-national politics, 163
post-positivist theory, 161–3
power, different forms of, 18
power-political analyses of international relations *see* geostrategic mediation
power relationships between states, 34–5, 48–9, 69–70, 95, 143
  asymmetry in, 59, 72–3, 75, 149

pragmatism, 98
praxeological analysis, 92
Princen, Thomas, 11, 17
principle, issues of, 14
PRIO peace institute, 129
problem-solving approach to mediation *see* facilitation theory
problem-solving workshops, 4, 13, 58–9, 64–75 *passim*, 157, 159
  efficacy of, 76
Pruitt, D. G.
  and Carnevale, P. J., 11–12, 15
  see also Kressel, K.
psychoanalysis, 65
psychological aspects of conflict, 17
public nature of diplomacy, 81

Qrei, Ahmad, 115
quarks, 38

Rabin, Yitzhak, 5, 106–7, 116–23, 130, 135, 138, 147
'radical intimacy of the hearth', 143–5
rationality, 3, 14–16, 19, 82–5, 92, 97–100, 157
Rawls, John, 2
Reagan, Ronald, President, 52
realist theory of international relations, 1–2, 15, 41; *see also* neo-realist approaches
reason *see* rationality
reconciliation, forms of, 7
reflection, 70
reflexivity, paradox of, 38
regional conflicts, 26, 53, 158
'regulative ideals', 86–7
Rehg, William, 98
religion, 99
reproduction of society and of state structures, 30, 40–1, 47, 53, 85, 151, 157–8
research on social conditions in Palestine, 109–10
Revolutionary Fateh movement, 115
Roderick, Rick, 70

Rogers, William, 50
Rogers Plan, 49
Rothman, Jay, 18, 23–5, 42, 60–2, 64, 66, 70, 72
Rouhana, N. N. and Korper, S., 72, 75
Roy, Sarah, 117, 121
Rubin, J. Z. *see* Bercovitch, J.

Sadat, Anwar, President, 50–1
Safty, Adel, 51
Said, Edward, 43, 51–2, 70, 73–4, 81, 122, 139–41
Sarpsborg document, 135–6
Sartawi, Issam, 110
Saudi Arabia, 115, 117, 119–20
Savir, Uri, 132, 135, 142
Sayigh, Yezid, 114, 137, 146
  and Shlaim, A., 48
Scali, Jo, 50
scientific community as arbiter of understanding, 38, 45–6
Second World War, 108
secrecy of negotiations, 112, 145, 157
security policy, Israeli, 64, 122, 136–7, 140, 150, 160–1
self-help behaviours, 39–40
self-sustaining solutions, 19
Shaath, Nabil, 109, 116, 132
Abd 'al-Shafi, 116, 148–9
Shamir, Yitzhak, 116
Sharif, Abu, 109
Sharon, Ariel, 50
Shlaim, Avi, 132–3; *see also* Sayigh, Y.
Shultz, Alfred, 62
Sinai desert, 50–2, 139
Sinai I and Sinai II agreements, 51
Singer, Joel, 135, 142
Six-Day War (1967), 49–50, 118
small states
  advantages as facilitators, 112–13
  weakness of, 144, 146
social conflict, protracted, 23–5
social engineering, 64
social learning, 82
socialization, 39

Index

sociological perspectives, 2, 91–2, 140, 143
South Africa, 74
sovereignty, 89–90
   conflicts about, 42
   Israeli, 142
   Norwegian, 144–6
   of nation-states generally, 162
   Palestinian, 105, 135–6
   unilateral declaration of, 144
Soviet Union, 48–51
   collapse of, 113–14, 121
   Jewish migrants from, 121–2
spin doctoring, 11
statecraft, 90–1
states *see* nation-states
Stoltenberg, Thorvald, 110
strategic rationality, 14–16, 19
structural anarchy, 1, 158
structuralism in international politics, 36–40
structuration theory of mediation, 75–6
Suez canal, 50
superpower rivalry, 48
Sweden, 109
symbolic meaning, 17
   of Oslo process, 132–3
Syria, 48–50

Tamari, S., 65
textual understanding, metaphor of, 59, 74
theories, assessing significance of, 45
third-party facilitators, 18
'throffers', 11
Thucydides, 36
torture, 122
totalitarianism, 29
Touval, S. and Zartman, W. I., 11, 13–15, 41, 43, 46
tradeable issues, 14
trusteeship, international (proposed), 134–5
'two-state' solution, 105, 115, 149, 163

understanding, process of, 61
United Nations
   Bush's speech to (1990), 114
   charter of, 9
   political structure of, 89–90
   Relief and Works Agency (UNRWA), 121
   Resolutions of, 49, 51–2, 107–8, 130, 134–5, 138–9, 160–1
   Security Council, 29, 148
United States, 107
   financial support for Israel, 51–2
   global foreign policy of, 4, 34, 113
   mediation in Middle East by, 158
   role in Israel-Palestine conflict, 3, 46–53, 81–2, 114
   Secretary of State, 34
   State Department, 49
universalisation, 68
universalism, 72
Usher, Graham, 117, 121–3
utilitarianism, 41

validity claims, 85–6
Valladao, A. G. A., 49
Vatican, the, 11
Vayrynen, T., 62–3, 70, 74
Vietnam War, 49
'volcano' model of social change, 63–4
voluntarism, 11

Waag, Hilde, 107–8
Walker, T. *see* Gowers, A.
Wallerstein, I., 34
Waltz, Kenneth, 45–6
Washington talks *see* Madrid-Washington process
weapons technology, 3, 26–30
'well-being' of states, 40
Wendt, Alex, 39, 161
West Bank (of the Jordan), 24, 51, 109, 116, 121, 131–2, 134–8, 140
Westphalian and post-Westphalian politics, 88–90, 97, 159
White, Stephen, 14, 66, 84

Index

Williams, Raymond, 1, 7
Wittgenstein, L., 16
world order 48, 82, 92; *see also* moral world order
world society, 63

Yassin, Ahmad, Sheikh, 117

Yeats, W. B., 26
Yom Kippur War (1973), 50
Yugoslavia, former, 3

Zartman, W. I. *see* Touval, S.
Zionist ideology, 131–2
Zolo, Danilo, 81, 97